# The North Coast 500

## Guide Book

### by Charles Tait

ISBN 9781909036604

# The North Coast 500 Guide Book

**First Edition**
© copyright Charles Tait 2017
Published by Charles Tait
Kelton, St Ola, Orkney KW15 1TR
Tel 01856 873738
charles.tait@zetnet.co.uk
charles-tait.co.uk

Text, design and layout © copyright Charles Tait, all photographs copyright © Charles Tait unless otherwise credited, old photographs from Charles Tait collection.

Mapping © Helen Stirling Maps 2017. Contains Ordnance Survey Data. © Crown Copyright and Database Right 2014

Printing by J Thomson Colour Printers, Glasgow

This book is dedicated to my father,
William Isbister Tait (1920-2011)

*Loch Borralan, Ledmore, Suilven and Quinag from the east*

# The North Coast 500

## Guide Book

### by Charles Tait

*Ardvreck, Castle, Loch Assynt*

## Welcome to the NC500

This tourist route takes in over 500mi (900km) of some of the UK's most stunning scenery. The North Coast 500 passes through the North Highlands of Scotland, starting and ending at Inverness. On the way it passes mountains, glens, beaches, cliffs, castles, ancient sites and picturesque villages.

This vast landscape encompasses the former shires of Caithness, Sutherland and Ross & Cromarty. It covers 5,200mi² (13,500km²) and had a total population of just over 94,000 in 2013. The main inhabited areas are Easter Ross and Caithness, which means that the population density in much of the area is very low.

This is a region of natural contrasts, caused by its complex geology. Much of Easter Ross and the Black Isle is fertile farmland, mostly given over to cereals. To the north, Caithness is gentle, rolling, green and fertile cattle grazing country, with sweeping sandy bays bound by rugged cliffs.

The north and west coasts are rugged with many inlets and are backed by high mountains. Here, tourism, crofting, forestry and fishing are predominant with small, scattered settlements. Inland the population is sparse but this was not always so. The empty glens of Kildonan, Strath Halladale and Strath Naver are testament to historic market forces.

Today the whole area, together with Inverness-shire and the Isle of Skye, is administered by the Highland Council. However, the former counties still very much exist in the minds of the inhabitants and are therefore referred to in this book. The gazetteer follows a clockwise trail around the NC500 which can be joined at any point, or indeed taken in an anticlockwise manner.

Access by road to Inverness (A9, A96 or A82) is via mostly single-carriageway roads, which can be very busy and slow. The A9 from Perth to Inverness is being slowly upgraded to dual carriageway throughout and has average speed cameras. There are rail

*Bealach na Ba road to Applecross*

| Sunrise & Sunset at Durness | | |
|---|---|---|
| 58.57°N 4.75°W | | |
| Date | Time | Azimuth |
| **June 21ˢᵗ** | | |
| sunrise | 03.59 | 037.2° |
| sunset | 22.29 | 322.7° |
| **Dec 21ˢᵗ** | | |
| sunrise | 09.08 | 137.6° |
| sunset | 15.26 | 222.4° |

*Blau Map of Scotland, 1654*

links via Inverness to Wick, Thurso and Kyle of Lochalsh. A wide range of connections are available from Inverness Airport and there is also an airport at Wick.

Ptolemy's 2nd century AD map is perhaps the first written reference to the North Highlands; it names several headlands and rivers. The oldest archaeological evidence dates

This question is often asked but very hard to answer since the area offers a great deal at every season. Because of the highly variable weather any recommendations can only be general. May and June are the driest, July to September the sunniest, but late September until early June are usually Midgie-free.

A persistent ridge of high pressure will bring fine weather at any time of year, sometimes for weeks at a time. Equally a continuous run of Atlantic depressions can yield long spells of wind and rain interspersed with glorious *"days atween weathers"*. The best advice is just to go anyway but to be prepared for anything.

**Daylight Hours** Seasons vary greatly in the number of daylight hours. In midsummer it never really gets dark with clear skies and the sun is above the horizon for about 18.5 hours. Conversely in midwinter it shines for only 6.5 hours. On a heavily overcast day it may seem dark all day.

The upside of this is a remarkable range of opportunities for wonderful sunrises and sunsets which vary over nearly 90° from midsummer to midwinter. *The Photographer's Ephemeris* app is an essential tool here.

*Stacks of Duncansby, Caithness*

*Suilven and Cam Loch*

*Inverness Castle marks the start of the NC500*

The first people to arrive left scant trace, mainly mounds of shells and some flint knives and scrapers. This is enough evidence to know when they were there and what they ate, but little else. No burials have been found from this time.

The first farmers arrived in the Neolithic Age. They built several hundred chambered cairns for their dead, mainly sited in fertile valleys where these people settled and grew grain and grass. They also kept cattle, sheep and pigs.

from over 8,000 years ago, at Sand in Applecross.

Most people come to experience the natural beauty and diversity of the landscapes. Many places of interest are described, some iconic, others less well known. There is a big range of interesting archaeological and historic sites to visit but only a small number of prime organised visitor attractions.

There was plenty of good timber here, so houses and farm buildings were usually built of wood. They did, however, build stone circles and alignments as well as erecting many solitary monoliths.

Bronze Age settlement remains, including hut circles, burial cairns and field walls are scattered on hillsides and in glens. No doubt further ruins lie hidden under the peat.

During the Iron Age sweeping changes took place. Large round buildings which we call brochs or duns were built all

*High Street, Dingwall*

*Wick in the height of the Herring season*

*The Old Smiddy, Berriedale, Caithness*

*Inverness in the early 19ᵗʰ century*

**THE HIGHLAND MIDGE**

**The Midgie** (*Culicoides impunctatus*; G *Meabh-chuileag*) is a small flying insect, prevalent in damp places like bogs and marshes in summer. Females form dense clouds and ferociously bite humans, as well as sheep, cattle, deer and other mammals.

They are at their most active just before dawn and around sunset but bite at any time of day. They are less of a problem when there is a light breeze or if humidity drops below c.70%. Below c.10C they become less active. Peak emergence times are early June and early August, in synchrony with the peak season for visitors.

over the North Highlands, especially in the fertile areas. These people were farmers and fishermen as well as expert stonemasons who used iron tools and weapons.

The Romans were the first people to describe the Picts. Many Pictish symbol stones have been found, mostly in Easter Ross, East Sutherland and Caithness. Evidence of several monastic sites and ancient chapels show that Christianity came to the North Highlands, in the 6ᵗʰ century.

The *Orkneyinga Saga* and Irish Annals describe many events in medieval times. Monasteries were sacked and bishops were killed but cathedrals were also built, notably at Dornoch which has the only intact 13ᵗʰ century church in the North Highlands. A much larger cathedral once stood at Fortrose but it was demolished for its lead, stone and timber.

After the 1745-46 Jacobite rebellion and its defeat at Culloden, the Government was forced to placate and control what they saw as the lawless Highlanders. The ancient traditions of clan life were seen as anachronistic and many people either emigrated to North America voluntarily, or were forcibly cleared from their ancestral lands.

*The Ord of Caithness 1950s*

*Strathpeffer Train Station*

*Durness in 1866*

*Suilven from Elphin*

Late in the 19th century, developments in harbours and fishing technology led to the Herring Boom which ended in collapse due to overfishing. In the 1950s an experimental fast breeder reactor was built at Dounreay in Caithness. The site is being decommissioned but remains at the forefront of nuclear technology.

**Landscape** The North Highlands offer a great variety of natural attractions. The complex geology makes for an interesting and beautiful landscape of mountains, lochs, rivers, moorland, bogs and fertile farmland.

The coast has everything from sheltered sandy coves and wonderful long sandy beaches with dunes and machair to some of the highest cliffs in Britain. Most are easily accessible, but others such as Sandwood Bay and Cape Wrath take some effort to reach. This only enhances the sense of achievement in reaching them.

Each of the mountains in the North Highlands is unique, carved from ancient rocks by erosion. Wind, ice, water, glaciers, rivers and sunshine have all played their part in breaking down the metamorphic and sedimentary rocks into the landscape of today. In addition to the elements, plants, animals and humans have contributed to the shaping of the scenery.

**Rivers** From the North Highlands, rivers flow into the North Sea and the Atlantic Ocean. In the west they are short and run into deep sea lochs through glacier carved valleys. Those that flow to the north and east tend to be longer and run into shallow firths. Many are famous for their Salmon and Sea Trout fisheries.

**Waterfalls** are very much a feature, from the impressive but

*Telford Bridge and Fishing Sheds, Helmsdale, Sutherland*

*Train at Garve, Easter Ross*

*Train in snow drifts, Dingwall*

small Falls of Shin or the Rogie Falls, where Salmon may be seen leaping, to the high Falls of Glomach. Most take a serious walk, but on the right day it is worth the effort.

**Woodland** Until medieval times, most of the Highlands were covered in forests of mature Scots Pine, while Oakwoods dominated in some areas. Many of these trees were used to make charcoal or cut down for timber. The largely bare landscape of today is maintained by grazing ungulates, mostly Sheep and Red Deer, which prevent regeneration of trees. In recent times deer fences and planting of native trees have started to mitigate this.

**Moors & Bogs** Another prominent feature of the North Highland landscape is the extensive bogs, marshland and moorland epitomized by the Flow Country. In these areas deep peat has built up. Lochs and pools develop in the hollows and hummocks are drier. The effect is to create a special habitat which supports a diverse range of wildlife.

*Main Road from Kylestrome to Durness*

*Lochinver and Suilven*

*Kyle of Lochalsh*

*Lochcarron in the 1920s*

*Bealach na Ba in the 1950s*

# Welcome to The North Coast 500

**Roads** Most of the main roads in this vast area are good, twin carriageway highways. However in many of the remoter places even 'A' roads are single track with passing places. It is important to obey the Highway Code regarding the etiquette of using such roads, especially regarding following traffic and the correct usage of passing places.

Please bear in mind that the speed limit outside towns and villages is generally 60mph. Local people, doctors, emergency services and others going about their business should be allowed to pass. The distances are long here. They do not like being held up behind slow moving vehicles, which should pull over to allow following vehicles to pass.

**Driving Times** in the North Highlands are in general far longer than in most other places, due to the long distances and slow roads. In some coastal and high areas fog is a frequent hazard. The table gives estimated times between places on the NC500. These do not allow for stopping to take photographs, short walks and the like. At busy times of year it may take much longer.

**Weather** Please be aware that snow and ice is frequent during the winter on the higher sections of roads and inland. Generally snow does not lie for long on the coast, especially in the west. The Ord of Caithness north of Helmsdale has snow gates; as does the Bealach na Ba which is frequently impassible for weeks at a time.

Also bear in mind that many of these roads traverse areas far from any population. During the winter getting stuck or sliding off the road can end up becoming a serious situation. Sleeping bags, blankets, a stove and food are essential, along with a torch and shovel. Winter tyres are strongly recommended.

*Those planning winter visits should check the weather forecast and plan their routes accordingly. In particular remote side roads may not be gritted or even cleared. Inland, temperatures can fall as low as minus 27C.* **Mobile phone reception cannot be relied upon in many of the remoter areas.**

## Distances And Estimated Driving Times

| | | |
|---|---|---|
| Inverness to Beauly | 12mi (19km) | 24min |
| Beauly to Garve | 15mi (24km) | 27min |
| Garve to Lochcarron | 37mi (60km) | 51min |
| Lochcarron to Applecross | 17mi (27km) | 42min |
| Applecross to Shieldaig | 24mi (39km) | 67min |
| Shieldaig to Gairloch | 37mi (60km) | 66min |
| Gairloch to Ullapool | 56mi (90km) | 82min |
| Ullapool to Lochinver | 36mi (58km) | 56min |
| Lochinver to Kylesku | 25mi (40km) | 72min |
| Kylesku to Durness | 35mi (56km) | 57min |
| Durness to Thurso | 73mi (117km) | 126min |
| Thurso to John o' Groats | 20mi (32km) | 31min |
| John o' Groats to Wick | 16mi (26km) | 24min |
| Wick to Helmsdale | 35mi (56km) | 48min |
| Helmsdale to Dornoch Bridge | 31mi (50km) | 45min |
| Dornoch Bridge to Dingwall | 31mi (50km) | 43min |
| Dingwall to Beauly | 9mi (14km) | 17min |
| Beauly to Inverness | 12mi (19km) | 24min |

**Side Trips**

| | | |
|---|---|---|
| Lochcarron to Eilean Donan | 21mi (34km) | 33min |
| Eilean Donan to Skye Bridge | 10mi (16km) | 14min |
| Skye Loop | c.150mi (240km) | 2-3 days |
| Lewis & Harris Loop | c.125mi (200km) | 2-3 days |
| North Sutherland Loop | c.30mi (50km) | 120min |
| Orkney Loop | 100mi (160km) | 2-3 days |
| Lairg & Bonar Bridge Loop | c.22mi (35km) | 60min |
| Black Isle Loop | 40mi (64km) | 64min |
| Loch Ness Loop | 67mi (109km) | half day |
| Inverness East Loop | 40mi (64km) | half day |

*Distances are by the most direct routes. Times may vary depending on traffic, time of day, weather, road works, drivers and vehicles.*

## Maps And Books Nc500

This book includes 1:250,000 Ordnance Survey based maps throughout to help navigation. Each area also has a smaller scale map to locate and describe it. The 1:250,000 OS Road Map 1 *"North Scotland, Orkney & Shetland"* is very good for navigation and route planning. NC500 produce a useful free map which is good for planning.

Many sites of interest have OS grid references of the style (XX123456). The UK is divided into 100km squares, each with a two letter code. These in turn are divided into 1km squares. Grid references are given with eastings followed by northings. It is assumed that visitors who are walking or cycling will be using the 1:50,000 Landranger Series or 1:25,000 Explorer Series maps. OS maps of the North Highlands are listed in the Bibliography.

Maps, GPS and compass should be carried when heading into remote regions. Digital offline OS maps are very useful on handheld devices because mobile phone signals are very patchy in most places. The use of a phone or GPS to geotag digital images will be found useful later when identifying images.

Suggested reading is included in the Bibliography. Local information centres and shops stock books related to the area as well as small booklets, brochures and other publications. VisitScotland produces information about accommodation, attractions, services and activities annually. The NC500 website is also an excellent source.

northcoast500.com

visitscotland.com

## Countryside Code

We are justly proud of our historic sites, wildlife and environment. Please help ensure that future visitors may enjoy them as much as you by observing these guidelines:

1. Always use stiles and gates, and close gates after you.
2. Always ask permission before entering agricultural land.
3. Keep to paths and take care to avoid fields of grass and crops.
4. Do not disturb livestock. Dogs must be kept under close control at all times, especially near livestock. Fields with cattle should be avoided.
5. Take your litter away with you and do not light fires.
6. Do not pollute water courses or supplies. Do not leave faeces or toilet paper.
7. Never disturb nesting birds.
8. Do not pick wild flowers or dig up plants.
9. Drive and park with care and attention. Do not obstruct.
10. Take care near cliffs and beaches, particularly with children and pets. Some beaches are dangerous for swimmers.
11. Walkers should take adequate clothes, wear suitable footwear and tell someone of their plans. In winter a torch, food and drink is recommended.
12. Above all please respect the life of the countryside, leave only footprints, take only photographs and pleasant memories.

*Notice: Whilst most of the sites of interest in this guide are open to the public and have marked access, many are on private land. No right of access is implied in the description, and if in doubt it is always polite to ask. Also, while many roads and tracks are rights of way, not all are.*

## Road Safety

is paramount on the NC500, as everywhere.
**1. The North Coast 500 is not a race** - take your time and enjoy it! Many of our roads are 'single track' which means that there are passing places to give way to oncoming traffic. If you are taking your time and enjoying the scenery, please be courteous and pull over to allow faster following traffic to pass.
**2. Watch where you stop** The route is full of beautiful views, but please remember to carefully consider where you pull over as it is not safe nor responsible to stop in a spot that may affect passing traffic. Always park appropriately and never in passing places.
**3. Speed** Although most rural roads may have a speed limit of 60mph always drive at a safe speed. The *"golden rule is that you must always be able to stop in the distance you can see to be clear ahead."* On winding narrow roads, the distance you can see to be clear ahead may be quite short. Also, always drive according to the weather conditions; in winter many stretches may become impassible in snow.
**4. Share the road** Many hikers, cyclists and bikers also use these roads. Obey the Highway Code and give them plenty of room when passing. Check your mirrors and blind spots for any oncoming bikers and allow them to pass.
**5. Share the road with animals** Sheep, cattle, deer and other animals are often encountered on these mostly unfenced roads. Take heed of any signs warning of animals, especially lambs. Hitting a Red Deer in the dark can be lethal. Do not sound your horn as this could frighten them and cause an accident!

*Inverness Castle and Flora MacDonald*

**Inverness Castle** marks the start of the NC500 route. Initially it follows the A862 westwards out of the city, crossing the River Ness and the Caledonian Canal before heading west along the southern shore of the Beauly Firth. There are panoramic views from Craig Phadraig (172m, NH640454) where there is an Iron Age vitrified fort.

*Beauly Town Square*

**Beauly** is an attractive village with an unspoilt centre of Victorian sandstone buildings. A stop here to explore its several interesting independent shops and cafés or the ruins of the 13th century Priory may be a good plan. From here the route heads north, then west, branching left just after Garve.

*Bealach na Ba*

**Applecross**, a remote settlement facing the Isle of Skye, is reached over the spectacular Bealach na Ba, at 629m the highest pass in Scotland. Not for the faint hearted this road offers spectacular views over Loch Carron and to the jagged Cuillin on Skye. The route is frequently impassible in winter due to snow and not advised for large vehicles or caravans.

*Torridon, Wester Ross*

**Torridon** has some of the finest mountain scenery anywhere in the UK. The imposing giants of Liathach (1064m) and Beinn Alligin (992m) rise steeply from sea level. Beinn Eighe (1010m) overlooks Loch Maree and is a National Nature Reserve. A visitor centre and network of paths make this an interesting stop.

**Gairloch** makes a good centre from which to explore Wester Ross. There are several very attractive beaches especially around Loch Ewe, as well as many narrow side roads to interesting places. Inverewe Gardens should not be missed, a barren hillside was transformed into particularly fine gardens and woodland.

*Sunset at Big Sand, Gairloch, Wester Ross*

**Ullapool** is the only large settlement in the whole of Wester Ross. It is the ferry port for Stornoway and has several very tempting independent shops. Ullapool is said to have some of the best fish and chips in the whole country. Fish is still landed here, especially prawns and scallops. North of Ullapool the lonely green mountains of the Coigach rear up to the west.

*Ullapool, Wester Ross*

**Assynt** is mostly wild country, dominated by Ben More Assynt and Quinag. From Elphin to Durness limestone outcrops cause unexpected greenery. Ardvreck Castle, on the shore of Loch Assynt, is a ruin. Lochinver nestles around its sheltered bay loomed over by Suilven (731m).

*Suilven looming over Lochinver, Sutherland*

*Kylesku Bridge, Assynt*

**Lochinver to Kylesku** via the B869 is a narrow, sinuous, switch back through remote countryside. With fine beaches and lovely views to the north and south this road can easily take half a day to traverse. It is not recommended for large vehicles or caravans. The curving Kylesku Bridge crosses the narrows of Kylestrome.

*Sango Sands, Durness, Sutherland*

*Stacks of Duncansby Winter Sunrise, Caithness*

*Sinclair & Girnigoe Castle, Noss Head, Wick*

*Achavanich Stone Setting, Caithness*

**Durness** is the most northwesterly settlement in Great Britain. Its dramatically situated campsite is well placed for exploring the many places of interest. These include Sandwood Bay, Kinlochbervie, Balnakeil Bay, Cape Wrath and of course the excellent beaches below the village. Balnakeil Craft Village is an old military base with eclectic shops.

**The North Coast** from Durness to John o' Groats is a slow road with many viewpoints and places to visit. Loch Eriboll, Tongue, Bettyhill and Melvich are a few. Thurso is the biggest town in the north and the ferry port for Orkney. The Castle of Mey was the northern home of the Queen Mother.

**John o' Groats** has had a major makeover in recent years. Nearby Duncansby Head and Stacks should not be missed. From here the road follows the coast to Wick, where dramatically sited Sinclair & Girnigoe Castle near Noss Head is an essential visit. Wick was once the Herring capital of Europe; its story is told in Wick Heritage Centre.

**Archaeology** South of Wick there are many good archaeological sites. These include the Grey Cairns of Camster, Achavanich Stone Setting and Yarrow Archaeological Trail. Whaligoe Steps were built to access the wharf in a large geo where Herring were once landed. They were gutted and packed at the top.

**Helmsdale** was mostly built in the 19th century as a planned fishing village. Timespan is a museum and art gallery near the old bridge which tells the story of the village and the sad events of the 19th century clearances. These are commemorated by the Emigrants Statue, which overlooks the village.

*Helmsdale with Whin (Gorse) in Bloom*

**Brora** has a wonderful beach where Jurassic fossils can be found in rocks at low tide. They also get washed out of the river banks and from the low cliffs to the south. Coal was formerly mined here which fired brickworks, salt pans and a distillery, still working.

*Dunrobin Castle, Golspie*

**Dunrobin Castle** is just north of Golspie. It has an enchanting appearance from a distance. Most of it dates from the 19th century, in the style of the Scottish Renaissance. The museum and gardens should not be missed. Falconry displays take place here.

*Dornoch Cathedral, Sutherland*

**Dornoch** is a lovely little town, built from warm coloured sandstone. Its cathedral dates from 1222, while its 16th century bishop's palace is now a luxury hotel. The former jail is now a large store selling all manner of Scottish items.

*Dingwall from Knockfarril*

**Dingwall** is now a tranquil settlement bypassed by the busy A9. Scotland's first champion haggis is made here, *"It boasts a nigh perfect melt in the mouth consistency which, quite simply, is never encountered elsewhere."*

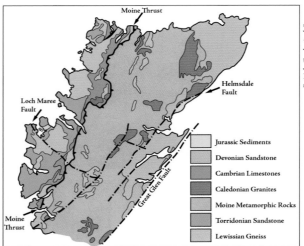

*British Geological Survey*

*Geology of the North Highlands*

Moine Thrust

Helmsdale Fault

Loch Maree Fault

Jurassic Sediments

Devonian Sandstone

Cambrian Limestones

Caledonian Granites

Moine Metamorphic Rocks

Torridonian Sandstone

Lewisian Gneiss

Great Glen Fault

Moine Thrust

**GEOLOGY** The highly varied and often spectacular scenery of the North Highlands is markedly influenced by the complex geology of the area.

**Lewisian Gneiss** forms the basement, but is only exposed west of the Moine Thrust. These Precambrian rocks formed deep in the Earth c.2,900Ma (million years ago). About 1,000Ma, as a result of erosion and uplift, they were exposed as the land surface. Today they give a rocky, ice-smoothed landscape, studded with lochans, which is very typical of north Sutherland.

**Torridonian Sandstone** was laid down from 1,000-750Ma as beds of red sandstone, conglomerate and grey shales up to 7km deep. The steep sided mountains of the northwest were formed by erosion of these hard sandstone beds. Applecross, Torridon and Coigach are typical of such landscapes.

**Moine Succession** East of the Moine Thrust another deep succession of sandstones and shales was deposited. Later, c.750Ma, they were metamorphosed deep within the Earth's crust. A rolling, rather

featureless landscape of hills, peatbogs and lochans results, forming most of the interior.

**Cambrian Quartzite**, Shales and Limestones were laid down in a shallow ocean near the coast. Many of the mountains of the west are capped by Quartzite, which shines brightly in the sun. Limestone outcrops at Elphin, Inchnadamph and Durness create havens of green grass and wild flowers.

**Caledonian Orogeny** In the Ordovician, c.500Ma, a major continental collision resulted in the formation of a huge mountain range called the Caledonides. The rocks were deformed and some were metamorphosed deep in the Earth.

**Moine Thrust** During the Caledonian Orogeny Moine rocks were pushed westwards over younger rocks to form the Moine Thrust Zone. This runs from the east of Loch Eriboll to Sleat in Skye. The North West Highlands Geopark covers the northern part of this zone.

**Old Red Sandstone** (Devonian) was laid down in thick beds as the Caledonides were

*Beinn Eighe*

*Loch Glencoul and the Moine Thrust*

eroded. This sandstone covers most of Caithness, the east coast of Sutherland and Easter Ross, including the Black Isle. The landscape is rolling and soils are fertile.

**Jurassic period** rocks were laid down in shallow seas. Sandstone, limestone and shale beds accumulated. The Brora coal seams and offshore North Sea Oil date from this time, while the Helmsdale Boulder Bed, best seen at Portgower, near Helmsdale, is slightly later.

**Fossils** exist in several places. Pipe Rock and Fucoid Beds in Torridonian Sandstone beds may be seen in road cuttings beside Loch Assynt. The Old Red Sandstones and Flagstones of Caithness are famous for their abundant fish fossils. Quarry waste at Achanarras (ND151545), north of Spittal, can be searched for fossils.

Jurassic rocks on the coast at Helmsdale, Brora, below Dunrobin Castle as well as at Balintore and Eathie on the Black Isle hold many plant and animal fossils. These range from tropical plants to corals, ammonites, molluscs and other marine animals.

**Glaciation** The results of the Ice Ages are evident everywhere, from the ice-smoothed, scratched rocks of the northwest to the smooth contours of much of the area. Glacial erratics are common, boulders have been carried often long distances by glaciers and then dumped as the ice melted. Hanging valleys, huge corries and box canyons are a few of the common features.

Only a few of the higher mountain tops in the west stood out from the ice sheet, their quartzite peaks shattered into scree by freezing and thawing. By 11,000BC most of the ice had gone, although there was a further advance around 9,000BC when glaciers again formed. Soon after, the climate warmed rapidly and all the ice melted.

*Lewisian Gneiss*

*Torridonian Sandstone*

*Cambrian Limestone*

| GEOLOGY SITES TO VISIT | |
|---|---|
| Assynt | 80 |
| Bealach na Ba | 54 |
| Brora | 144 |
| Caithness | 118 |
| Coigach | 78 |
| Contin | 182 |
| Cromarty | 176 |
| Durness | 98 |
| Geopark | 89 |
| Glencoul | 88 |
| Golspie | 147 |
| Great Glen | 193 |
| Handa | 94 |
| Helmsdale | 141 |
| Inchnadamph | 82 |
| Knockan Crag | 80 |
| Loch Eriboll | 106 |
| Torridon | 58 |

*Old Red Sandstone*

*Knockan Crag and the Moine Thrust*

*Puffins*

**BIRDERS** will find the NC500 very enticing in every season. Many otherwise rare species breed here, may migrate through or overwinter. The best places to see many of these birds are nature reserves with hides, which can offer good views without disturbance. It is important to avoid approaching breeding birds, especially those which are classed as Schedule 1 species.

**Raptors** include Golden and White-tailed Eagles, Red Kite, Osprey and Hen Harrier. Buzzards are common, while Merlin is more often seen in winter. Eagles are more likely to be observed in remote areas in the west. White-tailed Eagles are much less wary than their cousins. Loch Fleet is a good place to see Osprey; the Black Isle is the place for Red Kite.

**Mountains & Streams** Ptarmigan, Dotterel, Snow Bunting and Ring Ouzel breed on the high tops. Lower down, Dipper are frequently seen feeding underwater on the many streams. Where there are suitable banks, Kingfishers flash colourfully as they dive for fish while Yellow Wagtail patrol the margins.

**Lochs** The countless lochs and lochans are home to Red-throated and Black-throated Divers and many species of ducks including the rare Goosander and Pintail. The car can often double as a hide and allow good views over lochs without disturbance.

**Moorland** The vast areas of moorland here support large numbers of breeding waders, such as Greenshank, Redshank, Golden Plover, Oystercatcher, Curlew, Whimbrel and Dunlin.

**Woodland** species include Capercaillie, Black Grouse, Crossbill and Crested Tit. They are much more likely to be heard rather than seen.

**Seabirds** breed on small islands, such as Handa, but also on suitable cliffs all round the coast. Caithness and the north of Sutherland have the largest mainland colonies. Gannets do not breed here but are frequently seen plunge diving off the coast.

**Migration** Many species which breed in the far north pass through or overwinter in the North Highlands. Greylag, Greenland White-fronted, Pink-footed and Barnacle Geese may all be seen. Great Northern Divers overwinter, along with many species of waders and ducks.

Migrating seabirds can be observed from headlands. Tarbat Ness, Chanonry Ness, Rubdh Reidh, Point of Stoer, and Strathy Point are all good seawatching places and can also be good for cetaceans.

Many thousands of waders and waterfowl overwinter here. The estuaries and firths of Easter Ross are especially popular. Loch Fleet NNR is one of the best year round sites for water birds. Observation from the car parked near the shore at high tide is best.

*Red-throated Divers*

*Arctic Skua*

*Osprey*

*Ptarmigan*

*White-tailed Eagle*
*Black-throated Divers*

*Laurie Campbell*

## BIRDWATCHING SITES

### Easter Ross

| | |
|---|---|
| Black Isle (Red Kites) | 179 |
| Chanonry Ness | 174 |
| Cromarty Firth | 169 |
| Fairy Glen | 176 |
| Munlochy Bay | 174 |
| Nigg Bay RSPB Reserve | 168 |
| Struie Hill | 158 |
| Tarbat Ness | 166 |
| Tollie (Red Kites) | 182 |
| Udale Bay | 179 |

### Wester Ross

| | |
|---|---|
| Gairloch | 66 |
| Gruinard Bay | 71 |
| Inverewe Gardens | 69 |
| Loch Ewe | 70 |
| Loch Kishorn | 50 |
| Loch Maree & Beinn Eighe | 60 |
| Redpoint | 65 |
| Rubdh Reidh | 68 |

### West Sutherland

| | |
|---|---|
| Assynt | 81 |
| Handa | 94 |
| Lochinver | 84 |
| Point of Stoer | 86 |
| River Kirkaig | 84 |

### North Sutherland

| | |
|---|---|
| Forsinard Flows RSPB | 115 |
| Loch Eriboll | 106 |
| Melvich | 113 |
| Strath Halladale | 114 |
| Strathy Point | 112 |
| Torrisdale Bay | 111 |

### Caithness

| | |
|---|---|
| Berridale | 136 |
| Dunnet Bay | 122 |
| Dunnet Head | 124 |
| Duncansby Head | 127 |
| Noss Head | 128 |
| Scrabster Harbour | 122 |

### East Sutherland

| | |
|---|---|
| Achany Glen | 155 |
| Balblair Woods | 147 |
| Dalchork Bird Hide | 155 |
| Ferry Links | 147 |
| Lemore & Migdale Woods | 159 |
| Loch Fleet | 148 |

## BREEDING BIRDS

### Raptors

Golden Eagle
Hen Harrier
Osprey
Peregrine
Raven
Red Kite
White-tailed Eagle

### Mountains

Dotterel
Ptarmigan
Ring Ouzel

### Streams, Rivers & Lochs

Black-throated Diver
Dipper
Goosander
Red-throated Diver
Yellow Wagtail

### Seabirds

Arctic & Sandwich Tern
Fulmar Petrel
Gannet
Great & Arctic Skua
Guillemot Razorbill
Gulls
Puffin

### Woodland

Black Grouse
Capercaillie
Crested Tit
Crossbill

### Croftland

Corncrake
Skylark
Stonechat
Wheatear

### Waders

Common Sandpiper
Curlew
Dunlin
Golden Plover
Greenshank
Lapwing
Oystercatcher
Redshank
Ringed Plover

### Waterfowl

Eider Duck
Grey Heron
Pintail
Shelduck
Greylag Goose

*Loch a' Muillin*

**FLORA** The North Highlands are a botanist's paradise with a huge range of habitats, geography, micro climates and soil types.

**The Coast** extends for many hundreds of miles and ranges from very exposed beaches and headlands to sheltered bays and firths. The NC500 route passes close to the coast for much of its length, offering prime chances to explore seaside wild flowers.

**Limestone** outcrops in a band which extends from Durness and Loch Eriboll in the north to Loch Alsh in the south. Inchnadamph in Assynt has particularly extensive exposures. These limestone areas are immediately obvious with the sudden appearance of lush meadows after miles of moorland. Many interesting plants

*One-flowered Wintergreen*

grow here, which do not thrive elsewhere.

**Roadside Verges**, especially on minor roads which are not mowed frequently, provide a very good environment for many wild flowers. Meadows which are only lightly grazed and never fertilised are found away from the main agricultural areas in Easter Ross and Caithness.

**Farmland and Field Margins** can be excellent places to look for wild flowers, especially away from intensively cultivated areas. Much croftland is only lightly grazed and rarely if ever cultivated. Places where cattle graze are generally much more interesting botanically.

**Moorland** covers much of the interior of the North Highlands. This ranges from heather moors to the wetlands of the Flow Country. Limestone and Old Red Sandstone are permeable, but Lewisian Gneiss and Moine Schist are impermeable, and often peat covered. In late summer the moors are a riot of colour as Heather, Cross-leaved Heath and Bell Heather bloom.

Forsinard Flows RSPB Reserve is of particular interest for its plants, including carnivorous Sundews. Many lochans are covered with White Water Lilies in summer.

**Woodland** formerly covered vast areas of the Highlands. Most of this was Scots Pine and Oak. Very little natural woodland now remains except in isolated places which grazing sheep and deer cannot access such as small islands. Examples of ancient woodland can be found at Rassal in Kishorn and Loch a' Muillin near Kylesku.

Ledmore & Migdale Forest, near Spinningdale has some native trees and makes a very varied botanical walk with excellent views from the top. Struie Hill, southeast of Bonar Bridge provides access to a remote and scenic section of partially forested moorland and makes a fine diversion off the main A9.

Loch Fleet NNR is of great interest botanically. Balblair pinewood is planted but has been maintained rather than chopped down. It is situated on the north shore of Loch

*Creeping Ladies' Tresses*

Fleet near Littleferry. Rare species here include One-flowered Wintergreen, Twinflower and Creeping Ladies Tresses.

**Upland and Montane** areas can extend down to sea level here. Plants which usually grow in the high tops can be found on the seashore, especially in Limestone areas. In the north the Durness area and around Torrisdale Bay are good examples. The paths in the Beinn Eighe NNR are of great interest for wild flowers.

*Yellow Saxifrage*

*Oblong-leaved Sundew*

*Bog Cotton*

*White Water Lily*

*Globeflower*

### FLORA - SITES

**Coast**

| | |
|---|---|
| Cromarty Firth | 169 |
| Duncansby Head | 127 |
| Durness | 98 |
| Melvich | 113 |
| Sandwood Bay | 97 |
| Strathy Point | 112 |
| Torrisdale Bay | 111 |

**Limestone & Dunes**

| | |
|---|---|
| Durness | 98 |
| Elphin | 81 |
| Faraid Head | 103 |
| Inchnadamph | 82 |
| Raasal Ashwood, Kishorn | 51 |
| Torrisdale Bay | 111 |

**Moorland & Marshes**

| | |
|---|---|
| Forsinard RSPB Reserve | 115 |
| Loch Fleet | 148 |
| Munlochy Bay | 174 |
| Nigg Bay RSPB Reserve | 168 |

**Woodland**

| | |
|---|---|
| Balblair, Golspie | 147 |
| Beinn Eighe | 60 |
| Loch a' Muillin | 93 |

**Upland & Montane**

| | |
|---|---|
| Beinn Eighe | 60 |
| Beinn Wyvis | 47 |

### FLORA

**Coast**

Eyebright
Grass of Parnassus
Ladies Bedstraw
*Primula scotica*
Red Campion
Scots Lovage
Scurvy Grass
Sea Aster
Sea Campion
Sea Centaury
Spring Squill
Thrift

**Limestone**

Dark Red Helleborine
Mountain Avens
Yellow Saxifrage
Roseroot

**Inland, Verges, Farmland**

Broom
Early Marsh Orchid
Frog Orchid
Gorse
Kidney Vetch
Lesser Twayblade

**Moorland & Marshes**

Bell Heather
Bog Asphodel
Bog Cotton
Bog Myrtle
Bogbean
Butterwort
Cranberry
Cross-leaved Heath
Globe Flower
Heather
Sundew
Water Avens
White Water Lilies
Woodrush

**Pinewoods**

Bellflower
Creeping Ladies Tresses
One-flowered Wintergreen

**Upland & Montane**

Autumn Gentian
Alpine Ladies Mantle
Dwarf Juniper
Mountain Bearberry
Mountain Saxifrage
Mountain Sorrel

*Red Deer*

**LAND FAUNA**  Most of Britain's endemic species of mammals can be observed in the North Highlands. For many of them this is one of the best parts of the country to catch glimpses of rare mammals.

**Red Deer** are common. Stags and hinds are separate for most of the year, the former tending to roam higher into the mountains; the latter remain on richer pasture. In winter they move to lower ground, where they are easier to see. In the rut, from September to November, stags try to dominate groups of hinds with roaring contests, and antler fights. Calving is in May or June.

**Roe Deer** are smaller and prefer mixed woodland and lower ground. They are more solitary and have a white chin, black moustache and a cream-coloured rump. The males have small antlers with three or less points. During the rut, in July and August the males compete aggressively to mate with the females. Kids are born in late May. They are generally seen around dawn and dusk.

**Otters** are common around the coast, particularly near burn mouths. Their spraints are often left on small green mounds. The best time to see them is in early morning; with patience and by keeping quiet they can be seen at quite close quarters.

**Scottish Wildcats** are very timid and rarely seen. Larger than domestic cats with brown with black stripes, they hunt at night. Apart from mating, they are solitary and silent; like domestic cats, females caterwaul to attract males. Under 500 exist in the wild. They prefer forests, but hunt widely. Their prime threat is interbreeding with domestic cats.

**Short-tailed Vole**  The Vole is more stumpy than a mouse, with short rounded ears, and a short tail. It is normally darkish brown. They occupy moorland, marshland, grassland, field margins and ditches, where long runs are made from the nests. They are preyed upon by Hen Harrier, Short-eared Owl and Kestrel.

**Pipistrelles**, the smallest and commonest bats in UK, are mouse sized nocturnal insect feeders which use echo location to find their prey. They may eat several thousand midgies in a night. Bats roost in buildings or caves and hibernate in winter. They are most active in late evening just before dark in places with plenty of insects.

**Red Squirrels** are under threat elsewhere from the larger Grey Squirrel which has not gained a hold in the North Highlands. Their favourite food is pine cones; piles of chewed debris indicate their presence. They leave scratches on trees and

*Roe Deer*

*Otter*

*Laurie Campbell*

build large conspicuous dreys in tree forks. During courtship in spring or summer they become much more obvious as males fearlessly chase females.

**Mountain Hares** have a bluish grey coat well suited as camouflage. In winter it turns white, making them almost invisible in the snow. There can be three litters in a season; many leverets fall victim to Golden Eagles and Buzzards. In spring, they are conspicuous until their summer coat grows in; Mad March hares box each other and jump around, so they are much more easily seen.

**Foxes** can be seen almost anywhere in the North Highlands; although hunting with hounds is illegal, they are still heavily persecuted. Opportunistic hunters, they will eat almost anything, including eggs, nestlings, poultry and sickly lambs. Vixens have one litter of cubs in late spring. Foxes normally live in loose family units and are very shy of humans.

**Pine Martens** are members of the weasel family which inhabit Pine forests. About the size of a domestic cat, they were persecuted almost to extinction in the UK for their fur and because they prey on gamebirds' eggs and chicks. They are curious as well as aggressive hunters with darkish brown fur and a yellow bib. They are active around dusk and at night; a piece of bread and jam attracts them. They prey on Grey Squirrels and so may help the Red Squirrel.

**Badger** is present in the North Highlands. Normally nocturnal, they breed in winter; cubs are born in February in the sett. These underground dens are often traceable by trails left in the undergrowth. Sett watches are organised where people can observe these animals as they forage for food.

**Adder** Our only poisonous snake is recognizable from their zig zag patterned backs. They are often seen basking in the sun on large stones, or paths. They inhabit woodland margins or open heathland and prey on small rodents and young birds. Adders hibernate in the winter; in spring the males fight with each other for supremacy in the *Dance of the Adders*.

*Laurie Campbell*

*Pine Marten*

*Laurie Campbell*

*Red Squirrel*

*Laurie Campbell*

*Mountain Hare*

*Laurie Campbell*

*Adder*

*Wild Cat*

*Laurie Campbell*

| FAUNA - LAND |
|---|
| Adder |
| Mountain Hare |
| Otter |
| Pine Marten |
| Red Deer |
| Red Squirrel |
| Roe Deer |
| Scottish Wild Cat |

*Common Seal Mother & Pup*

**MARINE FAUNA** The North Highlands offer many opportunities to see seals, dolphins and whales. Boat trips are run all round the coast and offer the best chances of seeing cetaceans. Common Seals haul out in many places, but Grey Seals tend to be harder to find.

**Grey Seals** can be seen at all times of year, but most often during the breeding season. Females come ashore on small islands and sheltered coves from late September to pup and mate. The pups are weaned at about four weeks. The seals then leave the breeding grounds for the open sea.

.
Adult males reach 2.3m and up to 300kg, while females average 2m and 120kg. Males are sexually mature at 6 or 7 years, but do not gain the social status to breed until at least

10 years. They do not survive much beyond 20 years. Cows commence breeding at 6-7 years and may survive and bear pups until at least 35 years.

Pups are born with a silky white coat, and gain weight rapidly on very rich milk. The mothers identify their pups by smell, and they are very defensive. The pups moult at 3-4 weeks to a beautiful silver-blue-grey coat, and are ready for sea at 5-6 weeks. Cows mate at 3-4 weeks after giving birth and may copulate with several bulls. There are c.100,000 Grey Seals in Scottish waters, about 36% of the world population.

**Common Seals** are smaller, at about 1.9m, and more coastal in habitat. They may be seen all round the shores on skerries, small islands, and

sand banks at low tide. Pups are born in late June and July, in their adult coat, having moulted in the uterus. Though they can swim within hours of birth, it takes about 3 weeks before they become strong enough to haul themselves up the beach. They suckle for several weeks on the tide line and keep a close maternal relationship for an extended period.

There are over 20,000 Common Seals in Scottish waters, about 5% of the world population, but numbers have declined in recent years. The reasons are unclear but predation by Killer Whales, or disease, could be causes. In general the species is much less social than Grey Seals, although they do haul out in large groups in several places, especially round the shores of the Cromarty Firth.

**Cetaceans** About twenty species of whales have been recorded around the coasts of Scotland with increasing numbers in recent years. There is a good chance of seeing one or more species, either from various headlands, from a ferry or during a boat trip.

*Grey Seal Mother & Pup*

*Grey Seal Moulted Pup*

*Bottle-nosed Dolphin*

*Killer Whale or Orca*

**Blackfish** (smaller, toothed whales) usually live in groups. The Long-finned Pilot or Caain' Whale is mostly a pelagic species, rarely seen inshore. They used to be driven or caa'd ashore in large numbers as still is done in the Faeroes. They are jet black, with a small dorsal fin and reach up to 6m.

**Baleen Whales** or Rorquals can be sighted, the most common being the Minke. They may be seen from headlands, but more often at sea, especially around the Pentland Firth and in the Minch. They are quite distinctive, with a dorsal fin, small size and white striped flippers. Known by fishermen as the *Herring Hog*, most sightings are from April to October, especially July to September, when shoals of Herring and Mackerel come inshore.

**Humpbacks** are increasingly seen inshore, suggesting that numbers may be recovering. Other whales, such as Fin, Sei and Blue Whales are sometimes seen offshore as they migrate south along the continental shelf, but more usually when they come ashore dead.

**Sperm Whales** are seen most years, usually between September and January. The blow, head shape, small dorsal hump and back knuckles are diagnostic. Dead specimens are washed up sometimes, and there are occasional strandings.

**Dolphins** Several species of Dolphin frequent these waters, including Harbour Porpoise, often seen in bays feeding on small fish, or, from boats, usually in summer. White-beaked and Risso's Dolphin also occur

in the Minch and the Pentland Firth. White-sided Dolphin is pelagic, but is sometimes seen from boats or headlands.

**Bottle-nosed Dolphin** are present all year in the Moray Firth, but are regularly seen all round the coast, especially in the east and on the Pentland Firth, where they often chase shoals of Herring or Mackerel.

**Killer Whales or Orca**, prefer deeper water. They are seen off headlands, sometimes very close to the shore, usually in the Pentland Firth or the Minch. The tall dorsal fin, white chin and eye patch are unmistakable. Males average 7.3m and females 6.2m in length. Groups have different behaviours, some seem to prefer seals as prey while others prefer Herring and Mackerel.

*Humpback Whale*

| Fauna - Marine |
| --- |
| Grey Seal |
| Common Seal |
| Bottle-nosed Dolphin |
| Risso's Dolphin |
| White-sided Dolphin |
| Killer Whale (Orca) |
| Minke Whale |
| Humpback Whale |

# North Highlands Time Line

BC
c.11000 Ice retreats
c.6000 Grassland, Oak and Pine forest, Birch and Hazel-scrub
c.6000 First (Mesolithic) people Evidence at Sand, Applecross
c.4000 First known farmers Vegetation more open
3800 Climate deteriorates
3000 Chambered Tombs being used
2700 *Start of Great Pyramid Age*
2600 Trees in decline in many areas
c.2500 Bronze Age, Achavanich Stone Setting
1300 Peat bogs developing
1159 *Hekla in Iceland erupts*
700 Iron Age round houses
600 Oldest Broch deposits
c.325 Pytheas circumnavigates Britain
214 *Great Wall of China*
100 Brochs in peak period
AD
33 *Death of Christ*
43 Orkney submits to Claudius
83 Agricola's fleet visits the north
c.100 Brochs falling into disuse
297 Eumenius first refers to "Picts"
c.500 Celtic monks arrive Scotti moving over from Ireland
c.550 Portmahomack monastery
600 Norsemen appear in West
632 *Death of Muhammad*
c.673 Applecross Monastery founded
793 Major Viking raids begin
800s Norse migration
839 Major battle Vikings v Picts
843 Kenneth MacAlpin King Pictish/Scottish Kingdom
c.872 Harald Fairhair King Norway Sigurd of More, Earl of Orkney
995 Earl Sigurd the Stout baptised
1000 *Leif Erikson discovers America*
1014 Thorfinn, Earl of Orkney
1035 Battle off Tarbat Ness
1057 Death of MacBeth
1065 Earl Thorfinn the Mighty dies
1066 William - Viking takes England
1098 Magnus Barelegs expedition
1117 Murder of Magnus
1124 Diocese of Ross
1145 Diocese of Caithness founded
1151 Earl Rognvald to Holy Land
1153 St Duthac buried in Tain
1171 Sweyn Asleifson killed, Dublin
1197 Thurso Castle slighted by King William the Lion
1216 Rosemarkie a Royal Burgh
1221 Fearn Abbey established
1222 Bishop Adam burnt at Halkirk, Bishop Gilbert appointed
1224 Dornoch Cathedral started
1231 Last Norse Earl murdered

c.1235 First Earl of Sutherland
1263 Battle of Largs, Haakon dies
c.1264 Dingwall and Cromarty became Royal Burghs
1290 Margaret, Maid of Norway, dies
1300 Dutch already fishing herring
1314 Battle of Bannockburn
1379 Earl Henry Sinclair I
1398 Henry Sinclair visits America??
1455 Royal Burgh of Fortrose and Rosemarkie
1468 Orkney mortgaged
1470 Sinclair Earl resigns
1492 *Columbus reaches America*
c.1500 Jan de Groot starts ferry
1513 Battle of Flodden
1517 Battle of Torran Dubh, Rogart
1528 Battle of Summerdale
1529 Coal mining at Brora
1540 King James V visits North
1567 James VI becomes King
1586 Battle of Leckmelm
1588 Spanish Armada - many wrecks
1589 Wick became a Royal Burgh
1600s Herring fishery important
1602 Strome Castle blown up
1603 Union of Crowns
1607 Iron smelting at Loch Maree
1633 Thurso a Burgh of Barony
c.1660 Brahan Seer burnt to death
1666 *Great Fire of London; Newton realises gravity*
1698 Herring Fishing in Loch Broom
1715 First Jacobite Rebellion
1719 Eilean Donan castle blown up
1721 Kelp-making introduced
1723 Bernera Barracks, Glenelg
1725 Pirate Gow captured
1739 Reay Parish Kirk
1745 Second Jacobite Rebellion
1746 Inverness Castle blown up Battle of Culloden
1747 Hanoverians burn Coigach
1769 Whaligoe first mentioned
c.1770 Grass, clover and turnip seeds introduced, farming reforms
1772 Cromarty harbour developed
1773 First immigrant ship sails from Loch Broom to Nova Scotia
1776 *American Declaration of Independence*
1788 Ullapool village established
1790 Balblair Distillery established Telford survey of harbours
1794 Lighthouses Pentland Skerries Plockton founded
1798 Thurso new town laid out
1800 Over 200 boats at Wick First clearances at Strath Oykel
1801 Telford survey of roads
1802 Lybster development begins
1803 Wick Harbour developments

1804 Roadbuilding started
1810 Shieldaig Village started
1814 Helmsdale planned village
1816 The Mound constructed
1819 First pump room Strathpeffer
1822 Bealach na Ba road opens Caledonian Canal opens
1825 First flagstones leave Castlehill
1826 Old Pulteney Distillery
1828 Cape Wrath lighthouse first lit
1830 Collapse of Kelp Boom Sandside Harbour built
1831 Dunnet Head lighthouse lit Keiss Harbour built
1836 First Black Isle Show
1845 Croick Kirk clearance graffiti
1846 Inverness new Castle
1855 Steamer Stromness to Scrabster Inverness to Nairn railway
1856 Inverness to Perth Railway
1862 Peak of Wick Herring Fishing Inverewe Gardens started
1868 Kildonan Gold rush
1874 Railway to Thurso and Wick
1882 Thurso Esplanade
1884 Napier Report on crofting
1892 SS St Ola I starts long service
1894 Kyle Line opens
1898 Inverness to Perth Direct opens
1913 Brora gets electricity
1914 World War I
1915 HMS *Natal* blows up
1920 NZ Clover introduced
1937 End of Herring boom
1939 World War II,
1941 Anthrax on Gruinard Island
1951 MV St Ola II commissioned Beinn Eighe NNR
1952 Queen Mother Castle of Mey
1955 Dounreay NPDE work started
1956 Stroma evacuated
1959 Russia launches first satellite
1969 First landing on the Moon
1973 Ro-ro ferries start with Scrabster to Stromness and Ullapool to Stornoway
1974 Local Authorities formed
1975 Kishorn construction yard open
1976 Beatrice Oil Field
1979 Cromarty Bridge
1982 Kessock Bridge
1984 Kylesku Bridge
1991 Dornoch Bridge
1994 Dounreay shut down
1995 Skye Bridge opens
2002 new pier at Scrabster
2005 North Highlands Initiative
2008 Caithness Horizons opened
2009 North Highlands Guide Book
2014 NC500 route established
2016 First Maygen tidal turbine
2017 NC500 Guide Book

*Summer Sunrise over Sango Sands, Durness*

After the end of the last Ice Age, about 13,000 years ago, Mesolithic nomadic hunters arrived in Scotland. By 4000BC, Neolithic farmers were well settled here and for over 1,500 years their culture flourished. The houses, tombs and standing stones that we can see today are among the most spectacular Neolithic monuments in Europe.

The Bronze Age succeeded the Neolithic Age. These people left behind burnt mounds, middens, cists, and barrow graves as well as ruins of small houses. This period was marked by climatic deterioration and changes in society as well as the appearance of bronze tools and weapons.

From c.700BC the introduction of iron for tools and weapons was revolutionary. Large round houses started to be built; later the spectacular brochs, some with settlements, became fashionable. From c.AD43, as part of the Pictish Kingdom, the North Highlands had more outside cultural influence from Romans, Christians, the British and the Irish Scotti.

Beginning in the 8th century Scandinavian incursions started to occur in Scotland, probably not in huge numbers at first. Large scale migration took place during the 9th century, followed by the Golden Age of the Vikings.

The Norse domination of much of the North Highlands lasted for nearly 500 years and this influence can still be seen in many placenames today. The North of Scotland was of great strategic importance during Viking times, and the exploits of the Earls and their supporters are related colourfully in the *Orkneyinga Saga*.

Medieval times saw a large influx of Lowland Scots attracted by the rich lands of Easter Ross. However the remoter areas of the west and northwest remained so for centuries to come. Internecine clan warfare continued until the end of the 16th century. It was only in the mid 17th century before the trade in black

*Achavanich Stone Setting, Caithness*

*Sallachy Broch, Lairg, Sutherland*

*Culloden Visitor Centre*

cattle grew into a major export industry in the Highlands and Islands for a time.

The various Jacobite uprisings were the result of the Stuart King James II being overthrown by Parliament in 1688. He was replaced by William of Orange and his wife, Anne, nephew and daughter of the ousted King. The result was a constitutional monarchy and nearly 60 years of unrest

as various Jacobite supporters attempted to restore the Stuarts.

After the final Jacobite rout in 1746, at Culloden, the government realised the urgent need for accurate maps. King George II ordered Lieutenant Colonel David Watson to make a military survey of Scotland. This was completed in 1755 at a scale of 1:36,000 and led to the founding of the

Ordnance Survey in 1791. By 1823 most of the UK had been surveyed and mapped.

The government finally began to take the development of the Highlands and Islands seriously. At first this was from a military point of view. Fort George was completed in 1769, after 21 years of work and at a cost of £200,000.

The Clearances started as early as 1732 in Skye, but it was in the early 19th century that they really got under way. Tens of thousands of native inhabitants emigrated. As a result, many remote areas remain virtually uninhabited today.

Karl Marx observed in *Das Kapital*, 1867, *"The spoliation of the church's property, the fraudulent alienation of the*

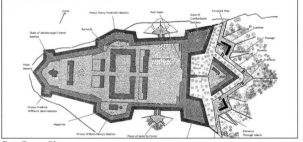

*Fort George Plan*

*Caledonian Canal at Fort Augustus*

*Bridge Street, Wick in the early 20th century*

*Ullapool in the early 19th century*

*State domains, the robbery of the common lands, the usurpation of feudal and clan property, and its transformation into modern private property under circumstances of reckless terrorism."*

Paradoxically, the start of the mass emigrations and clearances coincided with the beginning of massive inward investment to the Highlands and Islands. However these dramatic changes to civil society were not at first instigated by the government. In former times access to most of the North Highlands was easier by boat, which partially explains the lack of inland settlement.

Two developments catalysed progress. The Highland Society of London was formed in 1778 with *"the view of establishing and supporting schools in the Highlands and in the Northern parts of Great Britain, for relieving distressed Highlanders at a distance from their native homes, for preserving the antiquities and rescuing from oblivion the valuable remains of Celtic literature, and for promoting the improvement and general welfare of the Northern parts of Great Britain".*

In 1786 the British Fisheries Society was founded as a semi government body. With a capital of £150,000 the aim was to develop harbours and fishing stations around the coast. The main intent was to provide employment to those forced off the land by agricultural changes, as well as to provide a supply of seamen for the Royal Navy. In an astute move, Thomas Telford was appointed as its engineer.

*General Wade*

*Kessock Bridge*

# A Brief History

*Caledonian Canal*

ment brought heavy investment in services housing and infrastructure. However, the population has remained stubbornly low except around Inverness. Unlike in other areas, the impact of humans also remains minimal.

The region was further opened up with the advent of steam power in the 19th century when sea transport became more reliable and railways were built. During the later 19th and first half of the 20th century there have been the effects of the boom in Herring fishing and two World Wars.

Successful villages include Ullapool and Tobermory (1788). Pulteneytown, next to Wick (1808) grew to be the biggest fishing port in Britain during the Herring Boom. The government soon became involved and began decades of road and bridge provision, port construction and of course the Caledonian Canal. During this time 920 miles of road and 120 bridges were built under Telford's supervision.

In the 19th century, landowners such as the Duke of Sutherland and the Caithness Sinclairs, also invested heavily in harbours and planned settlements. Examples include many coastal villages, including Brora and Helmsdale in East Sutherland. Landowners were also expected to build roads themselves.

In the 20th century, wars and attempted industrial develop-

The Loch Ness Monster, for centuries the subject of folklore, came to the attention of the media with a supposed sighting in 1933. The publication of a supposed photograph in 1934 created huge interest and did much to stimulate interest in Loch Ness and the North Highlands. Huge numbers of tourists, journalists, scientists and Nessie hunters thronged to the scene, and continue to do so today.

After WWII there were great strides in agriculture,

*Urquhart Castle & Loch Ness Steamer*

*Fort Augustus Locks*

*PS Gondolier on the Caledonian Canal*

*Oil Rig off Invergordon*

## THOMAS TELFORD

The name Thomas Telford (1757-1834) crops up many times in the North of Scotland in connection with roads, harbours, bridges and churches. Born in Dumfries he was dubbed *"The Collosus of Roads"* in a pun by his friend, poet Robert Southey. Telford virtually invented the concept of civil engineering.

Having made his reputation in England, Telford was commissioned by the government to survey Scottish roads in 1801. Over the next 20 years over 900 miles of roads, 120 bridges and the Caledonian Canal were built. He oversaw construction of much of the road network in use today and built piers, harbours and even towns, such as Wick or Invergordon.

The "Parliamentary Churches" were built from 1823 in 32 places where none previously existed. Most of these standardly designed churches and manses survive today, despite being constructed as cheaply as possible. They were a symbol of the future of engineering and design.

especially in Easter Ross and Caithness. From the 1970s, North Sea Oil brought work in construction and offshore. An influx of large numbers of workers from England and the Lowlands helped to reverse the population decline.

In the 1970s and 1980s much public investment was made into infrastructure, especially roads and bridges. However this all ground to a halt, leaving half completed roads all over the Highlands. Work is in progress to make the A9 from Perth to Inverness fully dual carriageway. However many main roads in the west remain single track, unsuitable for heavy traffic.

In recent years Inverness has become one of the fastest growing areas in the UK.

Many hi-tech companies have chosen to relocate or etablish themselves here, so that the city now has a thriving and diverse economy. Elsewhere in the area, commerce still mainly depends upon natural resources, including agriculture, fishing, fish farming, whisky and crafts. Nevertheless, tourism remains the single most important industry here, depending on the vast unspoilt countryside.

*Thomas Telford*

*Fort Augustus*

*Jacobean Cruises, Caledonian Canal*

*Inverness and the River Ness from the Castle*

7. Kylesku to

6. Ullapool to K

5. Gairloch to Ullapool p66

4. Shieldaig to Gairloch p58

3. Garve to Applecross p48

2. I

Kyle of Lochalsh

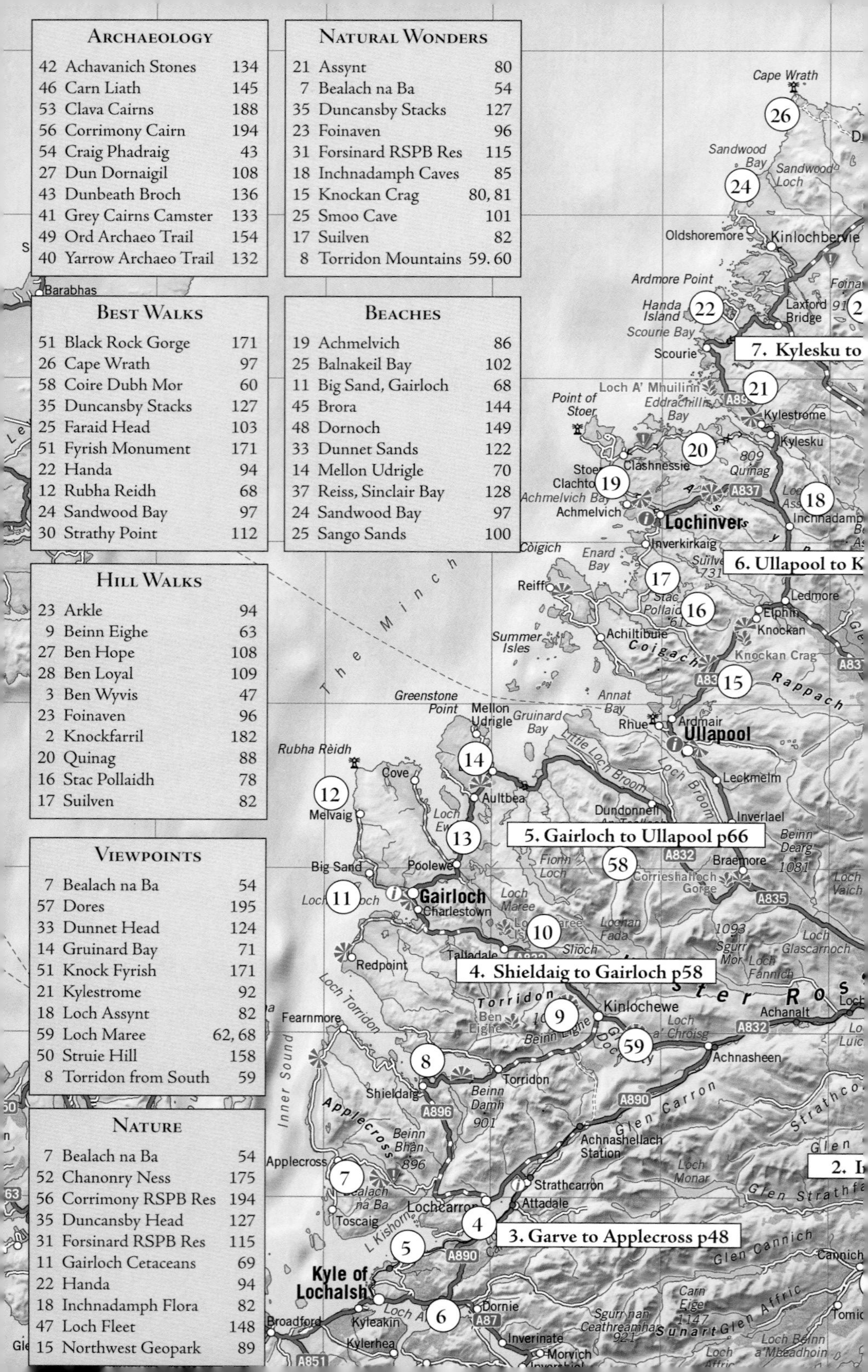

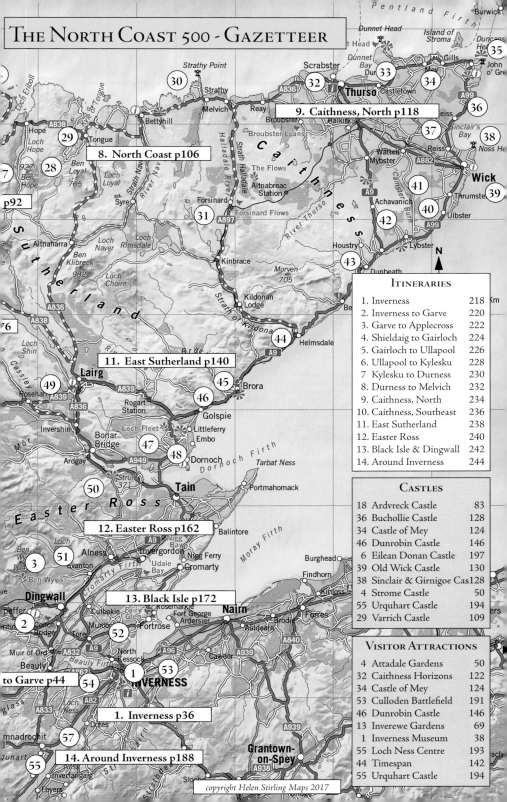

# The North Coast 500 - Gazetteer

**9. Caithness, North p118**

**8. North Coast p106**

**11. East Sutherland p140**

**12. Easter Ross p162**

**13. Black Isle p172**

**1. Inverness p36**

**14. Around Inverness p188**

to Garve p44

*copyright Helen Stirling Maps 2017*

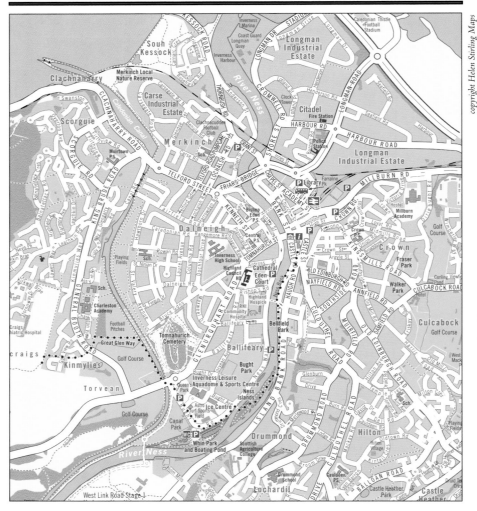

*copyright Helen Stirling Maps*

*Cladh na Cudainn*

**INVERNESS**, the capital of the Highlands, is one of the fastest growing and most dynamic cities in the UK. The Greater Inverness area had a population of over 59,000 in 2011, an increase of 18% since 2001. There is much to see and do in the city and surroundings.

**Inverness Castle** marks the start and finish of the NC500 route. At least three earlier castles occupied this strategic site. Although the building is not open to visitors, there are fine views over Inverness and the River Ness from its terrace. The statue of Flora MacDonald was unveiled in 1899.

Unfortunately there is very little parking at the Castle, so those wishing to start here

*Inverness and River Ness*

should leave their vehicle in one of the many car parks and include the start in a walking exploration. Inverness is very much a city best enjoyed on foot.

Most of Inverness dates from the 19th century with incongruous and rather brutal architecture from the later 20th century. The High Street is pedestrianised and has the usual chain stores of any British town. That said there are many independent shops in the side streets and in the restored Victorian Market.

*Clach na Cudainn* (G Stone of the Tubs) is an ancient sacred stone which now sits rather ignominiously below the Market

Cross outside the Town Hall. Washer women once rested their buckets on it; a seer used to sit on it when he made his prophecies. Earlier, in 1411, the *Sneckies* were relieved to find that it had not been damaged after Donald Lord of the Isles burned down much of the town. It is said that as long as Inverness looks after the *Clach*, it will prosper.

**The Visitor Information Centre**, below the Castle, stocks maps, books and guides. There is a large range of useful brochures about accommodation, eating out, attractions and things to do in the area. They have useful free maps of Inverness and round about as well as staff to answer questions.

*Old print of Inverness*

*Norman Wilkinson scene of Inverness from c.1930*

**Inverness Museum & Art Gallery** is on Castle Wynd, uphill behind the VIC. To quote one review, *"The museum is well worth a visit, beautifully curated and certainly good for kids. The art gallery has great exhibitions and we really enjoyed the current exhibition. Make sure you visit the cafe - the baking is very tempting!"*

The Museum has very well designed and presented displays on the geology, archaeology and history of the Inverness area. Everything from Jurassic fossils, Neolithic artefacts and Pictish symbol stones to modern times can be seen.

**Castle Gallery** *"is one of the best reasons to visit Inverness"*, according to the *'Independent'* newspaper. The Gallery holds exhibitions of fine and applied contemporary art by a wide range of new and established artists from all over the UK. The exhibitions change on a monthly basis.

**Kiltmaker Visitor Centre** Highland House of Fraser is on the west bank of the River Ness. The Visitor Centre explains the origins and history of the kilt. Skilled kiltmakers can be seen at work and explaining the workmanship that goes into their creation. Kilts and Highland Dress outfits can be purchased or hired here.

**The Victorian Market** in Queensgate dates from c.1890 and has an eclectic range of unique shops. With a fishmonger, butcher, baker, oriental food shop, florist, old fashioned watch maker, hairdressers and cafes among other interesting outlets the Market is well worth a perusal.

*Victorian Market*

*Castle Gallery*

*Pictish Bull in the Museum*

*Eden Court Theatre*

**Eden Court Theatre**, on the west bank of the River Ness, opened in 1976. The architect, Sir James Dunbar-Nasmith said, *"We were determined that it would not be just a good theatre but the best of its size currently being built in the world."*

It reopened in 2007 after a major revamp as the biggest arts centre in Scotland, with two theatres, two cinemas, two dance and drama studios and

three floors of purpose built dressing rooms. The venue hosts a wide variety of performances throughout the year and has a restaurant.

**St Andrew's Cathedral** is the seat of the Episcopalian Bishop of Moray, Ross and Caithness. It is constructed with Tarradale sandstone, while the columns of the nave are in Peterhead granite. It was completed in 1869, at a time when

*Flora MacDonald*

*Tartan Shop*

### INVERNESS CASTLE

The oldest records of a castle in Inverness are from the mid 11th century, when Macbeth was Mormaer of Moray. In 1056 Malcolm Canmore is said to have rebuilt the castle. There may very well have been a Pictish or Iron Age fort on the site earlier.

Around 1412 the Earl of Mar renovated it in stone. This fortification was attacked, destroyed and rebuilt several times during various clan wars. In the Civil War it was held by the Covenanters, but in 1649 the Royalists succeeded in taking the castle and slighted it.

In the aftermath of the 1715 Jacobite rebellion, General Wade greatly extended the castle as part of the British military presence in the Highlands. In 1718 the site was turned into a barracks for government soldiers; it became known as Fort George after the King.

The Jacobites occupied Inverness in February 1746. They besieged the castle and blew it up after the garrison surrendered. The French engineer who lit the fuse was blown up, his body being flung right across the river, though his poodle survived.

The present building dates from 1846, and is currently the Sheriff Court House. There are plans to turn it into a major Welcome to the Highlands Centre.

*Inverness Castle*

*Leakey's Bookshop*

most of the landed gentry were Anglicans.

By far the most impressive features of the church are the interior and the stained glass windows. The choir is especially impressive as are the reredos and altar, in Caen stone. The west window is perhaps the best of the beautiful stained glass windows.

**Eastgate Shopping Centre,** "with over 350,000ft² of fabu-

lous shopping, provides Inverness residents and visitors with an unequalled shopping experience. With over 50 speciality stores, a department store and 13 eateries, as well as two car parks offering 1350 spaces of covered parking, you will find everything you need right here – all under one roof."

This large shopping mall will either delight or appal those who are starting or have completed the NC500. If retail

therapy is your delight you will absolutely love it. Inverness Shopping, just east of the city on the A96 is another major shopping complex.

**Old High St Stevens** is the oldest church in Inverness. It is built on St Michael's Mound, where tradition says St Columba preached on his visit in c.565 when he met the Pictish King Bridei of Fortriu. Most of the building dates from the 18th century, but the lower tower is 14th century. With an Iona marble chancel and many memorials to illustrious Sneckies, this kirk is part of the Church of Scotland. The "Kirking o'the Cooncil" is held on the second Sunday in September. This tradition is over 400 years old and is a colourful event.

**Leakey's Bookshop** is based in St Mary's Gaelic Church in Church Street. Said to be the largest secondhand bookshop in Scotland, this is an essential stop for all book lovers. With over 100,000 books, rare prints, old maps, a log burning stove and café, there is a gem or two for every bibliophile. It is very easy to spend a long rainy afternoon browsing here.

*St Andrew's Cathedral*

*Beer Shop*

*Hootananny Bar*

*The Botanical Gardens*

### INVERNESS BOTANIC GARDENS

These charming gardens are on Bucht Lane, near the River Ness Islands, off the A82. For anyone interested in plants this is a marvellous place, compact but impressive. The glasshouses have contrasting habitats; tropical, arid desert.

The gardeners here cultivate a wide range of plants, many of which are available to buy. So keen horticulturists should not miss these seriously attractive gardens on their way home.

### NESS ISLANDS WALKS

Here is a secret few visitors know about. The islands are connected by suspension footbridges. An extensive network of footpaths covers these wooded islands, set in the River Ness. A short circular walk from below the Castle follows the river south to a suspension bridge and across the islands. The Botanic Gardens are near the south end of the walk. Return via the west bank to the city centre. Total distance c.3mi (4km).

**Pubs and Live Music** are very much part of the Inverness social scene. Several pubs have live music every night, including Hootananny, The Gellions Bar and Johnny Foxes.

For a more traditional pub atmosphere try Innes Bar, The Castle Tavern or The Waterfront. For a more upmarket experience try Nicky Tam's Restaurant & Bar, Bar One Inverness or Number 27.

**Cafés and Restaurants** Inverness has a vast choice of eating places ranging from simple cafés and coffee shops to fine dining plus a hugely diverse selection of restaurants. Chez Roux at Rocpool Reserve and Rocpool are both world class and need advance booking. There are also top class Indian, Chinese, Thai, Italian and Spanish restaurants, not to mention cafés serving traditional hearty Scottish meals.

*Lauders Pub*   *Rocpool Restaurant*

*Ness Islands Walks*

*Ness Islands Walks*

Caledonian Canal Lock

Muirtown Locks and Basin are on the A862 on the way to Beauly. With a swing bridge and four locks this an interesting place to watch the Canal in operation. The Sea Lock is at Clachnaharry. Nearby at the north end of Muirfield Basin another swing bridge carries the Far North Line railway.

**The Caledonian Canal** runs parallel to the River Ness until Torvean just southwest of Inverness. It then enters the Beauly Firth at Clachnaharry. The Canal was opened in 1822, having been constructed by the engineer, Thomas Telford. The 60mi (97km) waterway follows the Great Glen, joining Inverness and Fort William.

The Canal has 29 locks and cost £910,000 to build but only had a depth of 4.6m, too shallow for most commercial shipping even then. It was very popular with east coast fishing boats heading for the western fishing grounds. In the days of sail the Pentland Firth was dangerous, especially in winter.

Between 1995 and 2005 British Waterways carried out a major renovation project. The result is that the Caledonian Canal is busier than ever, and a very popular tourist attraction.

**Merkinch Local Nature Reserve** covers an area of coastal sand and mudflats between the River Ness estuary and the Caledonian Canal. A network of paths covers the reserve which is especially good for waders and waterfowl during migration times and winter. Access is from the carpark next South Kessock Pier.

**Ship Space** is a different sort of museum on the A862 west of Muirtown Locks. This interactive nautical museum has a 1/10th scale model of the *Titanic* as well as a selection of fishing boats, a *Watson* lifeboat and a deep sea submersible. There is no parking next to the museum. Please park at Telford Street Retail Park.

**Kessock Bridge** opened in 1982. Together with the Cro-

Merkinch Local Nature Reserve

Inverness Train Station

Post Office Avenue

*Muirtown Basin*

marty Bridge to the north, it transformed road transport north of Inverness. Previously the A9 wound its way around the Beauly Firth to Dingwall. This cable stayed bridge has a span of 240m and is protected against movement of the Great Glen Fault by seismic buffers.

**Inverness Airport**, at Dalcross 8mi (13km) east of Inverness on the A96, started in 1940 as RAF *Dalcross*. British Airways, easyJet, FlyBe, Loganair and KLM operate scheduled services within the UK and to Amsterdam from here. Several seasonal flights also operate.

**Highland Aviation Museum** is on the industrial estate near the airport. It has four complete aircraft, a Tornado GR1, a Buccaneer S1, a Nimrod MR2 and a Hunter F1. There are also several cockpits, including that of a Vickers Valiant. The building has interesting displays and a shop.

### CRAIG PHADRAIG

Craig Phadraig (G Patrick's Hill, NH638449, 172m) is a small hill which overlooks Inverness from the west. There is a large Vitrified Iron Age fort in a clearing at the summit which dates from c.500BC. The timber laced walls may once have been 8m high before the fort was destroyed by fire.

During the 6th century the site may have been occupied by the Picts. Traditionally it was here that St Columba met King Bredei in c.565AD, but it is perhaps more likely that they met on the site of the present day castle.

**Walk** On the A862 for Beauly, after the Muirtown Locks swingbridge, turn left into King Brude Road. Turn right to Leachkin then again into Leachkin Brae, signposted Craig Phadraig, and park in the Forestry Commission carpark. Follow the indicated route to the summit from where there are unrestricted views over the Beauly Firth. Glimpses of Inverness can be seen through the trees, 1.5mi, 2.5km, 1h.

*Kessock Bridge from South Kessock*

*Titanic Replica at Ship Space*

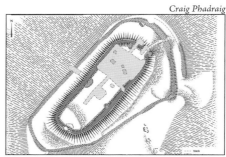

*Craig Phadraig*

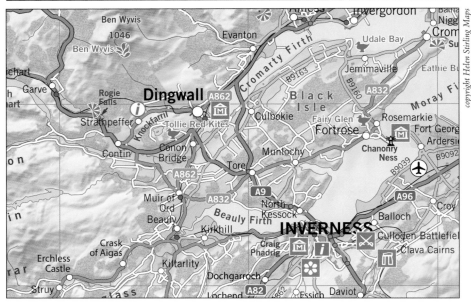

*copyright Helen Stirling Maps*

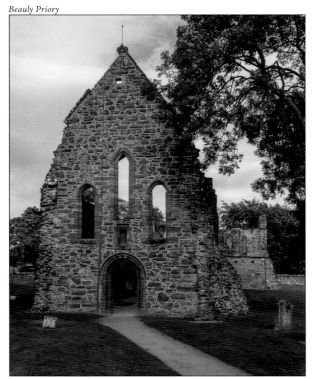

*Beauly Priory*

**STARTING POINT** The North Coast 500 starts from Inverness Castle in the centre of the city. Take the A862 west out of Inverness, following signs for Ullapool. The route passes the northern end of the Caledonian Canal over a swing bridge at the Muirtown Basin. Until the Kessock Bridge was opened in 1982 this was the main trunk road north to Caithness, the A9.

It then follows the south side of Beauly Firth to Lovat Bridge, built in 1814 by Telford as part of the new road to the north. Balblair Kirk is the home of Ffordes Photographic, an essential stop for anyone looking to buy new or secondhand camera gear. Beauly Gallery, on the ground floor, features local and internationally acclaimed artists and a coffee shop.

*Beauly Square*

*Lovat Bridge over River Beauly*

**Beauly** (Fr *Beau Lieu*, Beautiful Place) was probably named by the Valliscaulian monks of the Priory Church founded in 1230 by John Byset of the Aird. Although roofless, most of the church remains along with interesting grave slabs and some ancient Yew trees.

The village, through which heavy traffic once thundered, has a pretty central square with many attractive sandstone buildings and flamboyant floral displays in the summer. There are varied and interesting shops as well as cafés and several hotels. This is a good base from which to explore Easter Ross and the Black Isle.

**Muir of Ord** is the venue of the Black Isle Show, held in August. This is one of the largest and most popular agricultural shows in Scotland. Here, the route crosses the railway before turning northwest on the A832.

**Glen Ord Distillery** is situated on the edge of the village c.1000m from the turnoff. It was established in 1838 and now belongs to Diageo. The distillery has a large maltings unit which supplies malt to several other facilities.

The visitor centre is open all year. It offers a variety of tours around this large distillery, which get excellent reviews.

*Signpost on the A835 at Moy Bridge*

*Glen Ord Distillery*

| INVERNESS TO GARVE | |
|---|---|
| A862 (former A9) | 44 |
| Balblair Old Kirk | 44 |
| Beauly | 45 |
| Ben Wyvis | 47 |
| Conon Bridge | 181 |
| Dingwall | 180 |
| Garve | 47 |
| Glen Ord Distillery | 45 |
| Inverness Castle | 36 |
| Knockfarril | 182 |
| Loch Luichart | 47 |
| Lovat Bridge | 44 |
| Moy Bridge | 45 |
| Muir of Ord | 45 |
| Muirtown Locks | 42 |
| Rogie Falls | 46 |
| Strath Conon | 46 |
| Strathpeffer | 183 |
| Tollie Red Kites | 182 |

*Strath Conon and Marybank*

After the tour there is an opportunity to sample different expressions of the whisky and buy a bottle not available elsewhere. Booking is recommended Tel 01463 872004.

**The Rogie Falls** (ON *Roki A, Sparkling River*) are signposted off the A835 2mi (3km) west of Contin. They are well worth a visit when the river is in spate. A path leads from the Forestry Commission car park to several good viewpoints over the River Blackwater including a suspension bridge near the Falls. When the Salmon are running in autumn they can be seen leaping up the falls.

*Laurie Campbell*

*Male Salmon Leaping in the Falls of Shin*

**Strath Conon** is a long, lonely, beautiful valley which was cleared of its inhabitants in the 19th century. In the 1950s several remaining settlements disappeared underwater due to hydro-electric schemes. This strath is a good place to seek out the rare charm and peace of the Highlands.

*Winter dawn over Ben Wyvis*

*Ian Serjeant*

*Loch Garve*

It reaches well into Wester Ross. From Scardroy, at its head, it is only a few miles over the moor to Glen Carron. The windy, narrow road forces a slow pace but, on a fine day, the visit can be wonderful. Late August, with the heather in bloom, is the best time to go.

**Garve** itself may be just a collection of houses with a railway station, but the scenery round about is lovely, especially views over Loch Luichart in early summer with the gorse and broom in flower, then in autumn when the trees are turning. The aptly named Blackwater River is peaceful as it flows into Loch Garve compared to its rush down the Rogie Falls a few miles downstream.

**BEN WYVIS** (G *Uais*, awesome, 1046m, NH463684, pronounced *"weevis"*) stands in splendid isolation from the other mountains of the North Highlands, visible from miles around. Its whaleback ridge consists of Moine schist heavily moulded by the last Ice Age. The many mounds and ridges in the lower areas are glacial as are the erratic boulders dumped as the ice retreated.

**Flora** The ridge of Ben Wyvis is covered with Woolly Hair Moss, a greeny-yellow plant which forms a thick and springy carpet. There are at least 170 species of plants on the mountain, including alpine flowers, rare ferns, and lichens as well as dwarf willows and birch.

**Fauna** Red and Roe Deer, Mountain Hare and Pine Marten may be seen. The summit ridge holds breeding Dotterel in summer, as well as Ptarmigan, Golden Plover, Red Grouse and Ravens. Golden Eagles and Buzzards are frequently seen all over this area.

**Access** The route to the summit is from the Garbat Forestry Commission car park on the A836 4mi (6.5km) north of Garve (NH410671). The path is initially through the forest before climbing steeply up An Cabar (950m). The summit is 1500m to the northeast. Return distance is 9mi (14km), about six hours.

*Rogie Falls*

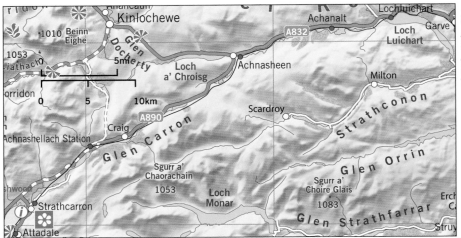

**WESTER ROSS** stretches from Lochalsh in the south to Inverpolly in the north and extends from the western watershed of Ross and Cromarty. The Atlantic coastline is over 300mi (500km) and is heavily indented with sea lochs.

This is an area of ancient mountains, tranquil coastal settlements, many single track roads and few inhabitants. It has some of the most stunning scenery of anywhere in the UK, a huge variety of wildlife and a very changeable climate.

**Geology** The diverse scenery of Wester Ross is due to the complex geology of the area. The base rock, ancient Lewisian Gneiss, is overlain by a succession of sedimentary strata, which include Torridonian Sandstone, Cambrian Quartzite and Limestone.

Here, the Moine Thrust runs from Glenelg in the south west to Knockan Crag in the north, adding to the geological confusion. Erosion over many millions of years has produced the spectacular landscape of today. Settlements in Wester Ross are sparse. Apart from the main centres such as Ullapool, Gair-loch or Lochcarron the villages are very small. Much of the landscape is unpopulated and frequently it is possible to walk all day without seeing anyone.

In this book Wester Ross is taken to begin at Shiel Bridge in the south and to include Lochalsh and Kintail, since anyone approaching from the south will pass this way. Whichever way one enters this area, the pace of life suddenly becomes slower.

Even some of the main roads are windy single tracks. There are spectacular views round every corner which vary with the season, weather and time of day. In winter, driving conditions can be hazardous, especially over high ground.

**West of Garve** take the left fork onto the A 832. From here the fast road through Strath Bran (G Raven Valley) follows the Kyle Line through very remote countryside to Achnasheen (G

*Achnasheen Train Station*

Field of Storms, 155m). The Telford road reached here in 1819, following the traditional route to Inverness from Skye.

Bear left at the roundabout for Lochcarron on the A890. Most of this highway was upgraded in the 1980s but the last few miles are along a very poor single track road which requires care.

*Glen Carron west of Achnasheen*

**Glen Carron** has a number of picturesque lochs, backed by high hills. It becomes increasingly pretty as the valley narrows and passes through woodland. Towards Strathcarron there are saltmarshes with glacial humps which can be explored by means of several paths along the River Carron. There are many patches of deciduous and conifer woodland to explore, some ancient. This area with its small lochs and marshes is good habitat for wetland wild flowers.

**Loch Carron** (P *Kars*, stone, rough) and Loch Kishorn (N *Keis Ord*, Big Headland) are sheltered by Applecross to the northwest and Skye to the west. Several laybys offer panoramic views over the loch.

**Lochcarron** is an attractive village, strung out along the northwest side of the loch. After 1813, when the Parliamentary Road reached here, the settlement grew considerably. This vibrant little village offers many facilities to visitors, including shops, a wide range of accommodation, cafes and restaurants, a good campsite, fuel, and a garage.

*Rowan Berries*

*Loch Carron from the Southwest*

*Lochcarron*

| GARVE TO LOCHCARRON | |
|---|---|
| Achnasheen | 48 |
| Attadale Gardens | 50 |
| Glen Carron | 49 |
| Kyle Line | 48 |
| Lochcarron | 49 |
| Loch Kishorn | 50 |
| Raasal Ashwood | 51 |
| River Carron | 49 |
| Strome Castle | 50 |

*Strome Castle*

Stromeferry offers fine views over Loch Carron and Applecross. A ferry ran across the narrows here for hundreds of years, but in 1970 it was replaced by a new road around Loch Carron. The best viewpoints are at Fernaig on the road to Plockton and from the hill above the village, Am Meallan.

**Strome Castle** is now a ruin, but from Norse times or earlier it was an important strategic site. The present building dates from the 15$^{th}$ century, when it was most likely a fortified tower house. It was fought over many times by the MacKenzies and the MacDonalds.

In 1602 the Lord of Kintail, Kenneth MacKenzie, laid siege to the castle. He was on the point of leaving when he heard that some of the women of the castle had been drawing water from the well. By accident they tipped the bucket into the gunpowder cask.

The MacDonalds surrendered, allowing the MacKenzies to gain possession, who promptly blew up the castle, leaving the gaunt ruins seen today.

**Attadale Gardens** are just south of Strathcarron. The house was first built in 1755 so the gardens of today have been cultivated for over 250 years. The mild climate has allowed a variety of themes. These include Water, Japanese, Sunken, Shade, Woodland and Kitchen Gardens as well as Rhododendron and Woodland Walks.

**Ardaneaskan** It is worth exploring further west to Ardaneaskan, for the fine views over Loch Carron to Plockton and west to Applecross. A track goes to nearby Loch Reraig and its wooded burn.

**Kishorn** is an area of scattered houses around the east side of the eponymous Loch. A minor road passes an arc of pretty cottages and a jetty. The views

*Lochcarron*

*Lochcarron Washing Line*

*Kishorn Seafood Bar*

across Loch Kishorn to Apple-cross are spectacular.

Kishorn Seafood Bar offers a wonderful menu after a day trekking and exploring. *"The emphasis is very much on local shellfish; with Oysters, Prawns and Squat Lobster from Loch Kishorn; Mussels and Queen Scallops from Lochcarron and Crab, King Scallops, Lobster, Smoked Salmon and Fresh Salmon also obtained locally".*

**Loch Kishorn** is very deep and was selected as a North Sea Oil yard. In 1975 a large dry dock and construction site to build oil platforms was opened here by Howard Doris. In 1977 over 3,000 were employed on the site and were accommodated on two old liners anchored in the loch.

The 600,000 tonne Ninian Central Platform was floated out in 1978. It remains the largest floating and movable structure so far created. By 1984 demand for huge oil platforms had dwindled and the site closed in 1987. The dry dock was used to build the footings for the Skye Bridge in 1992, but it is now derelict.

*Bealach na Ba from Loch Kishorn*

**Rassal Ashwood NNR** on the A896 north of Kishorn, is the most northerly in Scotland. The limestone outcrop here results in fertile soil. This supports a wide range of wild flowers. Apart from the Ash trees and their amazing lichens, there are Hazel, Rowan and Willows. The area has been used as grazing for centuries and many of the trees have been coppiced.

**Alternative Route** The A896 continues north from here over wild moorland via Glen Shieldaig to Shieldaig and Torridon. The Bealach na Ba is frequently closed due to snow and ice in winter, which make this remote route impassable. It should also be noted that the Bealach na Ba road is *"Not advised for learner drivers, very large vehicles or caravans after the first mile."*

*Loch Kishorn from Bealach na Ba*

*Loch Kishorn Saltmarsh*

*Rassal Ashwood NNR*

*Bealach na Ba and Loch Kishorn from the west*

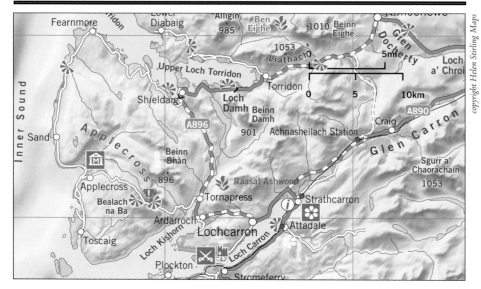

*copyright Helen Stirling Maps*

**APPLECROSS** (P *Aber Crossan*, Mouth of the Crossan) is a large mountainous peninsula composed of Torridonian Sandstone between Loch Kishorn and Loch Torridon. Though not unique in the Highlands for its remote situation, Applecross can only be reached by two long narrow roads or by sea. Nevertheless it remains a thriving community.

*Bealach na Ba* (G Pass of the Cattle), which reaches a maximum height of 626m, takes a very steep and windy route from Loch Kishorn. It climbs through the spectacular corrie of Coire na Ba between the crags of Meall Gorm (710m) and Sgurr a' Chaorachain (792m) to a viewpoint at Carn Glas (NG774426).

On a clear day there are panoramic views across the Inner Sound to Raasay, the Cuillin, Northern Skye and to the Western Isles. A track leads up to a radio mast (776m) and by skirting the crags and climbing a ridge to the east another viewpoint can be reached (792m). From here there is a panoramic view of the pass, Loch Kishorn and Loch Carron.

**The Parliamentary Road** over Bealach na Ba was completed in 1822, but it was not until the 1950s that it received a bitumen covering. Even today the pass can be blocked in winter for long periods and is unsuitable for caravans, coaches and large vehicles. There are plenty of places to pull over to admire the view.

*Loch Kishorn from the Bealach na Ba*

**Coast Road** It took until 1976 for the coast road to Shieldaig to be completed. The first section was opened by Princess Margaret on 11th May 1970, over 90 years after the Napier Report of 1884 recommended its construction. This was to serve a military development at Sand.

The road south of Applecross village passes through the unspoilt crofting townships of Camusteel with its tiny beach at Camusterrach. It ends at Toscaig Pier.

**Applecross Village** has a shop, campsite and hotel. There is a ruined broch next to the campsite. Applecross house dates from the 1730s, while nearby are two Top Barns which originally had heather thatched

*Bealach na Ba with Meall Gorm (710m) and Loch Kishorn*

roofs. They were used to store hay and unthreshed oats.

**A' Chomraich** In c.673AD the Irish monk St Maelrubha founded a monastery here. He was born in Londonderry c.642. The surrounding land was declared a Sanctuary (G,

A' Chomraich) and the name still survives in Gaelic. No trace remains today of this early Christian settlement, or of most of the Pictish cross-slabs which are said to have been broken up and buried by over zealous 19th century masons.

*Bealach na Ba hairpins from the top of the pass*
*Bealach na Ba from the eastern approach*

*Cuillin Ridge on the Isle of Skye from Bealach na Ba*

Next to the entrance of the graveyard a large cross-slab may commemorate Abbot Mor MacAogan, who died in 801AD at Bangor. The Vikings are said to have attacked the abbey around this time. Sadly no major archaeology has been done here yet to investigate this important early Christian site.

Apart from the impressive cross-slab there are a number of other ancient grave markers, some of which are inscribed. Most are either very weathered or obviously broken. The small chapel east of the church is 15th century while the present church was built in 1817, most likely on the site of a much earlier one.

The Heritage Centre near the church has displays describing the archaeology and history of the area. Artefacts, archives and old photographs can be seen here. It also has three parts of a broken carved cross which was found recently.

**Mesolithic Age** At the beautiful sandy beach of Sand (NG682488) on the coast road north of Applecross Bay, a mound in front of a rock shelter has yielded evidence of Mesolithic occupation around 6000BC. Shells (mostly Limpets), fish bones, bone and stone tools were found. Some of the stone tools were of bloodstone from Rum, others from Skye.

**Loch Torridon** North of Sand the road offers fine views over

*Glamaig from Bealach na Ba*

*Allt Beg, Applecross*

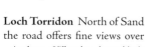
*Applecross Village has changed little*

Inner Sound to Raasay and the Trotternish Ridge on Skye. From Fearnmore eastwards it winds over rocky terrain with few habitations; increasingly dramatic panoramas open up to the north. The views over Loch Torridon and Loch Shieldaig with the Torridon Mountains in the background are some of the best on the NC500.

Skye from Applecross Beach

**Walking and Wildlife** This peninsula is one of the remotest places on the Scottish mainland. It is a great place for walking or cycling, whether gentle or extreme. Many paths lead into the interior and along the coast. Sea kayaking is available and there are guided walks led by Highland Council Rangers.

Applecross Beach and the Coast Road to Shieldaig

Golden and White-tailed Eagles, Red Deer and Otters are present here. The stands of mature Scots Pine around Applecross Bay are home to Pine Marten as well as many species of birds and plants. Common Seals regularly haul out on the shore, while Porpoises are often seen. Minke Whales and Dolphins are occasionally present.

Sand Viewpoint

Pictish cross slab

Applecross Hotel

Red Sand on Applecross Beach

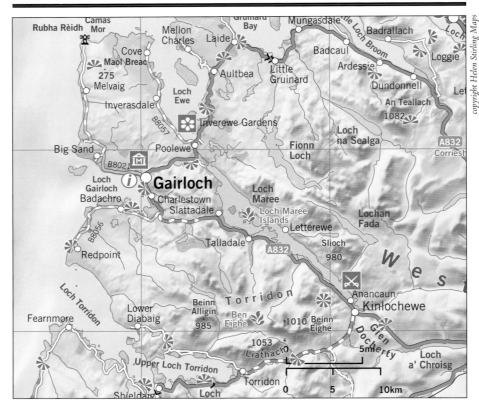

*copyright Helen Stirling Maps*

**TORRIDON** (ON Thorfinn's Township, or G Place of Transference) is full of scenic grandeur, its mountains rising dramatically from sea level to over 1,000m. They loom majestically over Upper Loch Torridon, and the little villages of Torridon, Inver Alligin, Alligin Shuas and Diabaig.

**Shieldaig** (ON *Sild Vik*, Herring Bay), a planned fishing village, built to encourage the development of fishing, is in a very sheltered position on Loch Shieldaig, a branch of Loch Torridon. The idea was to increase the supply of seamen for the Royal Navy, and building work commenced in

*Loch Torridon, the Torridon Massif and Shieldaig from the South*

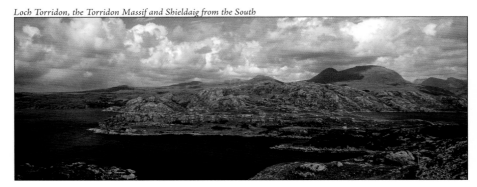

*Loch Torridon and the Torridon Massif*

1810, followed by the church in 1825.

Finance was provided for fishing boats, but as is often the case with such military-inspired things, the threat was long gone before any sailors were ready to fight. A new road was built to Kishorn, fish prices were guaranteed and salt provided duty-free. Prawns are still landed here, and Mussels farmed, but nowadays tourism has largely replaced fishing.

**Shieldaig Island** shelters the bay from westerly gales. It is covered with mature Scots Pine, planted in the 19th century to provide timber and spars for boats and fishing. It is home to White-tailed Sea Eagles, Grey Herons, Black Guillemots, Long-eared Owls and Kestrels. Seals and Otters frequent these quiet shores.

**Upper Loch Torridon** Approaching from the south, the A896 offers several panoramic views over Torridon. This link was only completed in the 1960s, previously a trip of over 60 miles was needed. By taking a walk over the moorland

*Spanish Cannon & Shieldaig Island*

*Shieldaig Lunch*

*Shieldaig from the South*

| Torridon to Gairloch | |
|---|---|
| Anancaun | 62 |
| Badachro | 65 |
| Beinn Eighe NNR | 60, 63 |
| Ben Alligin | 60 |
| Coire Dubh Mor | 60 |
| Deer Museum | 60 |
| Diabaig | 60 |
| Dubh-aird | 59 |
| Glen Torridon | 60 |
| Isle Maree | 64 |
| Kerrysdale | 64 |
| Kinlochewe | 62 |
| Liathach | 60 |
| Loch Maree | 62 |
| *Muc-sheilch* Monster | 64 |
| Redpoint | 65 |
| Shieldaig | 58 |
| Slattadale Forest | 62 |
| Slioch | 62 |
| Torridon | 58 |
| Upper Loch Torridon | 58 |

*Liathach reflected in Lochan an Iasgair*
from one of several viewpoints, the whole vista opens up.

**Dubh-aird Walk** A path also leads from the Torridon Hotel through woods along the shore to Dubh-aird, from where the whole expanse of loch and mountains can be seen. The loch is shallow with a muddy bottom, an ideal habitat for prawns. They are caught in special creels which do not damage the seabed.

*Deer Museum*

**Deer Museum** The National Trust Countryside Centre has displays, information on the area, its wildlife and current events as well as a small shop. The nearby Deer Museum explains the life cycle and management of Red Deer, a number of which can be seen in a nearby fenced enclosure.

**Diabaig** A minor road along the north side of the loch leads to Diabaig, a charming little harbour and village. It passes Inveralligin before reaching the steep Bealach na Gaoithe. There are dramatic views over Loch Torridon to Ben-Damph Forest to the south and Beinn Alligin to the east.

**Mountains** Beinn Alligin (G The Jewel, (986m), Liathach (G The Grey One, 1055m) and

*Lower Diabaig*

Beinn Eighe (G File Mountain, 1010m) form one of the most spectacular skylines in Scotland. Their cliffs, buttresses, corries and peaks look splendid from below and they offer some of the best hillwalking and climbing in the country.

**Glen Torridon** The road to Kinlochewe offers spectacular views of Liathach and Beinn Eighe. The scene changes constantly depending on the light and weather so that sometimes the mountains are shrouded in mist and at other times they are revealed in all their lofty splendour.

There is a fine view from above Lochan an Iasgair, which can be reached via a bridge and a path just east of the Glen Torridon car park below Liathach

*Glacial Hummocks in Glen Torridon*

*Ben Alligin and Loch Torridon from the South*

(NG958569). Perhaps best of all is the vista over Loch Clair, which is accessible on foot via the road to Coulin Lodge.

**Coire Dubh Mor** (G Big Black Corrie) runs northwest between the crags of Liathach and Beinn Eighe. A signposted 4mi (6km) path from the car park goes through the corrie to Coire Mhic Fhearchair on the back side of Beinn Eighe. Triple buttresses of red Torri-

donian Sandstone topped by Quartzite glittering in the sun is well worth the effort needed. The lochan in the foreground completes an idyllic scene on a clear day.

**Geology** The red Torridonian Sandstones were laid down about 900-750 million years ago (Ma) on top of much older (c.2,000Ma) Lewisian Gneiss. Many of the mountains are capped with Cambrian

### BEINN EIGHE NNR WOODLAND TRAIL

This type of woodland is *temperate rainforest*, where the flora and fauna are adapted to the cool, wet climate. In the last 50 years much has been done to regenerate these woodlands. The Woodland Trail is about a mile long and winds through the Scots Pinewoods which have existed here since after the end of the last Ice Age.

Birch, Bird Cherry, Rowan, Willow, Holly and Alder also grow here and large areas have been fenced off to keep out Red Deer and allow the regeneration of woodlands over a total of about 1,100ha.

The Pinewoods are ideal territory for Pine Martens, whose droppings are often apparent. Otters may be seen at the lochside or near streams and the Wildcat hunts here, but is rarely seen. Of particular interest are the 13 types of dragonflies which like the more open marshy places. Many species of lichen, liverworts, mosses and ferns live on the trees and rocks in these woods.

*River Torridon & Sgurr Dubh*

*River Torridon*

*Torridon from the southwest*

*Beinn Eighe from the top of the High Path*

Quartzite from c.200Ma later, which glints in the sun, especially if wet.

Spectacular cliffs rise up vertically from the valley bottoms to 900m in several places. These hard rocks erode slowly and do not produce fertile soils, thereby giving the landscape a somewhat savage beauty. Here, you will find, nature has an uncompromising splendour.

*Butterwort*

**Beinn Eighe** and **Slioch** to the north stand sentinel over Loch Maree. In 1951 the first National Nature Reserve was created here; 230ha of relict Caledonian Forest (G *Coille na Glas Leitre*, Wood of the Grey Slope) and over 4,000ha of mountain and moorland.

**Visitor Centre** The Reserve Visitor Centre near Kinlochewe has displays covering Beinn Eighe and Loch Maree, and helpful staff. It also has an outside picnic area.

**Loch Maree** (G *Loch Mma-Ruibh*, St Maelrubha's Loch) is one of the largest and most beautiful lochs in Scotland.

**Kinlochewe** is an ideal place to start any of several fine walks. A track goes up the valley of

*Lone Scots Pine*

Abhainn Bruachaig to narrow sided Gleann Muice. Another follows the Kinlochewe River to the end of Loch Maree, past Oakwoods to Gleann Bianasdail and eventually to Loch Fada. One route up Slioch (G Spear, 980m) goes from this path.

**Anancaun** (G Ford of the Heads) is on the Kinlochewe River. After a battle between Clans MacKenzie and MacLeod the heads of the latter were tossed into the river, and became stuck in the ford.

**Slattadale** has a car park and forest walks. There is a fine view back down the loch over the islands from a clearing near the car park. The nearby Victoria Falls were so named after the queen visited in 1877.

*Beinn Eighe Reflected in a Lochan*

*Loch Maree and Slioch*

**BEINN EIGHE NNR
MOUNTAIN TRAIL**

Starting from the Visitor Centre, this trail climbs to 550m and covers about 4mi (6km), passing through several climatic zones on the way. Climbing through the Pinewoods, there are many ancient trees which could be up to 400 years old, as well as younger, straighter ones. Scottish Crossbills may be seen or heard here.

**Loch Maree Islands NNR** includes the three large and about forty small islands in the loch. They hold ancient Scots Pine and mature Juniper, which have been protected from grazing.

Black-throated Divers nest on these islands. They can be heard frequently as they fly in with fish for their young. This is probably the best place in Scotland to observe them. They can be seen from the Loch Maree Hotel hide as well as places along the loch.

**Ironworking** using bog iron and charcoal was carried out around Loch Maree since the Iron Age. There were plentiful supplies of raw materials in the area, which encouraged Sir George Hay to set up furnaces at Letterewe in 1607. Wrought and cast iron were made here, and later at the Red Smiddy, Poolewe, in vast quantities until the trees had all been consumed. Iron ore was shipped in from England and it seems English workers were employed. The operations lasted for about 60 years.

The east side of Loch Maree can be accessed by a track which goes from Poolewe to

From the cairn at the top of the trail (550m) there are views over Loch Maree and Slioch to the north, to Ben Wyvis in the east and Kintail in the south, but the jagged ridge of Beinn Eighe to the southwest is the most impressive. Here only plants which are adapted to harsh conditions can grow. These include Juniper, Alpine Bearberry, Butterwort and Mountain Azalea as well as sedges and clubmosses.

Red Deer and Mountain Hares may be seen, as well as Golden Eagles and Ravens. Ptarmigan and Red Grouse are also present. Lower down the wooded Allt na h-Airidhe Gorge attracts woodland birds. Dippers hunt in the streams for insects and Great Spotted Woodpeckers may be seen or at least heard.

*Ptarmigan*

The north summit of Meall a' Ghuibhais (878m) could be included in this walk. It is about 1mi (1.5km) from the cairn mentioned above.

*Black-throated Divers*

Loch Maree

### THE SACRIFICE OF BULLS

The sacrifice of bulls continued on Isle Maree until 1678. This tradition seems to be ancient and probably long pre-dates Christianity. In the Highlands cattle were, for thousands of years, the basis of the economy.

The sacrifice of a prime bull to their god would have been a highly symbolic offering. Early Christians were adept at taking over existing customs and superstitions.Perhaps St Maelrubha did just this, except that henceforth the benefits of the sacrifice would work through the Christian God.

The Highlanders had a rite termed *taghairm*, where a seer or clairvoyant would don the hide of a newly sacrificed bull so that he might communicate with spirits to divine the future. This seems to have continued in some places into the 18th century. Doubtless the Church was very strongly opposed to such practices.

Kernsary then eventually all the way to Kinlochewe via Letterewe and its old ironworks.

**Isle Maree**, or *Innis Maree*, in contrast to the other islands, is wooded with ancient Oaks as well as Holly, Chestnut and other deciduous trees, suggesting that it is a pre-Christian religious site. The Wishing Tree, now dead, and studded with coins and nails driven into it for good luck, stands inside a small walled enclosure.

St Maelrubha is said to have built a chapel or cell on Isle Maree in the late 7th century, which was occupied by hermits for many years. Remains of the chapel and graveyard are inside this enclosure. It is here that

the Viking prince and princess of a tragic tale are buried. Their graveslabs lie end to end at the centre of the island, one marked with an angular cross, the other with a rounded one.

The holy well is now dry but still stands near the shore. The waters were reputed to cure mental illness. The cure involved rowing round the island three times in a clockwise direction and repeated immersion in the loch. Tradition does not record whether this worked.

**The *Muc-sheilch*** is a monster which is said to live in Loch Maree (G *Muc*, pig; ON *selkie*, seal). Another such beast is said to live in Loch-na-Beiste (G Loch of the Beast) near Aultbea. An 1850 attempt to drain the loch was an expensive failure for a Mr Banks from Letterewe. There have been no recent reports of these beasts.

**Kerrysdale** to Redpoint Just south of Gairloch the B8056 crosses the River Kerry, eventually reaching Redpoint. This winding single track road is very scenic and offers fine views. It passes a series of lovely little bays, sheltered by small

Loch Maree

islands and lined with woods.

**Badachro** is perhaps the prettiest bay. In former times Cod was dried on the shingle beaches. The local inn is a great place to stop for a meal and to watch the boating activities in the bay.

**Redpoint** The road continues though a suddenly fertile crofting landscape with fields of cattle and small farms. Dramatic vistas open up at Opinan, where there is a fine sandy beach. Skye and the Western Isles can be seen on clear days. The road ends at Redpoint car park, from where a path leads to a beach of red sand, backed by extensive dunes.

Redpoint itself hides another lovely south facing beach with an old fishing station. A path leads along the coast via a re-

*Harris Mountains and the Minch from Redpoint*

mote Youth Hostel at Craig, to Lower Diabaig in Torridon. There are fine views to Beinn Alligin and across Loch Torridon to the mountains beyond. The relatively fertile soils and red sand here are derived from Torridonian sandstone. Copious amounts of seaweed get washed up here and have long been used as fertiliser.

*Victorian Postbox*

Badachro

*Redpoint*

*Kerrysdale Tree*

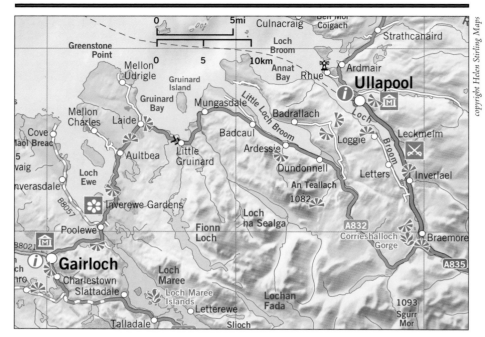

*copyright Helen Stirling Maps*

**GAIRLOCH** (G *Gearr Loch*, Short Loch) until recent times looked to the sea for access to the external world. It offers much of what the West Highlands visitor expects and is an excellent base from which to explore the area.

The village consists of a series of little settlements nestling round the shore of the loch. Charlestown is the first to be reached by the road from Loch Maree, and the site of the harbour, which was once the main route in and out of the area. In former times Cod and Haddock fishing was the main industry here. The fish were split, salted and dried for export to France and Spain.

The scenic A832 road from Slattadale to Gairloch follows the River Kerry and offers fine views over the Torridon mountains to the south. In Gairloch a viewpoint next to the golf course gives access to fine sandy beaches.

**Gairloch Heritage Museum** is in an old farm steading and tells the story of the area from the

*Sunset over the Minch and the Outer Hebrides from Big Sand, Gairloch*

*Loch Gairloch from the road to Big Sand*

first people to the present. It has Neolithic and Bronze Age artefacts, as well as a broken Pictish symbol stone with a fish and part of an eagle inscribed on it. Life on the croft, the school room, the village shop and an illicit whisky still are all illustrated. Also on display is the old lens from Rubha Reidh lighthouse, one of the largest in Scotland. Outside, old wooden fishing boats can be seen. The Museum has a small shop and a café.

The Harbour still has fishing boats which land prawns, crabs, and lobsters which may be available in local establishments. There are also boat trips in summer to see whales, dolphins, seals, and seabirds.

*Big Sand*

*Gairloch Beach*

| GAIRLOCH TO ULLAPOOL | |
| --- | --- |
| An Teallach | 72 |
| Ardessie Falls | 72 |
| Big Sand | 68 |
| Boat Trips | 69 |
| Camas a' Charaig | 70 |
| Camas Mor | 68 |
| Corrieshalloch Waterfall | 73 |
| Cove Road & Beaches | 70 |
| Dun an Ruich Ruadh | 73 |
| Dundonnell | 72 |
| Gruinard Bay | 71 |
| Inverewe Gardens | 69 |
| Leckmelm Arboretum | 73 |
| Little Loch Broom | 71 |
| Loch Broom | 72 |
| Loch Ewe | 70 |
| Mellon Charles | 70 |
| Mellon Udrigle | 70 |
| Pictish Stone | 68 |
| Poolewe | 68 |
| Rubha Reidh | 68 |
| Russian Convoy Mem | 70 |
| Tollie Viewpoint | 68 |
| WWII Loch Ewe | 70 |

*Loch Maree from the Tollie Viewpoint*

vaig. From here access is by foot only on the private road to Rubha Reidh 3mi (5km). A path follows the cliffs from the headland to the remote and enchanting beach at Camas Mor. The lighthouse was first lit in 1912, after a lengthy campaign dating back to 1853. The station was automated in 1986.

The Village offers a good range of accommodation, places to eat and shops. Undoubtedly, its biggest asset is its location and its wonderful scenery. The interplay of changing light on the sea, sky and landscape there is truly captivating.

Gairloch's history includes Neolithic, Bronze Age and Iron Age people, as well as Picts, Vikings and Scots. All probably came originally by sea, attracted by the sheltered harbour, good fishing and fertile land on the sand dunes.

**Big Sand** is a wide sandy beach, backed by extensive dunes and links. It is sheltered from the west by Longa Island, and is the site of an expansive and very fine campsite.

**Rubha Reidh** The road continues north from here to the end of the public road at Mel-

All along this road there are panoramic views to Skye and the Western Isles. About a mile before the lighthouse, a road goes up to radio masts on Maol Breac, (275m NG757900) for an even broader vista.

**Tollie viewpoint** At the north end of the loch, there are fine views from the A832 at Tollie. Nearby Tollie Bay is very picturesque with its deciduous woods.

**Poolewe** (ON *Bolstaðir*, farm, Farm of Ewe) is at the head of Loch Ewe where the River Ewe enters the sea from Loch Maree. The name Ewe is ancient, but may refer to Yew trees, always regarded as holy or, the *Tree of Life*.

**Pictish Stone** There is a Pictish symbol in the old graveyard near a ruined chapel. It is surrounded by iron railings. In contrast to Easter Ross, very few such stones have so far been found in the west. There are several other interesting stones here, including a knocking stone, an unusual graveslab with uprights at each end and three military graves.
**Inverewe Gardens** were cre-

*Gairloch Prawns*

*Inverewe Gardens*

*Inverewe House & Gardens*

*Loch Ewe from the southwest*

## Gairloch Boat trips

The waters of the Minch hold a substantial population of whales, dolphins, seals and seabirds. A boat trip is by far the best way of seeing them; several operators are based in Gairloch, using a variety of craft.

A converted ship's lifeboat with a glass bottom allows closeup encounters with wildlife in the bay. A conventional 31ft motor cruiser goes further afield, while a fast RHIB operates as far as the Shiant Islands. All run from Gairloch Pier; booking is strongly advised; all are weather dependent.

Details of these and other boat trips from the NC500 are listed in the What Do & See Section, page 207.

**Inverewe Gardens** were created by Osgood MacKenzie, who purchased the estate of Kernsary with help from his mother in 1862. From then until his death in 1922, he transformed a barren hillside into spectacular gardens and woodlands. His daughter, Mairi, continued until 1952 when she gifted them to the National Trust for Scotland, who maintain and continue to develop this enchanting place.

The mild climate and sheltered position have allowed the creation of a hugely diverse collection of plants from New Zealand, South America, China, Tasmania, South Africa and the Himalayas. MacKenzie is said to have had Irish soil shipped in and doubtless used seaweed and sand from the bay.

He planted over 100 acres of woodland for shelter, mostly Scots Pine, but also including many other species, local and exotic. A network of paths leads through an amazing selection of garden themes, from the original kitchen garden to the many imported flowers, trees and shrubs.

A visit is worthwhile in any season, while May, June and July are perhaps the best

*Inverewe House & Gardens from Poolewe*

*Camas Allt Eoin Thomais*

*WWII Heavy Anti Aircraft Battery*

*Loch Ewe NATO Fuel Jetty and Aultbea*

months. There is a visitor centre and restaurant. Inverewe House is now open for visitors *"a completely renovated, visionary and immersive 1930s house and visitor attraction."*

**Cove Road** The B8057 follows the west side of Loch Ewe to Cove. It passes through a crofting landscape and offers fine views across the loch to the mountains behind. There is a fine sandy beach, backed

by dunes and machair at Firemore. Camas Allt Eoin Thomais a little further on is more intimate and sheltered.

**Loch Ewe** North from Inverewe there are fine views to the west and to the Isle of Ewe. Aultbea and Mellon Charles are pretty villages with small harbours and Laide has an ancient chapel said to date from the 6th century. Further north, Mellon Udrigle has a very fine

beach, Camas a' Charaig, with white sands. The impossibly green-blue sea is sheltered by rocky headlands on both sides and backed by dunes. This is perhaps the most attractive seaside feature in Wester Ross.

**Loch Ewe in WWII** In 1939 the east coast ports of Rosyth and Invergordon were vulnerable to air attack and Scapa Flow was not yet secure. Loch Ewe and Loch Eriboll were selected as alternative anchorages. Extensive defences, including anti-aircraft, coastal batteries, a minefield and an anti-submarine boom were all eventually installed here. The lack of preparation was underlined when HMS *Nelson* was severely damaged by a magnetic mine in December 1939.

**Russian Convoys** The main wartime use of Loch Ewe was as a refuelling base for escorts and a rendezvous for ships taking part in the Arctic Convoys to Russia. The first of 19 left on 6th February 1942 and the last on 30th December 1944. Of 489 merchant ships that sailed from here only 16 were sunk, along with 5 escort vessels. Altogether over 100 mer-

*Loch Ewe from the North*

*Camas Allt Eoin Thomais*

*Russian Convoys Memorial*

chant ships and nearly 60 naval vessels were lost on both sides. A NATO refuelling base is still operational near Aultbea.

A multi site museum dedicated to the Arctic Convoys is in development. A display can be seen in the old school in Inverasdale but check hours first.

**Gruinard Bay** (ON *Grunna Fjordur*, Shallow Bay) runs in a wide sweep from Mellon Udrigle to Little Loch Broom. At its head a large area of sand is exposed at low tide. To the west the shore is shingly and is backed by a raised beach. At the viewpoint above Little Gruinard a scramble to the top gives a better view. Paths follow the Rivers of Little Gruinard, Inverianvie and Gruinard inland through forest and onto moorland behind.

**Gruinard Island** was the site of one of the most bizarre and irresponsible military operations ever conducted. Fears that the Nazis or Japanese might use chemical or biological weapons led to British research and trials. In 1941 a canister of Anthrax spores was exploded on the island near a group of sheep secured in wooden frames. All died in a few days. They were casually dumped over a cliff and covered in rocks. One drifted ashore on the mainland and infected other sheep.

For years signs saying *"Landing is Prohibited"* were displayed but finally the MOD was

*Gruinard Bay from south viewpoint*

shamed into action. In 1987 £0.5m was paid to decontaminate the ground with 280 tonnes of formaldehyde and to remove topsoil. Anthrax spores are extremely hardy and can survive for many years. Sheep seem to be able live on the island now, but it remains an object lesson in the arrogance and irresponsibility of the military.

**Little Loch Broom** is a long, narrow inlet north of Gruinard

Bay. The road goes through wild and lonely country with many opportunities to stop and admire the view. A short detour along the side road to Baduarlach (NH9983944) offers fine views over the loch. The little community of Scoraig can only be reached by boat from Badluarach or by walking in from Badrallach.

**Ardessie Falls** can be reached from the Ardessie car park

*Mellon Udrigle, Camas a' Chairaig*

*An Teallach from Loch Ewe*

The mountain has nine peaks over 950m, the highest two being Sgurr Fiona (The Fair Peak) and Bidean a'Glas Thuill (G The Sharp Peak of the Hollow). An Teallach is composed of Torridonian Sandstone with a cap of Quartzite. Its ascent is outside the scope of this book.

*An Teallach from Loch Toll an Lochain*

(NH053897) by a steep path which follows the Allt Ardessie for about 1,000m. There are several small falls and pools before the main waterfall. There are fine views down Little Loch Broom loomed over by Sail Mhor (767m).

**Dundonnell**, at the head of the loch, has a large area of salt marsh which is ablaze with colourful flowers in May and June. The Dundonnell River winds over Strath Beag and then further up it cascades down a narrow valley. From

*Corrieshalloch Waterfall*

a viewpoint at 279m there are fine vistas down the valley and over to An Teallach. The mixed woodlands, meadows and riversides are also full of wild flowers in summer.

The Dundonnell Yew may be the second oldest tree in Scotland, c.2,000 years old. It is in Dundonnell House gardens which are occasionally open to the public and has been cut back so that it is less irregular than most Yews. The gardens are very much worth visiting.

**An Teallach** (G The Forge, 1062m) may be named for mists rising like smoke from its heights. This ridge of high peaks, corries, buttresses and craigs dominates Little Loch Broom. To appreciate its splendour some hiking is needed as the spectacular main corrie is not visible from the road.

**Loch Toll an Lochain**, below the huge Corrie Toll, is easily reached without any climbing experience. The route starts a layby southeast of and Dundonnell (NH112858). The loch is situated at about 520m. The best time of day to go is early morning when the sun illuminates the corrie. This is a hard 6mi (10km) walk across rough moorland but worth the effort for the splendid corrie.

**Badrallach Detour** Near Dundonnell House a side road turns sharp left along the north side of Little Loch Broom to Badrallach. There are fine views of An Teallach. About 300m north of the high point of this road (NH099919, 236m) a track goes over the moor to Loch Allt na h-Airbhe. There are panoramic views over Ullapool, Loch Broom and the Coigach.

*Bleak Moorland near Dundonnell*

**Loch Broom** (G *Bhraion*, Place of Rain Showers) is a long, narrow sea loch formed during the Ice Age. After the bleak moorland the landscape suddenly becomes softer and greener with trees and some farms.

**Corrieshalloch** (G *Coire Shalach*, Ugly Corry) has a fine waterfall, *Eisan na Miasaich*, (G Fall of the Place of Platters) or the Falls of Measach. This 61m box canyon is south of Braemore, 12mi (19km) east of Ullapool. The car park and access is off the A832. The River Droma cascades for 46m, most impressive after heavy rain or when snow is melting.

The falls and gorge can be seen from a small suspension bridge situated directly over the waterfall. A path leads to a platform which juts out over the cliffs to give a dramatic view back up the gorge to the long narrow falls.

**River Broom** flows through the flat alluvial valley of Strath More. Its estuary has mudflats and a saltmarsh which are best viewed by taking the side road on the west side of the loch to Letters. This road passes several small settlements before ending at Blarnalearoch. There are fine views over Ullapool and Loch Broom from here.

**Dun an Ruigh Ruaidh** (NH149901) is built prominently against a cliff above Rhiroy. This C-shaped structure has been described as a

*Loch Broom & Ullapool from above Letters*

"proto-broch" and dates from the 3rd or 2nd century BC. There is a central hearth and an upper floor which rested on the prominent scarcement stones.

Much of the broch has been used to build a now abandoned sheep wash, but the remains of an intramural stairway and characteristic double wall construction can be seen. The front wall must have been straight rather than round, but has completely gone.

**Leckmelm Arboretum** (G *Leac Mailm*, Gravestone of Mailm) is an arboretum planted in the 1870s, 3mi (4km) southeast of Ullapool. The Victorians collected trees and shrubs from temperate zones around the world. It is best visited in early summer for foliage and flowers and in autumn for colours. The garden has large mature trees and flowering shrubs with paths winding through. It has a romantic, fairy tale feeling.

*Sunset down Loch Broom from Ullapool*

*Leckmelm Arboretum*

*Lochinver is dominated by Suilven (731m)*

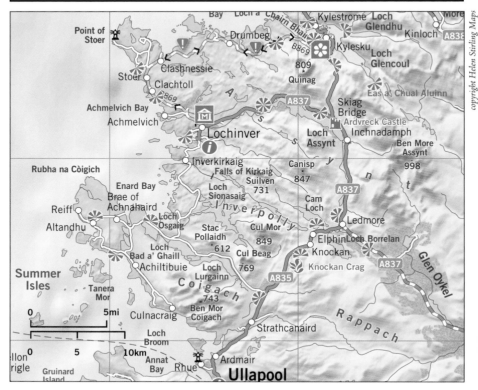

*copyright Helen Stirling Maps*

**ULLAPOOL** (N *Ulli Bolstaðir,* Ulli's Stead) is situated on a sheltered headland near the mouth of Loch Broom. The approach from the east on the A835 gives fine views of the village, with the white washed houses of Shore Street curving round the bay.

This attractive spot has probably been inhabited for thousands of years. Perhaps the oldest building is the roofless Catholic Chapel in the graveyard which may have associations with St Maelrubha. Ullapool is marked on a 1596 map, while a 1775 plan shows

over 20 buildings, roads and a mill, but no pier.

The village was planned by Thomas Telford in 1788 for the British Fisheries Society, which built the infrastructure needed for the Herring fishing and laid out the grid pattern of the streets. Buildings included the pier and the Customs House (to store salt). Houses were then built on plots by the villagers themselves.

Ullapool is the main settlement in the northwest. The harbour is the centre of activity, with fishing boats, the Stornoway ferry, tour boats and yachts coming and going. In summer

*Sunset over Ullapool & the Summer Isles*

this is a busy place, yet it never loses its charm despite the crowds. Out of season, especially on a fine autumn day, it is especially appealing. Ullapool Museum is based in a former Parliamentary Church designed by Thomas Telford and built in 1829. It *"tells the story of Lochbroom - the land and its people, through a blend of traditional and multimedia displays."*

There are displays on wildlife, the emigrants on the *Hector*, Ullapool's bicentenary and a special old-fashioned schoolroom. A large archive of documents and photographs is available including much of interest to genealogists.

**Herring Fishing** Loch Broom was famous for the abundance of Herring, so numerous that they were used to fertilize the land. In 1698 Sir George MacKenzie of Tarbat set up a fishing station on the Loch to process and export salt Herring.

However, it was to be nearly 100 years before the west coast fishery really got underway. The British Fisheries Society developed Ullapool, Tobermory on Mull and Lochbay on

*Ullapool Reflections*

Skye to encourage the development of a west coast fishery. The eventual result was over exploitation and collapse.

In WWII many east coast boats fished from here. Later, in the 1960s, Norwegian Klondykers (factory ships) arrived every year to buy Herring to process for export. In the 1970s and 80s Eastern Europeans came in substantial numbers to buy and process

*Ullapool Haddock & Chips*

Herring and Mackerel.

Although the Klondykers no longer come, local fishing boats catch prawns with creels. Lobsters, crabs and scallops are also landed. All may be found on local menus. Fish is

| Ullapool to Kylesku | |
| --- | --- |
| Achiltibuie | 79 |
| Achmelvich | 86 |
| Ardvreck Castle | 83 |
| Assynt | 80 |
| Ben Mor Coigach | 79 |
| Boat Trips | 78 |
| Bone Caves | 85 |
| Canisp | 82 |
| Clachtoll | 86 |
| Coigach | 78 |
| Drumbeg | 87 |
| Eas a' Chual Aluinn | 88 |
| Elphin | 81 |
| Inchnadamph NNR | 82 |
| Falls of Kirkaig | 85 |
| Geopark | 89 |
| Kerrachar Gardens | 87 |
| Knockan Crag | 80, 81 |
| Kylesku | 88 |
| Loch Assynt | 81 |
| Loch Glencoul | 88 |
| Lochinver | 84 |
| Point of Stoer | 86 |
| Quinag | 88 |
| Stac Pollaidh | 78 |
| Suilven | 82 |
| Summer Isles | 80 |

*Late 18ᵗʰ century Warehouses in Ullapool*

*Ardmair is just north of Ullapool*

still landed at Lochinver and Kinlochbervie in Sutherland, but nowadays it is Scrabster in Caithness that is the biggest northern fishing port.

**Walks** The Ullapool area offers many fine walks; some are

---

**ULLAPOOL BOAT TRIPS**

Boat Trips to the Summer Isles are run from the pier during the season. Seals, Dolphins, Porpoises, Minke Whales and many species of seabirds may be seen. A visit to Tanera Mor, which is still inhabited, is the climax.

Isle Martin lies just off Ardmair. It is unknown who Martin was, but an ancient graveslab, marked with a triple cross stands in the graveyard and is said to be his. In 1775 John Woodhouse from Liverpool set up a Herring curing station here. The fishing was very good but had collapsed by 1813. Today the island is owned by the Isle Martin Trust and it is unpopulated, except by birds and seals. In summer a small ferry runs to the island from Ardmair.

---

signposted from the village. The Braes of Ullapool have several paths from which there are fine views of the village.

**Rhue and Ardmair** Park at the sign for Rhue and head down the road to the lighthouse at Rubha Cadail. There are fine views over the Minch and Coigach from Meall Mhor (165m). Cul a Bhogha at Ardmair is a lovely shingle beach with some sand. Round the sheltering spit is the anchorage of Loch Kanaird.

**Loch Achall** A track runs up the Ullapool River from the bridge at Morefield. This follows the river to Loch Achall. Suddenly Ullapool seems many miles away. For a longer walk keep on the track to East Rhidorroch Lodge, then follow

*Knockan Crag*

---

a path through Strath Nimhe which reaches the main road near Leckmelm.

**Coigach** (G *na Coig Achaidhean*, The Five Ach's), the mountainous peninsula north of Loch Broom was divided into *Coig's*, or fifths. A single track road winds its way to Achiltibuie, or north to Lochinver. The road follows Lochs Lurgainn, Bad a'Ghaill and Osgaig, with many fine views of Cul Beag (769m), Stac Pollaidh (613m) and the mass of Ben Mor Coigach (743m).

None of these mountains is very high, but all are individually impressive. This is a quite inspiring and magnificent landscape. Though now all clothed in grass, the valleys and lower slopes were formerly covered in Pine and Oak woods.

Today, apart from Achiltibuie, Coigach is almost devoid of people, but in 1841 4,500 people lived here. Most emigrated to the New World after the clearances. For many centuries this area was famous for its black cattle, but today the lush grassland lies ungrazed except by a few Red Deer or sheep.

*The Heart of the Coigach, Loch Bad a' Gaill with Cul Beag and Ben Mor*

The former Coigach Forest has also gone, its last remnant allegedly burnt by Government gangs in 1747.

**Geology** Coigach consists of Torridonian Sandstone, which overlies much more ancient, hummocky Lewisian Gneiss. Only Cul Mor has a cap of Cambrian Quartzite. The mountains overlook an open landscape of rocks, bogs, lochs and lochans.

**Stac Pollaidh** (613m) may take its name from the River Polly just to the north. Its summit is only 500m above the car park (NC107095) via a very clear but steep path (3mi, 5km). The views from the ridge more than repay the effort. The western summit is only for mountaineers.

**Inverpolly Special Area of Conservation** is spread out before you. It covers the ground west of the A835, the Coigach lochs and ends at the Sutherland border. Loch Sionascaig is 3 miles long, but has a coastline of 17mi (27km).

**Ben Mor Coigach** (743m) is most easily climbed from Culnacraig, at the end of the Achiltibuie road (NC061041). The route is very steep and rocky and leads to a long summit ridge with dramatic northern cliffs. This c.6mi (10km) hike will take most of a day.

**Achiltibuie** (G *Achilidh bhuidhe*, High Yellow Place, NC025085) is a remote crofting and fishing township on the west side of Coigach peninsula. It is reached via a 14mi (22km) single track road off

*Stac Pollaidh & Loch Lurgainn*

*Stac Pollaidh*

*Loch Lurgainn and Cul Beag*

*View South Towards Torridon from Achiltibuie*

the A835, 10mi (16km) north of Ullapool. The Summer Isles Hotel brochure states that, *"There is a marvellous amount of nothing to do in Achiltibuie"*.

**Beaches** Achnahaird Bay is long and narrow, with a vast expanse of reddish sand at low tide. It is backed by dunes and machair, with extensive saltmarsh at its head. Garvie Bay is a lovely isolated cove, while Reiff faces southwest and is more rocky.

**Walks and Views** Before the road to Achiltibuie was built, access was by sea from Ullapool, or by the path from Strath Kanaird to Culnacraig. This 5mi (8km) coastal route makes a fine walk, but is extremely rough in places. The postman did this every day!

*Achnahaird Bay, Achiltibuie*

The low coastline and tranquil coastline here offers many pleasant walks. There are also several trails for more serious hikers with fine views from many places. These include south over the Summer Isles and Loch Broom to An Teallach and the Torridon Mountains, or north over Inverpolly to Suilven and Cul Mor.

Summer Isles Smokehouse is worth a visit to see the process of Salmon curing and smoking as well as to purchase some of their wide range of produce.

**Summer Isles** (G *Samhraidh*, Summer) This group of small islands is just off the coast of Achiltibuie. Tanera Mor (ON *Hafna-ey*, Harbour Isle) is inhabited with a cafe and issues its own stamps. There

are holiday lets and a sailing school on the island; boat trips run to these magical islands in summer.

The island was the site of a Herring station in the late 18th and early 19th centuries, The naturalist Frank Fraser Darling lived here 1939-1943 and it is the location for his book *"Island Years"*.

**Knockan Crag** (G *Creag a' Chnocain*, Crag of the Small Hill), is 13mi (21km) north of Ullapool on the A835. This site is famous for its geology as it formed part of the scientific debate about what is now called the Moine Thrust, where older rocks are thrust horizontally over newer ones.

**Rocks** Knockan Crag illustrates the succession of rocks discussed by geologists. It is a section cut through the underlying younger Cambrian limestone strata up into the older rocks of the Moine Thrust. From the bottom first is Pipe Rock, followed by Fucoid Beds, Salterella and then Durness Limestone, overlain by much older Moine Schist.

The interface of the Thrust itself is very sharply defined, although the rocks above and below it were heavily shattered by strong forces as the Moine Schist was pushed northwestwards over younger rocks.

**Assynt** (ON *Ass*, big rocky ridge) stretches from Elphin in the south to Kylesku in the

*Coigach from Knockan Crag*

north. It is a somewhat severe landscape of rolling rocky moorland with many lochs, all dominated by several unique mountains. In contrast, the Limestone at Elphin and Inchnadamph creates a softer, greener landscape. The coast is mostly low and rocky, with many big sea lochs, but also several fine sandy beaches.

**Elphin and Cam Loch** Elphin is a sudden patch of verdant grass, caused by a large outcrop of Limestone. A chambered cairn attests to ancient inhabitants. Crofts, animals and modern houses dot the landscape. Further on there are classic views of Suilven and Canisp over the Cam Loch. There are two more prominent cairns at Ledmore and Ledbeg.

**Loch Assynt** is 16mi (25km) long, and 80m deep. It is overlooked by the brooding

*Knockan Crag*

*Knockan Crag*
*Elphin Limestone with Lush Grass*

### KNOCKAN CRAG TRAILS

Park below Knockan Crag (NC190092) Here a combination of rock art, rock trails and a rock room, as well as extracts from poems by Norman McCaig give an alternative narrative of Scotland's geological past. The rock art pieces and poetry stones give a human view of the site.

**The Rock Room** is an open sided installation which explains the landscape by means of hands on models, touch screen computers, comic strips and a rock show. Although aimed at children, adults will find that it is in fact very informative.

**Rock Trails**   Three Rock Trails allow visitors to explore the Crag. The short and easy Quarry Trail takes only 20 minutes and involves no climbing. The Thrust Trail takes about half an hour. It shows how older rocks overlie younger strata in the Moine Thrust.

The Crag Top Trail continues from here to the top of Knockan Crag (386m) from where there are excellent views north to Assynt and west over Lochan an Ais to Cul Mor and Stac Pollaidh in Coigach. The path continues along the ridge, with fine panoramas over Loch Broom and south to Torridon before returning to the car park. This takes at least an hour, more if the vistas are to be savoured.

*Loch Assynt from the A837 east of Lochinver with Quinag in the Background*

masses of Quinag, Glas Beinn and Ben More Assynt, while Suilven and Canisp dominate the south. The surrounding moorland is mostly bare and rocky, but in former times it was heavily forested. The small islands on the loch show the effect of protection from grazing.

**Ben More Assynt** (998m) and Conival (987m) are the highest peaks in the district. Only the great western bulk of Conival is visible from the road. Both are capped by Cambrian Quartzite, grey on a dull day but bright in the sun. The ascent is normally made from Inchnadamph Hotel, but it is a serious expedition of 11mi (18km)and 1,750m of ascent.

**Suilven** (ON *Sula fjall*, Pillar Rock Mountain, 731m) is

perhaps Scotland's most iconic mountain, though far from its highest. It towers over its surrounding moorland and lochs, yet is a relatively easy climb, either from Inverkirkaig or from the north via Glencanisp Lodge near Lochinver. Both routes involve long walks.

**Canisp** (ON White Mountain, 846m) is to the northeast of Suilven and stands isolated 691m above its surrounding wilderness. The view from the top is regarded as being one of the best in Scotland, and which repays the long trek in from the Cam Loch, Loch Awe or Lochinver.

**Inchnadamph NNR** is something of a paradise for geologists and botanists. The former come to study the complex

rock formations of the Moine Thrust, while the latter are attracted by the amazing diversity of plants which grow on the limestone outcrops in this area. Even people with little knowledge of geology or botany cannot fail to notice the landforms and diversity of plant life.

Many alpine species grow here at low altitudes, including Mountain Avens, Purple Saxifrage, Yellow Saxifrage, Moss Campion and Alpine Meadow-rue. Several rare sedges, ferns, mosses and bryophytes are also present.

**Geologists** The Victorian geologists, Peach and Horne, based themselves at the Inchnadamph Hotel when they were surveying the area. They worked together for 40

*Loch Assynt*

*Suilven from Stac Pollaidh*

years. Their meticulous field mapping was to lead to the then spectacular explanation of the Moine Thrust, which led eventually to an understanding of plate tectonics.

**Roadside Geology** Roadside cuttings on the A837 between Inchnadamph and Lochinver offer good exposures of the various rock types.

At NC213251, Torridonian Sandstone lies on top of Lewisian Gneiss. The former is 800 million years old (Ma) and the latter at least 2,000Ma, an unconformity of at least 1,200Ma.

At least 600m of Torridonian Sandstone stretches nearly to the southern summit of Quinag from here, but the top

**ARDVRECK CASTLE** stands at the south end of Loch Assynt. This tower house dates from the 15th century, and was the seat of the MacLeods of Assynt. The circular, corbelled section enclosed the staircase while the vaulted basement held the kitchen, storerooms and dungeons.

Neil MacLeod gained notoriety for the kidnap and imprisonment (by his wife, Christine) of the Marquis of Montrose after the Battle of Carbisdale in 1650. Montrose was a staunch Royalist. MacLeod received £20,000 and 400 bolls of sour meal from the government.

Montrose was lashed backwards to his horse and taken to Edinburgh where he was found guilty of treason. Before being executed in the Grassmarket, he made a most eloquent speech.

There were constant disputes between MacLeods and MacKenzies; after a siege in 1672 the castle was abandoned. The last inhabitants were a pair of Ospreys in the 19th century.

*Ardvreck Castle, Loch Assynt*

*Calda House, Loch Assynt*

**Calda House** was built in 1726, by the MacKenzies using stone from the castle. It had 14 rooms, each with a fireplace, and a huge central chimney. During clan fighting the house was burnt down in 1737. The MacKenzie estates were made bankrupt in 1739 and in 1757 the Sutherland Estate bought up their lands.

*Inchnadamph Bone Caves*

is of white Cambrian Quartzite, an unconformity representing a 250 million year long gap.

**Quartzite** outcrops in several places near Skiag Bridge. The road cuttings at NC232246 and NC232246 expose light coloured Quartzite filled with vertical fossil worm burrows called Pipe Rock. In a fascinating cutting near Ardvreck Castle this rock is overlain by Fucoid Beds, which in turn lie below Salterella Grit.

**Durness Limestone** in turn overlies all of these. The crags at Stronchrubie (NC250200) above the roadside at Inchnadamph expose strata which span many millions of years. To the west lies the unaltered foreland, while to the east these rocks are jumbled up by

the Moine thrusts, which took place around 430 million years ago. The Cambrian Limestone outcrops from Loch Eriboll to Skye and is the reason for the vivid areas of greenery.

**Lochinver** is the only large village in Assynt, and owes its prosperity to its excellent harbour. Fishing boats land their catches of whitefish and shellfish here for shipment south. The imposing sugar loaf of Suilven, and neighbouring Canisp, provide a magnificent backdrop to the village.

Perhaps the best views are from the side road going west from the bridge at the north end of the street. A rocky knoll near the Highland Stoneware pottery is a good place from which to admire the scene.

The village offers a wide range of services including accommodation, eating out, fuel and shops. The Assynt Visitor Centre has displays on the area, tourist information and books for sale. It is the base for the Highland Council Ranger Service in Assynt, which organises walks and events all year. There is also a reference library for information on wildlife, geology and local history.

**Lochinver Larder** is a culinary delight, offering delicious pies, with savoury, vegetarian and dessert fillings. Additionally a full menu is available. Michael Winner enthused after a visit here, "*I had steak and ale pie and a chicken, cheese and potato one. Both absolutely tiptop. We eat in a large room overlooking the loch, an old church, wonderful scenery. Then I chose a chocolate fudge cake and a vanilla fudge cake. Totally, absolutely, incredibly historic.*"

Over 100 species of wild flowers grow here, along with a wide variety of lichens and mosses, which thrive in the moist, clean air. In the early morning or late evening an Otter or Pine Marten might be glimpsed.

**Inverkirkaig** (ON *Kirkju-Vagr*, Church Bay) is about 2mi (3km) south of Lochinver on the single track road that goes to Aird of Coigach. The River Kirkaig reaches the sea through a pleasant wooded valley at Inverkirkaig, where there is a fine pebbly, sandy beach. There is

*Lochinver from the North*

*Suilven Towers over Lochinver*

The Bone Caves face north from the foot of the limestone Creag nan Uamh overlooking Allt nan Uamh burn (NC268171). Excavations revealed many animal and some human bones, dating to about 2600BC.

also a double surprise for book lovers here, Achins Bookshop, where one can enjoy browsing the interesting books, and indulging in some nice coffee.

**Falls of Kirkaig** A path follows the river eastwards from here to the Falls of Kirkaig (about 2mi, 3km) through a woodland of Rowan, Hazel and Aspen. The falls themselves are only 18m high, but

after rain, they can be quite dramatic. In spring and early summer Salmon may be seen attempting to leap the falls, but they cannot pass here.

This walk may afford views of Dippers and Grey Wagtails on the river, while Pine Marten live in the woods. The path leads on to the Fionn Loch for wonderful views of Suilven. By continuing round the north

There were many bits of Reindeer antler dating from 8,000 to 47,000 years ago. Bones from at least 22 other species were also present, including Arctic species such as Polar Bear from 18,000 years ago, Arctic Fox, Brown Bear, Wolf, rodents and Lynx.

The bones may have been washed there by glacial meltwater or taken there by animals, or both. There is no evidence of human habitation. Reindeer formerly gathered to calf on the slopes of Breabag. Reindeer Cave and Bone Cave are connected by a narrow passage which children can crawl through.

The caves are a little over 1mi (1.5km) along a track from a signposted car park itself about 4mi (6km) north of Ledmore Junction. Great care should be taken on the paths leading up to the caves.

Along the burn there is much of botanical interest, including an intriguing spring about half way. Dippers and Grey Wagtail frequent the burn, while Buzzards and Golden Eagles can often be seen soaring above the crags.

*Lochinver Larder*

*Lochinver from near the Pottery*

*Inverkirkaig*

*Falls of Kirkaig*

side of the loch for another 3mi (5km), the southern approach to the mountain is reached. Waders such as Dunlin, Redshank and Greenshank breed on the moors and loch sides.

**Achmelvich** is about 3mi (4.5km) along the very twisty B869, north of Lochinver. This collection of wonderful sandy beaches backed by dunes and machair has some of the most enchanting sands in the north of Scotland. In early summer the machair becomes a riot of colour with wild flowers. This is a good area for walking, with paths over the moors back to Lochinver, north along the coast and northeast into the lochan dotted moorland. The camping and caravan site vies with Durness and Big Sand for the most enticing location.

**Clachtoll** is about 4mi (6km) further west and also has a fine sandy beach as well as exposures of interesting rocks. An abandoned Salmon fishing station bothy and ice house have been restored and have displays relating to the fishery. On the

south side of the Bay of Stoer, Clachtoll Broch still stands 2m high. The entrance has a massive triangular lintel and there are remains of an intramural staircase. On the east side a wall enclosed an area which may have been a settlement.

**Point of Stoer** A minor road continues for about 4mi (6km) to Stoer lighthouse, first lit in 1870 and another Stevenson design. It was automated in 1978 and the former keepers' accommodation is now let out as two holiday let flats. There are stunning views to the south and east taking in Canisp, Suilven and the Coigach mountains. The Western Isles can be seen on the western horizon.

**Old Man of Stoer** From the lighthouse it is a 2mi (3km) walk across moorland and past low cliffs to the Old Man of Stoer, a 61m high stack. There is a fine view from Sidhean Mòr (G Big Fairy Hill, 161m), the nearby hill with a radio mast. The Old Man can also be reached from Culkein.

This headland is a good place to look out for cetaceans, especially between July and

*Achmelvich*

*Stoer Lighthouse*

*Panoramic view east and south from the Point of Stoer to Canisp, Suilven, Cul Mor, Stac Pollaidh and the Coigach*

September. Porpoises, Minke Whales, White-sided Dolphins and Killer Whales may be spotted, especially if shoals of fish are about. Basking Sharks may also be present.

Culkein is another former Salmon fishing station. An unusual design of ice house sits near the ruined pier. There is a fine small sandy beach, sheltered except from northeast. The nearby headland of Rubh'an Dunain has a ruined dun, a natural arch and caves.

**Clashnessie** (G *Cleas an easidh*, Glen of the Waterfall) has a pretty little waterfall on the burn about 800m inland. Numerous lochans drain into this stream. Red and Black-throated Divers may be seen or heard as they fly in from fishing at sea. It also has a fine little north facing beach.

**Drumbeg** The B869 continues west through wild country via Drumbeg and Nedd to the A894 south of Kylesku. This road offers some of the best views in the northwest on a clear day. There are many good viewpoints as it winds over rocky moorland and patches

of woodland, one of the best being from the west end of Drumbeg.

**Ardvar Woods** in Glen Ardvar is a remnant of the forests that once covered much of the Highlands. These old woods are dominated by Birch but also have Rowan, Hazel, Wych Elm and Oak as well as a large variety of mosses and lichens.

*Quinag from the Drumbeg Road*

*Loch Drumbeg & Quinag*

**Kerrachar Gardens** are situated in a sheltered spot near the entrance to Loch a Chairn Bhain about 4mi (6km) west of Kylesku. There is no road or path, instead a small ferry runs from the pier at Kylesku.

The gardens have been developed since 1995 on abandoned croftland. They have featured

*Kylesku Bridge at Moonrise*

in gardening magazines and, in 2006, *The Independent* included Kerrachar in a list of 10 Best Gardens to Visit in Summer.

**Quinag** (G *Chuineag*, milking pail) is a large mountain (808m), which dominates the landscape all around it. Perhaps the most striking view is from the road north of the Kylesku Bridge. The mountain is composed of Torridonian Sandstone and the high peaks are topped by Cambrian Quartzite. Quinag is said to have some of the best hillwalking in Scotland.

**Loch Glencoul** The flanks of Ben Aird da Loch on the north side of Loch Glencoul very clearly show where older rocks were thrust over newer ones in the Moine and Glencoul Thrusts. There are several good view points along the road south of Kylesku.

*Loch a Chairn Bhain & Quinag*

*Quinag from the East on the A894*

**Kylesku Bridge** is an elegant curved structure which crosses the Caolas Cumhann. It is of pre-stressed box girder construction with a span of 276m and a height of 24m and was opened in 1984 by the Queen. It replaced a small car ferry and greatly improved access to the far northwest.

**Eas a' Chual Aluinn** (G Waterfall of the Beautiful Tresses, NC281278, 200m) is the highest waterfall in Britain. On the opposite side of the valley, Eas an't Strutha Ghil is higher (290m) but does not fall in one drop. They both cascade into Loch Beag at the head of Loch Glencoul and are at their best after there has been a lot of rain. They can be reached on foot by a long trek over marshy ground from south of Loch na Gainmhich, about 3mi (4.5km) south of Kylesku.

**Kylesku** is an attractive little village just off the main road, south of the bridge. The former ferry pier is the departure point for boat trips that are run in the summer to the Kerrachar Gardens and to see the

*Loch Glencoul*

waterfalls. These afford a good chance to see wildlife such as seals, Otters or Golden Eagles. From here on north the NC500 enters the wildest and most spectacular country of the whole route, indeed of the whole of the UK. With very few habitations, lovely bays and lochans as well as dramatic scree topped mountains and rock strewn landscapes, these are the Lonely Lands. Here there is a vista or a secret fairy place around every corner.

*Kylesku Prawns*

*Northwest Highlands Geopark*

*Kylesku Bridge*

## NORTHWEST HIGHLANDS GEOPARK

Most of the area has been designated as the North West Highlands Geopark, whose eastern boundary roughly follows the Moine Thrust from Loch Eriboll south to Ben More Assynt. Coigach and the Summer Isles are also included.

These "Lonely Lands" have some of the most spectacular scenery in the whole of Britain. This starkly beautiful landscape is lovely on a fine day, but dour when the weather is bad. Many roads are single track and require care, but they also force you to slow down and afford a new vista around every turn.

Much of the landscape is ancient Lewisian Gneiss, this is overlain by Torridonian Sandstone in several places. The mountains of Suilven, Canisp and Quinag are examples, as is the Stoer Peninsula, Handa Island and much of the Parph Peninsula.

Outcrops of limestone at Durness, Inchnadamph and Elphin are lush in comparison to most of the area. Many of the mountains are capped with Cambrian Quartzite, which gleams in the sunshine when wet.

This complex geology leads to a diverse range of habitats, making it a compelling place for naturalists. One can spend the entire day without seeing anyone, or any sign of human habitation.

Cape Wrath Lighthouse from the east

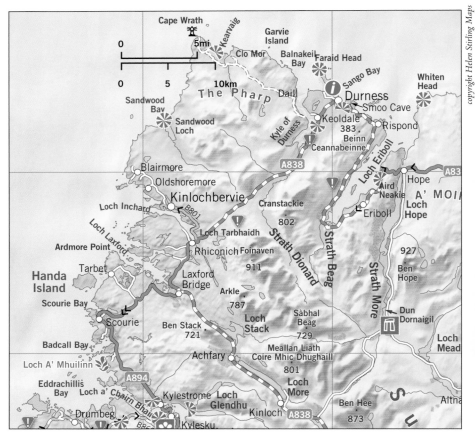

*copyright Helen Stirling Maps*

**The Lonely Lands** Kylestrome, just north of the bridge, is an attractive place to explore. Otters are often seen in the gloaming along this shore. A two mile (3km) path leads east-

*Duartmore between Kylesku and Scourie*

to the waterfalls at the Maldie Burn, not so high as the more famous ones, but much easier to reach and to view. There are good views of the Moine Thrust east from here.

**X-craft Memorial** The XII[th] Submarine Flotilla operated out of Lochs Glendhu and Glencoul from 1943. X-craft miniature submarine crews trained here before going to

Norway where they succeeded in disabling the German battleship *Tirpitz*. The memorial north of the bridge honours the 39 men who died as well as the local people *"who knew so much and talked so little."*

**Loch a' Mhuilinn NNR** is situated on the coast south of Badcall Bay. It is the most northerly patch of native Oak woodland in UK. Dominated by Birch, it has Rowan, Hazel, Aspen and Willow trees as well as a large flora of lichens and mosses. It is a peaceful and pleasant place to stop.

**Edrachillis Bay** is one of the most enchanting of the many fine bays on this coast. It is strewn with small islands and a summer evening stroll can be very romantic, just so long as the midges are not out! A Salmon fishing station formerly operated here. The old buildings and jetty date from about 1840; a Salmon farm now occupies the site. The nearby old manse is now the highly rated Eddrachillies Hotel.

**Scourie** (G *Scobh Airigh*, Shieling by the Little Wood)

*Eddrachillis Bay*

is a small village situated at the head of Scourie Bay. A small sandy beach is backed by an area of machair. Now partially bypassed by the A894, the village is a good place to stop and also a fine base from which to explore the far northwest. Most of the cottages date from the 19th century.

All around there are dramatic exposures of twisted and convoluted Lewisian Gneiss, with later Scourian Dykes, where molten rock has infiltrated cracks. The low rocky shores offer fine walking as well as lovely views to Handa and over Eddrachillies Bay.

**Tarbet and Fanagmore** are reached by a small side road north of Scourie which crosses rocky moorland and many lochans on the way. Divers breed on these lochans and waders in the marshy areas.

*Loch a' Mhullin*

| Kylesku to Durness | |
|---|---|
| Arkle | 94 |
| Badcall Bay | 93 |
| Ben Stack | 96 |
| Cape Wrath | 97 |
| Carnstackle | 96 |
| Foinaven | 96 |
| Handa | 94 |
| Kinlochbervie | 96 |
| Kyle of Durness | 97 |
| Kylestrome | 92 |
| Loch a' Mhuilinn NNR | 93 |
| Loch Inchard | 96 |
| Loch Laxford | 94 |
| Loch Stack | 94 |
| Oldshoremore | 96 |
| Polin | 96 |
| Sandwood Bay | 97 |
| Scourie | 93 |
| Srath Dionard | 97 |
| Tarbet | 93 |
| X-craft memorial | 92 |

*Scourie from the South*

*View South from Handa*

appearance it gets its name. Black-throated Divers nest around the lochs here, Greenshanks and other waders may be heard calling and Dippers may be seen by the river.

**Handa** (ON, *Sand-ey*, Sandy Isle) is a small island near Scourie famous for its birds and wild flowers, taking its name from its beaches. It is composed of Torridonian Sandstone which gives it a totally different character from much of the nearby mainland, and which weathers to make the ledges so liked by birds.

**Loch Laxford** (ON *Lax, Salmon*) is larger than Badcall Bay, but also strikingly beautiful, with its many islands and rocky headlands. The River Laxford is fed by Loch Stack and both are famed for their Salmon angling. Road cuttings on Laxford Braes show interesting patterns in the Lewisian Gneiss rocks.

Near Laxford Bridge, mudflats, sandy areas and saltmarsh attract many waders. Grey and Common Seals are often present and this is prime Otter territory. The many small patches of woodland attract small birds.

**Loch Stack and Arkle** There are fine views of Arkle (ON *Ark Fjell*, Flat-Topped Hill, 787m) from the A838 around Loch Stack. The mountain is made of Cambrian Quartzite from whose glistening

Although now uninhabited, over 60 people lived here until 1848, when they all emigrated to Nova Scotia. They were not cleared, but left as they had become over reliant on potatoes; blight caused crop failure. This seems unlikely to be the entire reason as there is a wealth of birds and fish as well as fertile land to grow other crops.

**Birds** In summer the island is home to about 100,000 nesting seabirds. The high cliffs (120m) and the Great Stack hold thousands of Guillemots, Razorbills, Puffins, Shags, Kit-

*Port an Eilean, Handa*

*Assynt & Coigach from Handa*

*Great Stack of Handa*

tiwakes and Fulmars, while Great Skuas, Arctic Skuas and gulls nest on the hill. Handa is easily the best place in the area to see breeding seabirds in large numbers.

**Wild Flowers** The combination of sandstone rock, lots of bird droppings and low grazing pressure means that Handa has a very interesting selection of wild flowers. Probably they are at their best in late June when Thrift, Spring Squill, Grass of Parnassus, Sea Plantain and many others give a wonderful display of colour.

Handa was undoubtedly used by the Vikings because of its sheltered landing and ease of access from the Minch. This is one of the better places to pull up a longship on this hard and inhospitable coast. There is an

ancient ruined chapel in the graveyard, where traditionally people from the nearby mainland were buried so that they were not dug up by wolves.

The ruined settlement has an ancient and slightly mysterious feeling about it, especially on a misty day. According to folklore the ancient inhabitants had their own queen, the eldest widow, and a parliament which met to decide on daily chores.

*Arctic Skua*

*Puffin*

*Great Skua*

**HANDA BOAT TRIPS**

A ferry runs from Tarbet slipway during the summer on demand and depending on the weather. Follow the A894 for about 3mi (4km) then turn off onto a signposted side road Tarbet is a further 3mi overlooking a sheltered little harbour.

Handa is a Scottish Wildlife Trust Reserve. There is a small visitor centre with a composting toilet above the beach. From here a board walk leads across the hill to the spectacular northwest cliffs and the Great Stack. In early summer the ledges are occupied by thousands of breeding Guillemots and Razorbills. Puffins nest in burrows on top of the stack, and on the cliffs opposite.

The path follows the high cliffs before it drops to a rocky shoreline then past the old settlement to the sandy beach. There are spectacular views north to Cape Wrath, east to the mountains of Assynt and south to the Stoer Peninsula and Coigach.

Handa is a somewhat romantic place with its ancient graveyard and ruined settlement near the landing place. The best time to visit is late May and June to see the nesting seabirds and wild flowers. In July and August the moorland becomes resplendent as the heather blooms. Cetaceans may be seen offshore at this time also.

*Foinaven and Arkle from Loch Inchard*

**Loch Inchard** (G *Innis Ard*, Pasture Head) is the last sheltered inlet before Cape Wrath. In former times this area was famous for its yellow cattle and was heavily forested. Parts of the landscape remain very green today and there is evidence of ancient settlement.

**Kinlochbervie** is now a major landing port for white fish trawlers and the fish market makes an interesting visit during an auction. The flurry of activity as the catch is landed, sorted, sold and despatched on trucks is in great contrast to the relaxed atmosphere which pervades most of the time.

Apart from a number of inshore boats which catch shellfish, most of the trawlers are from the northeast and base themselves here to save fuel, the crews returning home at the weekends. Sadly the Fishermen's Mission is now closed.

Before the roads were built in the 1830s, all access was by sea. In 1936 a new pier was built for the MacBrayne's steamer, which called regularly with supplies. After WWII, road improvements meant that this service stopped. Harbour developments continued over the years as have road improvements which have sustained Kinlochbervie's port status.

**Oldshoremore** The road west of Kinlochbervie passes the crofting townships of Oldshoremore, Oldshore Beg, Balchrick and Sheigra. Each has an attractive beach, backed by dunes and machair. They are different in character, but all have lovely sands, sheltered on each side by rocky headlands.

Perhaps the finest beach is the one at Polin. There are very interesting rock exposures especially in the low cliffs of Oldshoremore. In summer the machair is covered by a colourful carpet of over 200 species of wild flowers.

**Foinaven** (G *Fionne Bheinn*, White Mountain, 908m), along with the peaks of Ben Stack (721m), Arkle (ON *Arkfjall*, Ark Mountain, 787m), and Carnstackie (800m) dominate the eastern horizon. Ben Stack is composed of Lewisian Gneiss while the others are all composed of Cambrian Quartzite which gleams in the sun, especially after rain.

*Kinlochbervie*

*Oldshoremore*

## Sandwood Bay

*Sandwood Bay Panoramic*

Sandwood Bay (ON *Sand Vik*, Sandy Bay) is a 4mi (6.5km) hike across a moorland path. Park at Blairmore near the end of the road from Kinlochbervie. There are public toilets here. This beach is nearly 2mi (3km) long, with rugged cliffs at each end.

These mountains may not be very high but they present spectacular views along the A838 on the road to Durness. They have steep scree covered slopes, and great corries, where frost shattered quartzite has tumbled downwards. Gentler slopes allow access to walkers. All but Ben Stack involve long and arduous treks over rough ground, very steep in places and often covered in scree.

**Srath Dionard** runs southeast between Carnstackie and Foinaven. A track follows the river up the valley, from which there are dramatic views of the eastern corries of Foinaven and the screes of Conamheall (482m). The lonely A838 continues north through a bleak landscape which suddenly becomes green and lush near the Kyle of Durness when the outcrop of limestone at Durness is reached.

It is said to be the home of a mermaid, which lures seamen with her hauntingly beautiful songs. Many ships were certainly wrecked here in the days of sail and sometimes people have a feeling of a slight shiver down their back, an unease that makes them eager to leave.

Certainly the roofless house is said to be haunted by the ghost of a drowned mariner. After northwesterly storms ribs of some of the wrecks may be exposed. They are soon covered with sand again on this very active beach.

A stack, *Am Buchaille* (G *The Shepherd*), stands to the south, while Cape Wrath is 8mi (13km) of hard trekking to the north. The beach is backed by a large area of sand dunes and machair which is best in early summer for rare wild flowers.

A large expanse around Allt Briste above Sandwood Loch has been fenced off to exclude deer and sheep. It has been planted with thousands of native trees to regenerate some of the forest that formerly stood here.

*Sandwood Bay and Am Buchaille*

*Fionaven reflected in Loch Tarbhaidh*

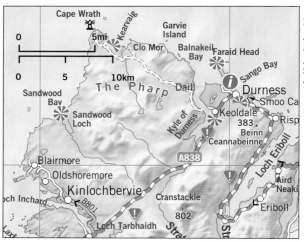

*copyright Helen Stirling Maps*

The north of Sutherland is an ideal place for nature lovers, its varied habitats harbouring many interesting species of birds, mammals, insects and plants. Perhaps the diversity of wild flowers is the most remarkable feature of this landscape.

**Durness** is the most remote and least populated parish in the UK, with only 2.4 people per square mile. Despite this it has a vibrant community and a long history. Most of the coastline is cliffs, reaching 190m at Clo Mor. The major inlets of the Kyle of Durness and Loch Eriboll are different in character. The former is shallow and sandy, while the latter is much larger and very deep.

**Geology** To the west, the plateau of The Parph is composed of Lewisian Gneiss overlain in places with Torridonian Sandstone. It is mostly peaty moorland with rolling hills. Between the Kyle and Eriboll a range of Quartzite hills stretches from Foinaven (908m) to Beinn Ceannabeinne (383m). The Moine Thrust follows the east slopes of Loch Eriboll in a southeasterly direction.

**THE NORTH COAST OF SUTHERLAND** goes from Cape Wrath in the west to Strathy Point and Melvich in the east. It is a gentler coast than that of the west, with three large indentations, the Kyle of Durness, Loch Eriboll and the Kyle of Tongue. Apart from Ben Hope (927m) and Ben Loyal (764m) in the west, much of the hinterland is low lying with blanket peat bog.

The landscape is dotted with many lochs, large and small. Strath More, Strathnaver and Strath Halladale were all formerly inhabited. Evidence can

be seen of this in the form of chambered cairns, brochs and more recent ruined farmsteads and settlements.

Most of this area is made up of the former Pictish and Norse province of Strathnaver. It was MacKay or Reay country and was for centuries the scene of disputes between the MacKays and their neighbours, the Sinclairs, Sutherlands, MacLeods, and MacKenzies. Eventually it was nearly all bought up by the Sutherland Estate, which introduced large scale sheep farming in the 19th century.

*Kyle of Durness*

*Kyle of Durness*

Durness itself is located on a large outcrop of Limestone, making for fertile soils and thus attractive for settlement. There are also outcrops of Limestone on the east side of Loch Eriboll.

East of the Moine Thrust the rocks are Moine Schists, which are very hard and result in a vast area of peat bog with a few hills and mountains. Ben

Hope is the highest and rises to 927m. It is the most northerly Munro (mountain over 3,000ft, 914m).

**Archaeology** Most of the ancient sites visible today are concentrated on Limestone areas. These include several Neolithic chambered cairns, Bronze Age cist burials, Iron Age houses, souterrains, brochs and duns. Apart from a Norse burial at

## DURNESS
### Origin of the name

In the Sagas and old manuscripts the parish is always referred to as *Dyrnes* (ON *Dyr Nes*, Deer Headland). Until 1724 it extended from Kylesku to the Water of Borgie. Now the parish only encompasses Durness itself, the Parph district to the west and the Moine, including Eriboll to the east. Many of the placenames are of Norse origin, suggesting that this area was well settled by the Vikings. Some are undoubtedly pre-Norse, including *Parph*, *Moine* and *Loyal*. These names may be Pictish or even handed down from the original settlers.

*Chambered Cairn*
*Kyle of Durness from Ferry House*

*Millennium Stone*

| DURNESS AREA | |
|---|---|
| Balnakeil Bay | 102 |
| Balnakeil Craft Village | 102 |
| Beinne Ceannabeinne | 98 |
| Cape Wrath | 100, 104 |
| Clo Mor | 105 |
| Duslic Rock | 105 |
| Durness | 98 |
| Faraid Head | 103 |
| John Lennon Memorial | 101 |
| Kearvaig | 105 |
| Keoldale | 105 |
| Kyle of Durness | 100 |
| Loch Eriboll | 106 |
| Pharp | 98, 105 |
| Rispond | 106 |
| Sandwood Bay | 97 |
| Sango Beg | 104 |
| Sango Bay | 100 |
| Smoo Cave | 101 |
| Srath Dionard | 97 |
| Traigh Allt Chaligeag | 104 |

*Summer Sunrise over Sango Sands*

Balnakeil, there is no physical evidence of the Vikings. However there is an abundance of Old Norse placenames, which attest to settlement.

**WWII** RAF Sango Chain Home Low radar station was established in Durness in 1940. This was part of an early warning system all around the coast. The facility required hundreds of personnel and some of the many buildings remain in use today, notably the Youth Hostel. Many ruinous concrete structures remain from this time.

A new radar station was planned after the war, but was abandoned in 1954 before it became operational. Since 1932 Garvie Island, the adjacent coast and sea have been used as a live firing range by warships and aircraft. Access to Cape Wrath is curtailed at times.

**Kyle of Durness** The sandbanks and channels in the Kyle change from year to year. There are stunning views from the road between Ferry House and Daill, which change with the tides, weather and light. At high tide the greens and blues can be particularly striking.

**Sango Bay** (ON *Sand Gja, Sand Geo*) is nearly 1,500m of beautiful sands, sheltered by cliffs and facing northeast. Small rock stacks greatly add to the beauty of this bay. During the summer it is perfectly situated for sunrises. The tops of Hoy in Orkney can be seen, over 60mi (100km) away over the Pentland Firth.

*WWII Chain Home Radar Station*

*Youth Hostel in Old WWII Huts*

*John Lennon & Family at Durness*

*Sango Sands with Faraid Head in the Distance*

**Smoo Cave** (ON *Smuggja*, rocky cleft) has the biggest entrance of any sea cave in the UK. It is about 15m high, while the main chamber is 60m by 40m. Allt Smoo plunges 25m down a sink hole into an inner cave. The waterfall can be observed from a platform. Further caves can only be reached by means of boat tours.

Geodha Smoo and the caves can be accessed from a nearby car park. After heavy rain Allt Smoo swells and flows into the underground pool with a mighty roar. Trips into the inner cave are available subject to the water level.

**John Lennon** had a cousin in Durness and, as a child, used to come here for summer holidays. In 2002 an area next to the village hall was landscaped, part of which was dedicated to the memory of Lennon. He was last here in 1969 with Yoko Ono, Julian and Kyoko.

**Walks** The Durness Path Network booklet describes a number of interesting walks in the area. These cover most of the places of interest. Many are coastal, but others follow peat roads into the moorland.

**Wildlife** The landscape is largely devoid of trees, partly due to exposure and partly because excessive grazing by sheep and deer prevents any regeneration of saplings. However, the Limestone areas support an extremely diverse range of over 500 species of plants. Alpine plants grow at sea level here. The clifftops support maritime heath, with *Primula scotica* and other rare plants.

*Moonrise over Sango Sands*

*Smoo Cave Waterfall*

*Smoo Cave Interior & Entrance*

*Balnakeil Bay at Low Tide*

Divers are present on many of the lochs and Corncrakes are still heard calling here in summer. Durness can also be a good location to seek rare species during migration times.

Badgers, Otters, Foxes and Wild Cats live in the area. Grey Seals haul out to have their young on shingle beaches below Whiten Head, the largest colony on the Mainland.

**Balnakeil Craft Village** is housed in an abandoned Cold War military site about 1,000m west of the Spar shop on the way to Balnakeil Bay. It was part of a new radar system but was abandoned in 1954 before being completed. These utilitarian concrete buildings remained derelict for many years before being taken over in the 1970s by New Age optimists.

A wide range of businesses here range from Cocoa Mountain, a chocolate café and factory, to a whole variety of other creative outlets, art galleries and hairdressers. On no account let the stark military architecture put you off.

**Balnakeil Bay** (G *Baile na Cille*, Township of the Chapel) is a beautiful 1.5mi (2.4km) west facing arc of sand north of Durness. It is backed by sand dunes and machair which is a sea of colour with wild flowers in summer.

**Balnakeil Kirkyard** is the site of a very early Culdean Christian settlement. A ruined chapel here may be on the site of one established by St Maelrubha in the 7th century. The now roofless church was built around 1619 on the site of a

*Cocoa Mountain*

*Balnakeil Craft Village*

*Balnakeil Bay & Faraid Head from the South*

*Old Photograph of Durness from the East*

## Faraid Head Walk

**Longer** The longer route starts at Durness village centre and follows a path around the cliffs above Sango Bay then along the east side of An Fharaid to Faraid Head. Return via the dunes and Balnakeil Bay and follow the road back to Durness, visiting Balnakeil Craft Village along the way, total 8mi (12km).

**Shorter** Drive to the carpark below Balnakeil Kirkyard and follow the beach right around to the north end. Take the road that leads to the military base then climb to the top of the cliffs, following the fence. Return along the east cliffs and sand dunes to the beach and carpark, total 5mi (8km).

much earlier one. There was a monastery here in former times which was rich enough to contribute funds to the Third Crusade in 1190.

There are a number of interesting tombstones, including that of Donald MacMurdo, a local villain who died in 1623, and Rob Donn, who was a bard and composer of Gaelic songs, who died in 1828.

**Balnakeil House** is built on the site of a 7th century monastery. The Bishop of Caithness had a residence here in the 12th century but by the 16th century the house belonged to the chief of Clan MacKay, later Lord Reay.

In 1744 the house was rebuilt in Georgian style. It incorporates parts of the original

towerhouse and remains substantially unchanged today. The farm steading was built in 1801 but destroyed by fire in 1995. The ruinous mill is also 19th century.

**Faraid Head** (G, *am Faire Aite*, the Watch Place, 100m, NC390719) shelters Balnakeil Bay from the north and east. The headland is composed of highly resistant Lewisian Gneiss and Moine Schist, giv-

*Durness from Faraid Head*

*Mather's Shop Today*

*Mather's Shop in the 1980s*

*Cape Wrath & Lighthouse from the East*

ing way to Durness Limestone on the south side of the bay. Puffins breed on the east side of the headland. Many rare wildflowers, including orchids and *Primula scotica* may be found on the maritime heath.

The MOD control centre on the headland is part of the Cape Wrath Range. A road leads through the dunes but it frequently disappears beneath drifting sand. The facility monitors the surrounding area during live exercises to ensure the safety of commercial aircraft and shipping.

**Fossils** The shoreline below the Golf Course has many exposures of stromatolites. These fossil cyanobacteria, or blue-green algae, are some of the earliest forms of life on Earth. Here they date from

480 million years ago, and were responsible for producing our oxygen rich atmosphere.

**Shinty at New Year** In former times Shinty (a form of hockey) was played on the sands of Balnakeil on Old Christmas and Old New Year's Day. Up to 100 players took part on each side, cheered on by their womenfolk and older men. The game continued until dark and often took to the sea. It was occasionally violent but, as in other traditional events, animosity ended with the game.

**Sango Beg** and Traigh na Chailgeag, to the east of Smoo Cave, are also very attractive coves, much less frequented than Sango Sands but similarly sheltered by cliffs except from the northeast.

**Cape Wrath** (ON *Hvarf*, Turning Point, 100m, NC260748) is the most north-westerly point of the Scottish mainland.

**Lighthouse** The engineer in charge of building Cape Wrath lighthouse was Robert Stevenson. It was first lit in 1828, and has an elevation of 122m. Stone for the tower and dwelling houses was quarried at nearby Clais Charnach, near the jetty and landing place used for supplies. The road from the Kyle of Durness also dates from 1828.

The gaunt building on the hill above the lighthouse is Lloyd's Signal Station which operated from about 1903 until 1932. Passing ships radioed details of their cargoes, destinations and estimated time of arrival.

*Duslic Rock*

*Lloyds Signal Station*

*Cape Wrath from Seaward*

**CAPE WRATH**
**Origin of the name**

The name Cape Wrath is a map-maker's invention. The Sagas refer to it as *Hvarf*. Ptolemy's map has a *Torvedunum* which may be this prominent headland. It is interesting that the hill behind the lighthouse is called Dunan. *Parph* and *Dunan* may well be ancient pre-Celtic names, perhaps also meaning turning point, thus giving the name Ptolemy quotes.

**Kearvaig** is a beautiful sandy bay about 3mi (5km) east of the Cape. There is a lovely walk from the lighthouse along the clifftops to this enchanting bay. The Vikings are said to have pulled up their boats here.

The rock at the east end of the bay is nicknamed The Cathedral on account of its twin spires. The beach has fine white sand with shingle at the top. Another mile to the

east the dramatic Torridonian Sandstone cliffs of Clo Mor are the highest on the UK mainland at nearly 200m.

**Duslic Rock** is a dangerous reef which lies about 0.7mi (1km) northeast of the lighthouse. Small vessels keep in mid channel but large vessels keep well offshore here. Waves break spectacularly here and on the rocks below the lighthouse during storms.

**CAPE WRATH VISIT**

A small passenger ferry runs in summer from the jetty at Keoldale to another jetty on the Cape side. From there minibuses take visitors the 12mi (19km) to the lighthouse. If the weather is fine there is a spectacular walk back along the cliffs to Kearvaig 4mi (6km), 4 hours.

Military exercises take place regularly on the Cape Wrath Range. Live firing of munitions by warships, and by the Army of artillery, mortars, and missiles is carried out on the Range. Aircraft practise bombing and test fully armed bombs, missiles, and cannons on Garvie Island.

Access to Cape Wrath and adjacent areas may be restricted during these exercises, which are necessary, *"to maintain the skills our armed forces need to carry out the tasks which they may be called upon to perform."*

*Kearvaig Bay East of Cape Wrath*

*Cape Wrath from Dùnan Mòr*

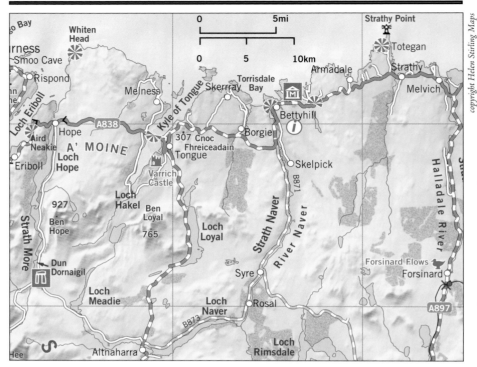

**Loch Eriboll** (ON *Eyrr Bolstaðir*, Ayre Farm), from the tombolo at Ard Neakie, is about 10mi (16km) long, with a depth of 30m to 120m. It has for a long time been used as a safe anchorage by ships, including the Royal Navy. Traditionally, when crew members were given leave to go ashore, they set out the names of their ships in stones on the hillside.

Norwegian King Haakon and his fleet anchored here on their return from their unsuccessful mission south in October 1263. In 1937 HMS *Hood* moored in the loch for 9 days, during which the crew left its name on the hillside. During May 1945 the loch was the site of the surrender of over 30 German U-boats. The servicemen of WWII called it *Lock*

*'Orrible* due to the lack of shore facilities.

**Rispond** has the only harbour in the area. It was developed in the 1780s by Peterhead merchants trading in fish and kelp. Until the roads were built in the 1830s it was the landing place for supplies, most of which came from Orkney.

*Ard Neakie and Loch Eriboll showing the tombolo*

Ard Neakie is joined to the east shore of the loch by an ayre. In the 1870s the Reay Estate opened a quarry and built lime kilns on the island to supply fertiliser for its land reclamation projects.

Whiten Head, at the east entrance to Loch Eriboll, rises to over 170m. The Quartzite cliffs gleam white in the sun and have many caves. The largest mainland colony of Grey Seals in the UK comes ashore to pup here each autumn. There is no path to Whiten Head, which is a 5mi (8km) hike along the cliffs north of the road.

Strath Beag is an attractive little valley at the south end of the loch. It runs inland for about 2mi (3km). A path goes up the eastern side, then follows the

*Whiten Head from near Rispond*

river to deciduous woodland. Pine Martens live in the woods and Otters may be seen here. Dippers and Wagtails feed on the river, and Golden Eagles frequently quarter the ground. Red and Black-throated Divers breed on the high lochans.

A' Mhoine (G Peaty Ground) is a rather monotonous area of rolling hills, lochans and peat bog between Loch Eriboll and

Tongue. The rocks are hard Moine Schist, derived from sandstones and mudstones which were metamorphosed before being once more thrust to the surface.

*Shepherd with his Flock, Loch Eriboll*

*A' Moine Moorland with Ben Loyal*

| North Coast | |
|---|---|
| A' Moine | 107 |
| Altnaharra | 109 |
| Ard Neakie | 107 |
| Ben Hope | 108 |
| Ben Loyal | 109 |
| Bettyhill | 110 |
| Clearances | 113 |
| Dun Dornaigil | 108 |
| Dunviden | 112 |
| Farr Bay | 111 |
| Loch Eriboll | 106 |
| Melness | 110 |
| Melvich | 113 |
| Old Split Stone | 114 |
| Portskerra | 113 |
| Rispond | 106 |
| RSPB Forsinard Flows | 115 |
| Strath Halladale | 114, 107 |
| Strathnaver | 110 |
| Strathnaver Museum | 111 |
| Strath More | 108 |
| Strathy | 112 |
| Strathy Point | 112 |
| Tongue | 108 |
| Torrisdale Bay | 111 |
| Varrich Castle | 109 |
| Whiten Head | 107 |

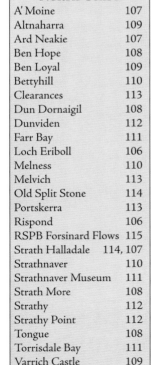

Loch Hope is c.5mi (8km) long, and drains to Loch Eriboll by the short River Hope. It is famous for its Sea Trout and Salmon angling, the most highly regarded of all Scottish lochs. The road passes good farmland with grazing cattle as well as abundant evidence of ancient human occupation.

*Ben Hope from the North*

## BEN HOPE

Ben Hope (ON *Hjop*, Bay, 927m) is the highest mountain in the north. Its northern and western aspects are dramatic and craggy. It can be climbed by taking the single track road south along the east side of Loch Hope to Alltnacaillich (NC459457).

A well marked, but steep and rocky path up Allt na Caillich burn with several cairns leads to the summit. Total distance is about 5mi (8km) return. The panoramas all around on a clear day are well worth the climb. They also give a good impression of the vastness of the *"Lonely Lands"* of the far northwest, with hardly a habitation in sight. Many alpine wild flowers grow on the mountain.

The Moine Thrust takes its name from the a' Moine area. From Whiten Head to Strath Beag there are exposures all along the eastern slopes of Loch Eriboll of features of these massive earth movements, where older rocks were thrust over younger strata. The Arnaboll thrust subsequently carried Lewisian Gneiss over this already complex sequence.

Strath More The main road from Eriboll to Tongue passes through the plateau of a' Mhoine. It offers fine views of Ben Hope, Ben Loyal and the Kyle of Tongue, often with pretty lochans in the foreground. A much more scenic route is the narrow side road down the east side of Loch Hope to Altnaharra, passing the west flank of Ben Hope on the way to remote Altnaharra.

Dun Dornaigil (NC457450) is a well preserved broch, still rising to 6.7m. It has an impressively large triangular lintel stone, and is well situated to guard the fertile valley of Strath More. In the 19th century the interior was filled with stones to stop it falling down, so it is obscured.

Strath More continues south of the broch over lonely moorland. There are particularly fine views over Loch Meadie to the southwestern flanks of Ben Loyal. The road passes several isolated farms and follows the River Mudale to Loch Naver. This narrow single track road is remote and offers an opportunity to see Red Deer and Golden Eagles.

Tongue (ON *Tonga*, Tongue) is a sheltered village on the east

*Ben Hope & Loch Hope*

*Dun Dornaigil*

*Alltnaharra & River Mudale*

*Ben Loyal by William Daniell (1815)*

## ALTNAHARRA & BEN LOYAL

**Altnaharra** (G *Allt N Herra*, Stream of the Parish) is one of the remotest villages in the UK. It holds the record for the lowest temperature, of minus 27.2C in December 1995. It is a popular base for anglers, deer stalkers, climbers and hill walkers. From here the A836 goes north to Tongue and south to Lairg. The B873 follows Loch Naver and then Strathnaver to Bettyhill. At Syre the B871 heads east to Kinbrace.

**Loch Loyal** The lonely road north to Tongue passes Loch Loyal and the eastern ramparts of Ben Loyal. The many lochs here are the haunt of Red and Black-throated Divers, while Greenshank, Golden Plovers and Dunlin also breed.

**Ben Loyal** (perhaps pre-Celtic, 764m) is a Syenite volcanic intrusion with four summits. Its most spectacular aspect is probably from the north from the car park on the Kyle of Tongue causeway. Another fine viewpoint is over Lochan Hakel on the old road round the Kyle.

side of the Kyle of Tongue. For centuries this whole area was Reay territory, which stretched from Kylesku to Melvich, but by 1830 all this land had been bought up by the highly acquisitive Sutherland Estate.

**Kyle of Tongue** A causeway and bridge across the Kyle was opened in 1971 as part of road improvements to the far northwest. This means that visitors no longer have to negotiate the winding 10 miles around the head of the Kyle. However

those who wish to explore this quiet road will find chambered cairns, cup-marked stones and a broch. There are also wonderful views over Ben Loyal.

**Varrich Castle** stands on a promontory above the Rhian Burn. It is probably Norse and may be the *Beruvik* of the *Orkneyinga Saga*. Later it was a MacKay stronghold. A path leads up to it from the village. There are fine views of the Kyle from here, and even better from An Garbh Chnoc (124m).

The normal ascent route follows a track from Ribigill Farm about 2mi (3km) south of Tongue (NC583548). A track and then a path go south across the moor before a steep pathless climb to the grass covered summit ridge, 10mi (16km) 6 hours; fantastic panoramic views.

*Ben Hope from the Tongue Causeway*

*Varrich Castle overlooks the Kyle of Tongue; Ben Hope in Background*

**Cnoc Fhreiceadain** (G Watch Hill, 307m) above Coldbackie offers fine views across the Kyle and the Pentland Firth. This little hill is notable for its rounded top. Nearby Ben Tongue (300m) has good vistas to the west.

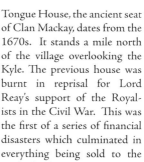
*The Farr Pictish Stone*

**Dun na Maig** (NC553530) is a ruined Iron Age broch at the head of the Kyle. The walls are still 3m high, with an intramural staircase, entrance passage with guard cell and ramparts. There are fine views down the Kyle from here.

Tongue House, the ancient seat of Clan Mackay, dates from the 1670s. It stands a mile north of the village overlooking the Kyle. The previous house was burnt in reprisal for Lord Reay's support of the Royalists in the Civil War. This was the first of a series of financial disasters which culminated in everything being sold to the Sutherland Estate.

Clan Mackay has an illustrious military past, during the 30 Years War, in 1715 and 1745 on the government side, in the

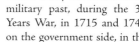
*Melness is on the Northwest of the Kyle of Tongue*

Crimean War and famously at Waterloo, where the lone piper was a Mackay.

**Melness** (ON *Melr Nes*, Sand Headland) The single track road which heads north around the Kyle passes a number of crofting townships including Melness, Midtown, Skinnet, Talmine, Portvasgo and Midfield. Many of these crofts were created in the 19th century for displaced tenants.

There are several fine beaches and a small harbour, which the road winds through. With fine views over the Kyle and many good places for walks this tranquil area is well worth visiting.

**Strathnaver** The Province of Strathnaver originally stretched from Kylesku to Caithness. There is evidence of long settlement here from ancient times with Neolithic chambered cairns, stone circles, Bronze Age cist burials and Iron Age brochs. A mixture of Gaelic and Norse place-names as well as many ruined farmsteads and settlements evoke more recent times.

The Strathnaver Trail runs 26mi (42km) from Farr Old Parish Kirk to Loch Naver. There are 29 marked sites along the way which take in over 5,000 years of settlement in this lovely valley. The river, moorland and lochs are home to many birds and plants.

**Bettyhill** takes its name from the Countess of Sutherland

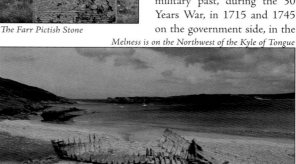

*Farr Bay, Bettyhill*

### JACOBITE REBELLION

In early 1746 the ship *Prince Charles* was chased into the Kyle by the Royal Navy frigate HMS *Sheerness*. The Jacobite ship was in fact the commandeered Royal Navy ship, HMS *Hazard*, and was carrying £13,000 in French gold to pay the rebels as well as supplies for Inverness.

After a three hour gun battle, the rebel ship was disabled and grounded on a sandbank off Melness. The crew got off with the gold in the dark but were stopped near Loch Hakel. The MacKays soon rounded up the crew and the ship's valuable cargo. Meanwhile a force of 1,500 men was sent north by Bonnie Prince Charlie, only to be apprehended en route by the MacKenzies. It has been said that the outcome at Culloden may have been different if the men in Inverness had been paid and stores had arrived.

who created the village to accommodate evicted tenants. It occupies the peninsula between the estuary of the River Naver and Farr Bay. For many years there was a large Salmon netting fishery at Navermouth. Today only an icehouse, pier, and ruined buildings remain.

**Strathnaver Museum** is in the Old Parish Kirk of St Columba, built in the 1700s. It has many interesting displays related to the clearances, archaeology, and history of the area. The Clan McKay Room is upstairs. It has information and exhibits which tell the story of the clan.

The Farr Stone dates from the 8$^{th}$ century, a large wheeled cross with many symbols. It stands on the west side of the kirkyard. Unfortunately it was misguidedly cleaned of its centuries of lichens which has greatly diminished its splendour. There are three other Pictish inscribed stones inside.

**Farr Bay** to the east of the village is a lovely sandy beach, backed by dunes and machair. In summer there is an abundance of wild flowers which support several species of bum-

blebees, some of which are rare. The beach is popular with surfers who take advantage of the big swells which often come into the bay.

**Torrisdale Bay** is a smaller version of the Kyle of Tongue, with large areas of tidal sandbanks fed by the River Naver. The area between the mouths of the Rivers Naver and Borgie is famous for its diversity of flora, which results from its various habitats and exposed situation. Plants which are normally alpine flourish near sea level here.

These include Crowberry, Mountain Avens, Bearberry, Moss Campion and dwarf shrubs. The banks of the River Naver are quite accessible and full of floral interest in summer. The former NNR itself

can be accessed on foot from Invernaver or south of Torrisdale.

**Sites to visit** The minor road to Skelpick has chambered

*Strathnaver*

*Torrisdale Bay, West of Bettyhill*

cairns at Achcoillenaborgie (NC716590) and Skelpick (NC722568). Both are ruined but the chambers and outlines are visible. There are also ruined brochs near both sites, as well as a clearance village overlooking Loch Duinte.

**Dunviden** (NC727519) on the B871 about 6mi (9km) north of Syre is another long inhabited site. The standing stones near the broch are the remains of a chambered cairn, perhaps the stones being used to build the now ruined broch. Nearby a cleared village consists of five houses with outbuildings, an intact corn kiln and field walls. Bronze Age hut circles and a burnt mound as well as another nearby broch show the longevity of occupation here.

**Strathy** In 1790 an Edinburgh lawyer by the name of Honeyman bought the Strathy Estate and promptly started the process of clearances and agricultural improvement which were to be so ruthlessly carried out by the Sutherland Estate. The old traditions and culture of the Highlanders were viewed as anachronistic in the Age of the Enlightenment.

The tenants were relocated in coastal settlements, with small patches of land; many emigrated to the New World instead. Their former lands were turned into large sheep runs and leased to farmers from the south. Sheep farming on this scale did not last.

**Geology** Outliers of Old Red Sandstone mean that some of the land here is quite fer-

tile, especially around Strathy itself, Portskerra and eastwards from Bighouse. This explains the sudden appearance of fields in an otherwise barren landscape.

**Strathy Point Lighthouse** was built in 1958, the last manned one to be built in Scotland and the first to be powered by mains electricity. It was automated in 1997. There are fine views along the coast from here. The clifftop vegetation includes many rare plants including *Primula scotica*. Puffins and other seabirds nest here.

Strathy is a small crofting settlement at the mouth of the River Strathy. Strathy Bay has a fine sheltered, but north facing sandy beach. The coastline of Strathy Point has spectacular low cliffs.

*Farr Bay, Bettyhill*

*Looking towards Orkney over the Pentland Firth*

*Strathy Point*

A track follows the River Strathy for about 10mi (16km) into the moorland, passing Strathy Forest and many lochans and marshy areas. This is prime territory for a variety of rare birds, including Greenshanks and divers.

**Portskerra** is northwest of Melvich. It was created during the clearance of Strath Halladale as a fishing village. There is a small sheltered harbour with a slipway at Portskerra and a modern but rather exposed pier on the west side of Melvich Bay.

A memorial here commemorates the loss of fishermen in three accidents, in 1848, 1890 and 1918, when at least 26 men were lost in total. The coastline to the west is heavily indented and has pretty coves, natural arches, geos and Puffins.

*View West from Strathy Point*

*Portskerra, Melvich*

## CLEARANCES

The clearance of Strathnaver, by the Sutherland Estate, to create sheep farms began in 1814. This was overseen by the Estate factor, one Patrick Sellar, who later faced trial for his actions.

Donald MacLeod of Rosal said, *"The consternation and confusion were extreme. Little or no time was given for the removal of persons or property; the people striving to remove the sick and the helpless before the fire should reach them; next, struggling to save the most valuable of their effects. The cries of the women and children, the roaring of the affrighted cattle, hunted at the same time by the yelling dogs of the shepherds amid the smoke and fire, altogether presented a scene that completely baffles description, it required to be seen to be believed."*

*"A dense cloud of smoke enveloped the whole country by day, and even extended far out to sea. At night an awfully grand but terrific scene presented itself - all the houses in an extensive district in flames at once. I myself ascended a height about eleven o'clock in the evening, and counted two hundred and fifty blazing houses, many of the owners of which I personally knew, but whose present condition - whether in or out of the flames I could not tell. The conflagration lasted six days, till the whole of the dwellings were reduced to ashes or smoking ruins."*

*Halladale River Estuary at Melvich*

**Beaches and Walks** There are fine sandy beaches at Armadale, Strathy and Melvich. All three bays have rivers flowing into them and are sheltered by low cliffs to east and west which are interesting to explore. Melvich Bay, with a large area of dunes, machair and river bank is perhaps the best for wild flowers and bumblebees.

**Melvich** lies on the west side of the estuary of the Halladale River. This fertile crofting township includes a large area of machair links. In former times, there was a large Salmon fishery here; nets were set in the rivermouth and in the bay.

**Bighouse** (ON *Bygdh hus*, Village House) to the east of Melvich dates from the 1760s. It was built and owned by the Mackays until it was sold to the Sutherland Estate in 1830.

The main buildings include the Lodge, Barracks, Icehouse and a walled garden.

**Old Split Stone** On the A 836 east of Melvich, the Old Split Stone marked the boundary with Caithness. Folklore says that an old woman was returning from a shopping trip and was chased by the devil. She ran round the stone three times to escape. He became very angry because he could not catch her, and split the stone in two.

**Strath Halladale** (ON Holy Valley) is a lovely river valley which extends over 15mi (24km) inland from Melvich to Forsinard. It was not completely cleared in the manner of Strathnaver, perhaps because the Sutherland Estate acquired it after the main clearances. The remote A897 passes at least five ruined brochs, many isolated houses and several modern farms, making a splendid alternative route south.

The Halladale River is a classic spate river, with the best catches usually after heavy rain. The main fish run is in July and August. Smolts are released every year from a hatchery to help maintain the fish population. The river is short at 22mi (35km) but, fed by the vast Flow Country, rarely runs low.

*Portskerra*

*Old Split Stone*

*Forsinard Train Station*

*Strath Halladale*

**The Flow Country** of Caithness and Sutherland is a vast area of blanket peat bog, the largest in the UK and covers about 1,500mi² (3,885km²). The bogs build up as Sphagnum moss accumulates in areas with poor drainage underlain by impervious Moine Schist rocks. The rolling landscape provides a wide range of habitats with pools, hummocks, ridges and hills. This in turn ensures a varied flora.

Between 1979 and 1987 large areas of the Flow Country were drained and planted with conifers, rich investors taking advantage of tree planting grants and tax breaks. By 1988 it was becoming clear that these activities were destroying this great wilderness and the grants were stopped. The RSPB have created a unique nature reserve at Forsinard. Many trees have been felled and the bogs are returning to their natural state.

## FORSINARD RSPB RESERVE

**Forsinard RSPB Reserve** (NC891426) is open at all times. It is situated on the A897 single track road through Strath Halladale, 14mi (23km) south of Melvich and 24mi (39km) north of Helmsdale. There is a flagstone trail which winds through the moor past lochans and peat bog.

**The Visitor Centre** in the railway station is open from April to October and has audiovisuals and live nest watch displays. Guided walks are regularly available. There are many roadside viewing sites in the area.

**Wildlife** Birds such as Greenshanks, Dunlins, Golden Plovers, Arctic Skuas, Common Scoters, Red and Black-throated Divers breed on the moors or around the lochans. Hen Harriers, Short-eared Owls and Golden Eagles may also nest here.

Otters are quite common here and many Salmon spawn in the rivers and burns. Red Deer are also seen, especially in winter when they come down from the hills to feed. There are rare Water Beetles and Dragonflies, while the scarce freshwater Pearl Mussel survives in a few places. Insectivorous Butterworts and Sundews are common, while some lochans put on a dazzling display of Water Lilies in summer.

*Emerald Damselfly*

*Sundew*

*The Flow Country at RSPB Forsinard Reserve*

Castle Sinclair & Girnigoe, Noss Head, Wick

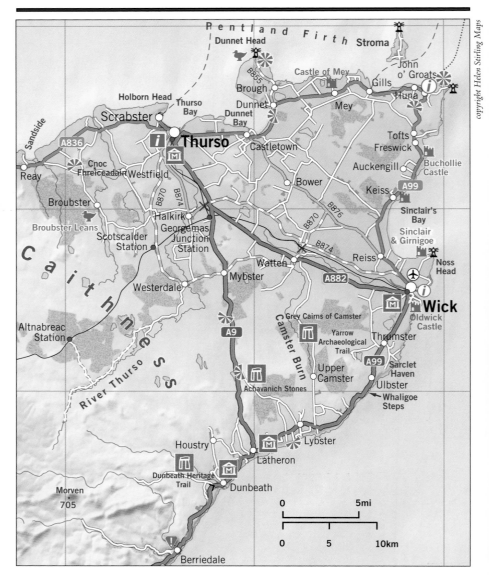

**CAITHNESS** (ON *Katanes*, Headland of the Cats, a Pictish tribe; G *Gallaibh*, Land of Foreigners) is the northeast extremity of Scotland. The landscape is in contrast to that of most of the rest of the North Highlands.

East of a line running from Reay in the northwest to Berriedale in the southeast, the underlying rock is Old Red Sandstone, so that the topography resembles that of Orkney and parts of Easter Ross. To the west, lie the impermeable Moine rocks of the Flow Country.

Much of the coastline is cliffs, in places quite high, without any sea lochs. There are several large bays with wonderful sandy beaches, backed by

*Stacks of Duncansby in Winter*

dunes and machair. The rolling countryside is generally given over to beef cattle farming, though sheep are also reared. Silage and barley are grown in large quantities for winter feed.

coastline, farmland, moorland, rivers, lochs, bogs, and hills, Caithness is home to a large variety of birds, plants and animals. Although the Flow Country is indeed special, the rest of the county has many treats in store, such as *Primula scotica* and other unusual plants on coastal maritime heath.

**Archaeology** Caithness has a wealth of sites to visit, although very few are formally managed. These range from Neolithic chambered cairns and standing stones, Bronze Age houses, burnt mounds and cists to Iron Age roundhouses and many brochs. Pictish symbol stones, Norse settlements, keeps and churches as well as medieval castles, all give a fascinating insight into the past.

**Heritage** Caithness is cultur-

*Primula scotica*

**Wildlife** With a wide range of habitats ranging from its varied

*Round Cairn of Camster*

| CAITHNESS | |
|---|---|
| Achavanich Stones | 134 |
| Badbea | 137 |
| Berridale | 136 |
| Buchollie Castle | 128 |
| Cairn o' Get | 133 |
| Caithness Horizons | 122 |
| Castle of Mey | 124 |
| Castlehill | 124 |
| Clan Gunn Centre | 135 |
| Cnoc Fhreiceadain | 120 |
| Dounreay | 120 |
| Dunbeath | 136 |
| Duncansby Head | 127 |
| Dunnet Bay | 122 |
| Dunnet Bay Distillery | 123 |
| Dunnet Head | 124 |
| Freswick | 128 |
| Gills Bay | 125 |
| Grey Cairns of Camster | 133 |
| Herring Fishing | 131 |
| Hill o' Many Stanes | 133 |
| John o' Groats | 126 |
| Keiss Castle (old) | 128 |
| Laidhay Croft Museum | 136 |
| Latheron | 135 |
| Lybster | 134 |
| Mary Anne's Cottage | 124 |
| Old Pulteney Distillery | 130 |
| Old St Peter's Kirk | 121 |
| Old Wick Castle | 130 |
| Ord of Caithness | 137 |
| Pentland Firth | 125 |
| *Primula scotica* | 119 |
| Reay | 120 |
| Sandside Bay | 120 |
| Sarclet Haven | 132 |
| Shortest Street | 129 |
| Sinclair & Girnigoe Cas | 128 |
| Sinclair's Bay | 128 |
| Stroma | 126 |
| Thurso | 120 |
| Waterlines Visitor Cen | 135 |
| Whaligoe Steps | 132 |
| Wick | 129 |
| Wick Heritage Museum | 130 |
| Yarrows Archaeo Trail | 132 |

*Sandside Harbour*

with its cottages and storehouse built about 1830, suffers from silting up with sand.

**Dounreay Nuclear Power Development Establishment** was commenced on the site of a WWII airfield in 1955 to develop Fast Breeder Reactors. Electricity generation ceased in 1994 and decommissioning is expected to take well into the 2030s. Dounreay is still a major employer.

ally distinct from the rest of Scotland, sharing some placenames, surnames and dialect words with Orkney and Shetland. It was part of the Orkney Earldom for hundreds of years and retains a sense of its Norse heritage today. A few Pictish names have survived while to the west and inland Gaelic placenames predominate.

**Reay** (ON *Ra*, Boundary Mark) is the most westerly Caithness settlement. From Drum Hollistan there are fine views over the Pentland Firth. The church dates from 1739. It has a fine tower accessed by an external stair. It retains its 18th century layout with the pulpit on the south wall, communion table and pews.

**Sandside Bay** is a fine wide sandy beach, backed by extensive sand dunes. Signs indicate possible danger yet, despite this, local people still walk on the beach. The pretty harbour,

**Cnoc Fhreiceadain** (G Watch Hill, ND012653) has two long chambered cairns. The south cairn is known as *Na Tri Shean* (G The Three Fairy Mounds). It is about 70m long with a higher mound at each end and "horned" forecourts. The northern one has a round mound and a forecourt at its south end. There are fine views over Reay, Dounreay and the Pentland Firth from here.

**Forss Mill** is a particularly fine 19th century grain mill in a lovely situation overlooking waterfalls and surrounded by Beech trees. Now converted to housing, it has retained much of the workings.

*Old St Peter's Kirk, Thurso*

*Dounreay Nuclear Power Development Establishment*

**Thurso** was an important settlement in Norse times as it is mentioned frequently in the *Orkneyinga Saga*. Both the Earl and the Bishop had castles here. The present ruinous castle dates from the 1660s.

With a population of just under 8,000, it is the largest town in Caithness and the most northerly in mainland Britain. It has a distinctive aspect, facing north to the Pentland Firth and Orkney. The town grew rapidly in the 19th century due to the success of the flagstone industry and, again in the latter half of the 20th century with the development of Dounreay.

*Sir John's Square, Thurso*

The original village was on the west side of the river and, until recently, was known as *Fishers' Biggings*. Many of the houses here date from the 17th and 18th centuries, and have been renovated rather than demolished. Sir John Sinclair of Ulbster laid out the new town in 1798 to provide homes *"for all sorts and conditions of men"*.

**Old St Peter's Kirk** dates from the 13th century, or earlier, with later additions. It is said to

have been founded by Gilbert de Moravia, who was appointed Bishop in 1222. The tower is set at an angle to the rest of the building between the east and south aisles. The graveyard has many interesting old memorials. A runic stone cross, found here in the 19th century, is in the museum.

**The Esplanade** was first built in 1882. It is a good viewpoint for observing the impressive waves which break here in cer-

### THURSO
#### ORIGIN OF THE NAME

The name "Thurso" may derive from an ancient river name, represented by *Thiorsa* in Old Norse. It is probably reflected in Ptolemy's supposed name for Holborn Head, *Tarvedum* or Bull Head, from the Celtic roots *tarv*, bull and *dun*, fort. The headland has a series of ramparts defending its landward approaches.

*Ulbster Pictish Symbol Stone*

*Surfer in Thurso Bay*

*Scrabster Harbour*

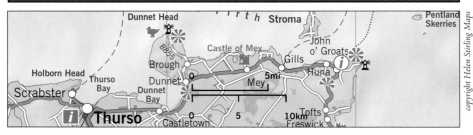

*copyright Helen Stirling Maps*

tain conditions. There are fine views over Thurso Bay and the Pentland Firth to the Orkney island of Hoy.

**Surfing** is a popular sport in Thurso. The Pentland Firth is famous for its strong tides and ferocious seas; winds and tides create large waves which break on the east side of Thurso Bay, an ideal surfing environment.

**Caithness Horizons** is located in the former Thurso Town Hall and adjacent Carnegie Library. It incorporates a mu-seum, interactive exhibitions and displays, lecture and pres-entation facilities, a tourist information centre and a café. The development of Dounreay is covered in an interesting dis-play. The centre delves into all that Caithness has to offer.

**Scrabster** (ON *Skara Bolstaðir*, Steading on the Edge) nestles in the shelter of Holborn Head on the west side of Thurso Bay. In 1855 a regular steamship ferry service to Stromness in Orkney commenced. Holborn Head lighthouse was first lit in 1862, but is now redundant. The harbour has grown great-ly to cope with ferries, com-mercial and leisure craft. The port has also become one of the busiest fish landing ports in the UK, due to its northerly position.

**Thurso Lifeboat** was first based here in 1860. Eleven vessels have so far served here, and there have been many heroic services involving the rescue of over 600 people. In 1956 the lifeboat shed and the brand new lifeboat Dunnet Head were destroyed by fire.

**Holborn Head** is exposed to the full fury of the Pentland Firth. The Old Red Sandstone cliffs have been eroded into a dramatic series of caves, geos, gloups, blowholes, stacks and natural arches. The headland is protected by large geos on each side, and by ramparts built across the narrow part. This exposed location is most likely to have been a spiritual rather than a military site.

**Dunnet Bay** has a fine 2mi (3km) stretch of sand, backed by high dunes. Massive waves break here which are attractive to surfers. The beach is popu-lar for walking, sand yachting

*Scrabster Harbour*

*Fossil Fish*

*Dounreay Fast Reactor*

and other pursuits. Dunnet Ranger Visitor Centre, at the caravan site, has displays about the wildlife here.

**Dunnet Forest** is a community woodland. A number of paths and trails for walkers, horses and mountain bikes have been developed. The forest is managed to encourage wildlife.

**Dunnet Bay Distillery** was established in 2014. A traditional copper still, Elizabeth, is used to produce their acclaimed Rock Rose Gin and Holy Grass Vodka. Situated beside the Northern Sands Hotel, the distillery has a small shop and runs tours in the tourist season.

**Dunnet Kirk** may date from the 12th century, though most of the building is 16th century.

*Dunnet Sands*

Timothy Pont was minister here from 1602 to 1610. He surveyed Scotland for Blaue's 1654 *Atlas Novus*. The church retains the traditional layout of pews with the pulpit on the

*Castlehill Harbour*

*Dunnet Bay Distillery*

*Dunnet Parish Kirk*

*Dunnet Head Lighthouse*

*Dunnet Bay Distillery*

*Dunnet Head*

home to breeding seabirds. The clifftops are carpeted with wild flowers in early summer.

**Mary-Ann's Cottage** is a 19th century crofthouse at West Dunnet. It was the home of Mary-Ann Calder until 1990 when she was 93. Built by her grandfather, John Young, in 1850, the buildings, rooms, fittings, artefacts, tools and implements are all original.

south wall. The tower was added c.1700 and overlooks an interesting graveyard.

**Castlehill**, the old name for Castletown, developed as a result of the growth of the Flagstone Industry. In 1825 James Traill shipped his first cargo of paving stones from Castlehill Harbour. During the next century over 400,000 tons of stone were shipped worldwide.

*Castlehill Windmill Base*

**Castlehill Heritage Centre** holds themed exhibitions and workshops. The nearby Flagstone Trail follows the story starting at the quarry. The windmill powered water pumps to empty the quarry and the dam drove a waterwheel to power saws which cut the flags. In 1861 steam power was introduced which allowed for a higher production rate. The nearby mill was used to thresh and mill grain as well as flax. Castletown retains many pretty houses from this period.

**Dunnet Head** (127m) is the most northerly point in mainland Britain. The lighthouse was built in 1831 by Robert Stevenson atop the 90m cliffs of Easter Head. The viewpoint offers fine vistas over the Pentland Firth to Orkney and Stroma. In summer it is

**Scarfskerry** (ON *Skarf*, Cormorant), further east, has a small harbour, The Haven. The coastline here is low and rocky but pretty with many chambered cairns, a broch and a chapel site. Further east at Harrow there is another exposed jetty in Wester Haven.

**The Castle of Mey** was built between 1566 and 1572 by the Earl of Caithness. It was renamed Barrogill Castle in the 18th century and extensive additions were made in the 19th century. By the 1950s it had fallen into severe disrepair.

In 1952, after the death of King George VI, the Queen Mother purchased and restored the castle. When she took over

*Mary-Anne's Cottage*

*Dunnet Sands from Castlehill Harbour*

*Castle of Mey*

Castle of Mey

*The Queen Mother at Home*

there was neither electricity nor running water. The castle is the product of her own taste and she acquired many items from shops such as the Ship's Wheel and Miss Miller Calder's Shop in Thurso.

In 1996 she formed The Queen Elizabeth Castle of Mey Trust and endowed it with the castle, and estate. The interior remains set out very much as she left it. Knowledgeable guides make tours interesting and enjoyable with anecdotes and explanations. Two cannons on the front lawn probably came from the Mey battery; they have a 6.5in bore and are 94in long. One carries a George IV mark and date from c.1820.

The Animal Centre in the old granary includes a variety of interesting poultry. Rare

breeds of sheep, goats and pigs can be seen. In spring children can feed the lambs and also see newly hatched chicks.

**The Pentland Firth** (ON *Pettaland Fjordur*, Pictland Firth), together with the islands and parishes on both sides, is frequently mentioned in the *Orkneyinga Saga*. It separates Orkney from Caithness. The distance from Burwick to John o' Groats is about 6mi (10km).

At the meeting point of the North Sea and the Atlantic Ocean, the strong tides of 10 knots or more are impeded by islands, skerries, the sea bed and weather, all of which combine to create complex eddies and, sometimes, dangerous seas.

**Gills Bay** (ON *Gil*, ravine) is named for the many small clefts in the low banks above the shore. It is the terminal

*The Duke of Rothesay (Prince Charles) at the Mey Games*

*Castle of Mey Feeding Time*

*Geo of Nethertown, Stroma*

*John o' Groats*

There were numerous alterations until the station was automated in 1994.

**Canisbay Kirk** is dedicated to St Drostan and is built on top of a prehistoric mound, perhaps a broch. It is first mentioned in 1222 but the present building mostly dates from the 17th century. The tower is said to have replaced an earlier circular one. St Drostan was a 6th century missionary to Pictland.

**John o' Groats** is 876mi (1,402km) from Lands End, the furthest distance apart of any two places on the UK mainland. Ever since the American Elihu Buritt completed the walk in 1865 there have been all manner of record breaking and charity fund raising traverses of Britain.

John o' Groats has been extensively renovated with a range of self catering accommodation, a hotel, cafes and interesting shops, one of which is the tourist information centre. Unlike at Lands End, parking is free as is the distance pointer.

Traditionally, the ferry ran from John o' Groats to Bur-

## JOHN O' GROATS
### Origin of the name

Jan de Groot, a Dutchman, had his house here in the reign of James IV (1488-1513). His seven sons disagreed about precedence so he built an octagonal house with 8 doors, and an 8-sided table so that no one had the head of the table. He ran a ferry to Orkney and charged 2d a trip. This coin became known as the 'groat'. He is buried in Canisbay churchyard where his tombstone stands in the porch. Locally he became known as John o' Groats, and the area took on his nickname.

for the year round Pentland Ferries service to St Margaret's Hope, operated by the catamaran, *Pentalina*.

**Stroma** (ON *Straumey*, Stream Island) lies 1.5mi (2.5km) off Canisbay on the south side of the Pentland Firth. Uninhabited since 1962, 375 people had lived here in 1901. The Stroma men had a reputation for being exceptional seamen and had an almost innate knowledge of the tides. They fished mainly for Lobsters, Cod and Herring, depending on the season.

**Pentland Skerries**, 4mi (6.5km) northeast of Duncansby, is another hazardous place for shipping. Many ships have foundered here in the past, especially in foggy weather. Sailing ships were particularly prone to be grounded on calm days with poor visibility. The two lighthouses were erected in 1794. One was 24m high, the other 18m, and used a total of 66 catoptric reflectors.

*John o' Groats Fingerpost*

*Sannick Sands*

wick on South Ronaldsay. The first recorded ferryman was Jan de Groot, appointed by James IV about 1496, to ensure communications with his recently acquired islands. Today, the short sea crossing is run in the summer months by the *Pentland Venture* which carries up to 250 passengers. Day tours to Orkney are very popular.

**Duncansby Head** (ON *Dungal's Boer*, Dungal's Estate) is called *Veruvium Promantarium*, or Clear-cut Cape on Ptolemy's map. Many drive to the car park, take a look and leave, which is a pity as the coastal walk south from the lighthouse should not be missed.

The finest views of the Duncansby Stacks are from the vantage points on the path, south from the lighthouse. The cliffs offer excellent views of breeding seabirds in early summer. From May to July there is a sea of colour from the carpets of wild flowers which change as the various species come into bloom.

The Long Geo of Sclaites is a collapsed cave, while the Knee is a stack where Puffins may

*Stacks of Duncansby in Winter*

be seen during the breeding season. Whales and dolphin are regularly seen from here. Duncansby lighthouse was established in 1924. It was automated in 1997.

The Ness of Duncansby is one of the best beaches in the North Highlands for those wishing to collect shells, especially *Groatie Buckies* (Cowrie Shells). There is a very good walk along the shore from John o' Groats to the Bay of San-

nick. The fine views, mixture of sandy beaches, Old Red Sandstone boulders, fossiliferous rocks and flower-covered links are quite sublime on a summer's evening.

**Viewpoint** There is a panoramic view over the Pentland Firth to Orkney from Warth Hill (ND371699, 124m). Park near an old quarry off the A99 3mi (4km) south of John o' Groats and walk 200m to the summit for the best view.

*Duncansby Head from the South, Midwinter Sunrise*

*Duncansby Head Lighthouse in Midsummer*

*Stacks of Duncansby in Summer*

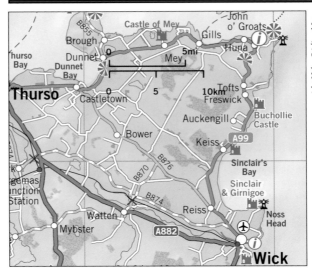

add to the pretty scene. The harbour is reached from the main part of the village by passing an attractive terrace of cottages. Old Keiss Castle is a romantic 16th century ruin which can be reached by following the coast for 800m north from the harbour. It is perched on the edge of low cliffs and is slowly disintegrating. Keiss and Whitegate Brochs are passed along the way.

Sinclair's Bay has a 3mi (4km) stretch of sand, again backed by extensive dunes and machair links. It is accessed via car parks south of Keiss and at Reiss. Ackergill Tower dates from the 15th century; extensively altered in the 19th century, it is now a luxury hotel.

**Castle Sinclair & Girnigoe** is located 900m west of Noss Head lighthouse, 5mi (6.5km) north of Wick. This is one of the most spectacular castles in Scotland. It is sited right on the edge of a 30m high promontory and it is protected on the landward side by a large geo (ON *gja*, narrow sea inlet).

It was built in the 14th century and partially demolished in

**Freswick** (ON *Tres Vik*, Tree or Driftwood Bay) is about 4mi (6km) south of John o' Groats. The long sandy beach is backed by sand dunes and machair. The area has been occupied for at least 2,500 years, as shown by the presence of four brochs. Remains of an extensive Norse settlement have been excavated in the links. The house of Freswick probably started life as a Viking castle. It was enlarged in the 17th century and later. It has variously been called both a castle and a manor.

**Lambaborg, or Buchollie Castle** (ND383658) at Kingans Geo is built on a large rock which sticks out into the sea. It was the site of one of Sweyn Asleifson's many exploits detailed in the *Orkneyinga Saga* where he escaped from Earl Rognvald by means of swimming and a small boat. It was re-named Buchollie by the Mowat family in the 15th century.

**Keiss** has a fine harbour built in about 1831. A stone fishing store and a small icehouse

*Freswick*

*Buchollie Castle or Lambaborg*

c.1680. The castle was protected by a deep ditch, drawbridge and barbican on its west side. It is internally divided by another dry moat into an inner and outer bailey. The entrance to the latter is by means of a 14<sup>th</sup> century vaulted passage which leads to a courtyard. A second drawbridge then led to the 3-storey tower house and ranges of outbuildings which extend to the end of the promontory. From here a stairway descends to a sea gate giving access to the shore.

It was originally lime-washed, and must once have been an extremely prominent and impressive structure. Its purpose was less military and more symbolic of prestige and power. All that remains of the West Gate House is the structure around the chimney stack, its appearance gave rise to the idea that this was 'Castle Sinclair'. 'Castle Girnigoe' was deemed to have been built for strength and 'Castle Sinclair' for beauty.

**Wick** (ON *Vik*, Bay, popn. 7155 in 2011) The town developed along the north bank of the Wick River, which is tidal until well upstream of the

*Castle Sinclair & Girnigoe*

present Bridge Street. This would have afforded early navigators a safe haven on a hard coast.

It became a Royal Burgh in 1589, but it was not until the early 19<sup>th</sup> century that Wick's dramatic development as a town and harbour began. By 1800, there were about 200 boats working from here. There were also sixteen firms processing and packing Herring into barrels.

Engineers such as Telford, Bremner and the Stevensons had many technical problems, due to the exposed location. Sir William Pulteney persuaded the British Fisheries Society to buy 390 acres south of the river for development.

The world's shortest street is Ebenezer Place. At 2.06m it has only one door and one address, Mackay's Hotel's No 1 Bistro. It was officially declared a street in 1887 and

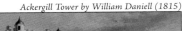
*Castle Sinclair & Girnigoe by William Daniell (1815)*

*Old Keiss Castle*

*Ackergill Tower by William Daniell (1815)*

*Wick River is Tidal*

entered the Guinness Book of Records in 2006. The menu is highly recommended.

*1 Ebenezer Place*

**Old Pulteney Distillery** was established in 1826. It produces a Highland single malt Scotch using unusually shaped pot stills. It reputedly gains its characteristic nose due to exposure to the sea air. The water comes from the Mill Lade, a burn flowing from Loch Hempriggs. There is a visitor centre in Huddart Street. The distillery is now owned by Inver House Distillers Limited.

**Wick Heritage Museum**, in Bank Row, was opened by the Wick Society in 1981. Displays include a 1920s dwelling house, with rooms typical of the period, a Herring curing yard and a cooperage. Many artefacts, documents and photographs pertaining to Wick and Caithness can be viewed. The story of Caithness Glass, the original lighthouse workings from Noss Head, and the story of Herring Fishing at Wick as well as a host of interesting machines, tools and objects are all on display.

*Isabella Fortuna* is a fine example of a traditional "Fifie", built in 1890 at Arbroath for the Smith family, who worked her until 1976. She was acquired by the Wick Society in 1997 and has since been fully restored. Still powered by a 1932 Kelvin, she is berthed in Wick Harbour in the summer.

**Old Wick Castle**, known to seamen as the Old Man of Wick, is on a peninsula between two deep geos a mile south of Wick. It probably dates from the 12$^{th}$ century, when under the Norse Earls of Orkney. It has a rock-cut ditch

*Wick Harbour from the South*

*Wick During the Herring Boom*

*Old Wick Castle*

## THE SILVER DARLINGS

Herring Fishing was a boom industry in the late 19th and early 20th centuries and Caithness led the way for a long time. The peak year for Wick was 1862, when 1,122 boats were based here during the fishing season.

*Old Pulteney Distillery has Distinctive Stills*

on the landward side defended by a rampart and gatehouse and is surrounded on the other three sides by steep cliffs.

The keep had four floors, with access from outside by ladder. On the seaward side a range of buildings extends to a small courtyard. From the 14th century onwards it was held by various Scottish families and was abandoned in the 18th century. It is the best preserved of many such castles in Caithness.

**Wick John o' Groats Airport** is the most northerly on mainland UK and is run by Highlands and Islands Airports. Eastern Airways operates flights to Aberdeen and Loganair to Edinburgh from here. The airport was established in the 1930s and taken over by the RAF in 1939.

The A99 to the south of Wick passes through farming countryside on the way to Lybster. The coast consists of

The fishermen, coopers, gutting girls, shore workers, schooners' crews and others expanded the population by over 10,000 during this time. It is said that when a really good catch was landed no less than 500 gallons of whisky was drunk in one day. There were 22 pubs in Wick and 45 in Pulteneytown.

As catches from near waters fell, Zulus and Fifies were replaced with steam drifters and, later, seine netters. These innovations only accelerated overfishing and the demise of the vast shoals of Herring that once swam here. By 1937 the local industry was finished, never to revive. Today only a tiny fleet of seine netters and small lobster boats is based at Wick.

The Old Fish Market on Harbour Quay was built about 1890. Prior to this catches were auctioned straight from the boats, but increasing landings meant that a mart had to be set up. The nearby cannon was donated by the MP in 1881 for use as a fog signal. The east coast is very prone to sea haar in the summer months.

*Wick Harbour Today with the Isabella Fortuna in the background*
*The Cannon, now Restored*

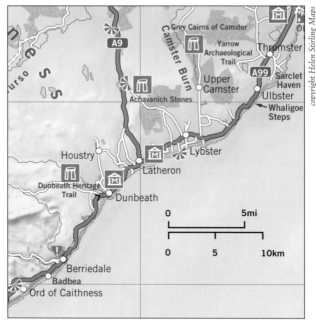

*copyright Helen Stirling Maps*

years. There are three ruinous Neolithic chambered cairns, Bronze Age and Pictish houses as well as an Iron Age broch.

The Broch of South Yarrows is one of the best in Caithness and sits on the edge of the loch, partially flooded. The walls are over 2m high in places, with intramural stairs and passages still visible. The entrance has a guard cell and lintel still in place. The broch is surrounded by banks and ruined buildings which may be Pictish. In Caithness these are called wags (G *Uaimhach*, little cave). They are partially sunk into the ground and the roofs were held up on large upright stones.

Whaligoe at Ulbster has 300 steps (ND322403) which lead down to a large geo with deep water which was used to land and ship Herring, Salmon, whitefish and shellfish. The curing house at the top dates from 1813, and replaced a much older *corfhouse*, where Salmon was processed. Schooners even docked here to load cargoes. In 1855 there were 35 boats and 140 fishermen; by 1928 there were only 8 boats.

low cliffs with many geos and stacks. Several of these inlets have been used for centuries to keep boats and land fish. During the early years of the Herring Boom these tiny harbours saw a huge increase in landings. However as the boats got larger, landings were increasingly made at Wick.

**Sarclet Haven** and village were developed in the early 1800s. There were salt pans here in former times. Today all that remains is a fish curing shed and an old windlass. The Haven is a very pleasant place for a picnic and is a good starting point for coastal walks to the north or south.

**Yarrows Archaeology Trail** is signposted off the A99 near Thrumster. From the car park (ND306435) a circular walk takes in a variety of interesting sites spanning at least 3,000

*Sarclet Haven*

*Whaligoe Steps*

Great care should be taken when visiting Whaligoe as the steps can be treacherous if wet. There is a good viewpoint from the south side clifftop. Wester Whale Geo is also worth a visit. The curing house is now The Whaligoe Steps Café.

**Cairn o' Get** or Garrywhin (ND313411) is signposted off the main road at Ulbster opposite Whaligoe. It is a small Neolithic chambered cairn. The roof has gone but the passage and chamber are otherwise intact.

On excavation in 1866 the walls were still over 2.5m high. A 0.5m layer of ashes, burnt wood and bones covered the chamber floor. Large amounts of flints and pottery shards were also present. A row of skulls lined the east wall.

**Hill o' Many Stanes** at Mid Clyth (ND295384), about 3mi (4km) north of Lybster, is the best-preserved of a type of stone setting only seen in Caithness and Sutherland. Over 200 stones are arranged in 22 or more rows on the south side of a hill. They run

north to south in a fan shape with their broad faces aligned with the rows. The stones are less than 1m high.

The site may once have had 600 stones and was possibly an ancient lunar observatory. Forty-five metres west a fallen standing stone could have been part of this. Though assumed to have been laid out about 2,000BC, this is purely conjecture.

**Grey Cairns of Camster** (ND260440) are located on a minor road 5mi (8km) north of West Clyth just east of Lybster, signposted off the A99. These Neolithic chambered cairns date from c.3000BC. They were excavated and conserved and are reached by boardwalks over the boggy ground. The cairns are among the best pre-

**ARCHAEOLOGY**

Caithness has an abundance of archaeological sites from many periods. No more so than the route from Wick to Latheron, near which are many of the most impressive and accessible monuments. Yarrows Archaeological Trail has Neolithic chambered cairns, Bronze Age houses and an Iron Age broch all in a small area.

The Grey Cairns of Camster and the Cairn o' Get are also very impressive Neolithic chambered cairns. The Hill o' Many Stanes has unique and enigmatic stone rows of small standing stones. At Achavanich, an unusual U-shaped stone setting has the most impressive standing stones in Caithness.

Hill o' Many Stones

Broch of South Yarrows

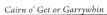
Cairn o' Get or Garrywhin

Camster Round. Both entrance passages face eastwards. The chamber roofs are not original as they were destroyed in the 19th century, but they retain a strong sense of grandeur.

**Achavanich Stone Setting** (G The Monk's Field, ND187417) is about 5mi (6.5km) north of Latheron near Loch Rangag off the Cassiemyre Road (A9). It can also be reached via a side road on the west side of Lybster. The standing stones form a U-shape with their narrow faces aligned inwards. About 40 stones remain of a probable 54. They vary in height between 1m and 2m. The setting is thought to date from before 2500BC.

*Long Cairn of Camster*

served in Britain. Both have intact chambers and passages with rooflights so that no torches are needed.

**Camster Round** is about 20m in diameter and 4m high. The east-facing entrance has an impressive facade and leads to a passage about 6m long. The chamber has a nearly intact corbelled roof. It is divided by 3 pairs of upright slabs. The roof is one large monolith and is over 3m above the floor.

**Camster Long** is a huge extended pile of stones over 60m long. There are horns at each end and a large forecourt at the north end. The retaining wall has been repaired to represent the original appearance. The monument started off as two separate round cairns which were subsequently joined and extended southwards.

The north chamber is lined with vertical slabs, while the south one resembles that of

**Lybster** (ON *Hlith Bolstadir*, Slope Farm) developed as a Herring station in the 19th century. By 1838, 101 boats worked from the harbour, by then the third biggest Herring port in Scotland. The Reisgill Burn (ON *Hris Gil*, Brushwood Ravine) enters the sea here through a deep cleft. The Norse called the bay *Haligeo*, suggesting a possible early monastic settlement.

*Achavanich Stone Setting*

*Camster Round Cairn Interior and Passage*

*Long Cairn of Camster Central Interior*

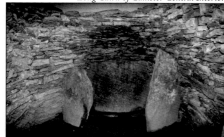

The village was planned by Patrick Sinclair and developed from 1802. He had been in the army in Canada and retired as a Lieutenant General. The wide Main Street was his idea as was the name "Quatre Bras" after a battle in which his sons served in 1815.

*Lybster Harbour, Waterlines Visitor Centre on Left*

The harbour continued to be developed right through the Herring Boom, and the lighthouse was built in 1884, by which time the fishery was in decline. Today a small number of boats fish for lobsters and crabs from here. Lybster also welcomes many yachts every year, either cruising or racing.

**Waterlines Visitor Centre** is in the restored building above the harbour. It has an exhibition on Lybster Harbour's history and natural heritage. There are also demonstrations of traditional boatbuilding, and other regular events. As well as a coffee shop there are facilities for visiting yachts.

**Latheron** (ON *Hlith-tun*, Sloping Enclosure) is at the south end of the Cassiemyre road, where the A99 and the A9 meet. By tradition there

was a monastic site near the Old Church. Pictish symbol stones have been found in the area suggesting that there may be some truth in this.

**The Clan Gunn Centre** is situated in Latheron Old Parish Church which dates from 1734. It tells the story of the clan from Norse times against the background of the history of the north of Scotland. It also contains a substantial Clan archive and shop.

**Latheronwheel** (ON *Vathill*, ford) was planned by the laird, Captain Dunbar, as another Herring harbour. The hotel was the first building and is universally known as *"The Blends"* since the 1890s when the then proprietor did his own whisky blending. Incoming tenants were allocated 2 acres of ground and the right to fish from the small harbour.

Over 50 boats once fished from the attractive but exposed little

*Clan Gunn Museum at Latheron*

*Latheron Coastline from the South*

*Latheronwheel Harbour*

*Dunbeath Broch is well preserved*

harbour. The old road followed the coast more closely, crossing a fine old bridge which may date from 1726, no doubt replacing the ford across the Latheronwheel Burn.

**Dunbeath** (G *Dun Beithe*, Fort of the Birches) was developed from the 1790s. Over 80 families were cleared from the Strath. Many settled at the mouth of the river and became involved in fisheries.

The main street dates from the 1840s. The old bridge was built by Thomas Telford in 1810, now replaced by a large curving concrete viaduct. By the 1840s up to 100 boats worked out of Dunbeath. The attractive harbour remains, but few boats fish from here now.

**Dunbeath Heritage Centre** is situated in the old school to the south of the river. Neil M Gunn (1891-1973) was born

and raised in Dunbeath. He is one of Scotland's most acclaimed 20th century novelists. "*Highland River*" and "*The Silver Darlings*" are two of his most popular works.

The Ballachly Stone was found when a 19th century farm building was demolished. It may date from the 7th century and is the upper part of an upright cross-slab.

**Laidhay Croft Museum**, north of Dunbeath, is a 19th century croft, comprising a dwelling house, byre and barn in one long-house. The furnishings are typical of the period with box beds, cupboards, tables and chairs. The "ben" end was the sitting room and the kitchen would have been where most activity went on. The byre leads directly off the kitchen, while the barn has multi-timbered cruck frames.

**Berriedale** (ON *Bergi dalr*, Cliff Dale) and its steep Braes is at the mouth of the Berriedale and Langwell Waters. Nearby the Old Smithy displays many antlers. A small road leads along the river to a range of cottages set on a raised

*Dunbeath Harbour*

*Prisoner's Leap, where Ian McCormack Gunn escaped*

*Laidhay Croft Museum*

*The Ord of Caithness in Spring with Whin (Gorse) in Bloom*

### DUNBEATH STRATH HERITAGE TRAIL

Dunbeath Strath Heritage Trail starts at the car park beside the Meal Mill. It goes upstream past Chapel Hill and across a footbridge and through woodland.

Dunbeath Broch sits prominently above the confluence of the Houstry Burn and Dunbeath Water. The entrance with its guard cell and a corbelled cell in the opposite wall are intact. The walls are still over 3m high. It is best visited in winter when the vegetation has died back.

Prisoner's Leap is a deep glacial ravine. Tradition says that Ian McCormack Gunn was being held in Forse Castle by the Keiths, who wished to kill him. He came from Braemore on the south side of the river and claimed he could jump the gorge.

Sure that he would fall to his death the Keiths agreed that he would be freed if he succeeded, which of course he did. He was said to have been an orphan and weaned on hind's milk, which gave him the ability to jump so far.

beach. Further old cottages line the shore on the north side over a small suspension bridge.

**Badbea** (ND488200), south of Berriedale, is the sad remnant of a village formed by 28 families evicted from nearby Langwell. The steep, poor ground above precipitous cliffs made the settlement untenable. A memorial does nothing to alleviate the sadness.

**The Ord of Caithness** (G *Aird*, steep headland) is on the border between Caithness and Sutherland. This area of high moorland is beautiful with flowering Whins in spring. It is frequently shrouded in sea fog at any time of year. In winter it is often blocked by snow, when snow gates may be shut between the section of the A9 from south of Berriedale to north of Helmsdale.

*Berriedale Today*

*Berriedale by William Daniell (1815)*

*Ruined Houses at Badbea*

Loch Fleet National Nature Reserve from the Mound

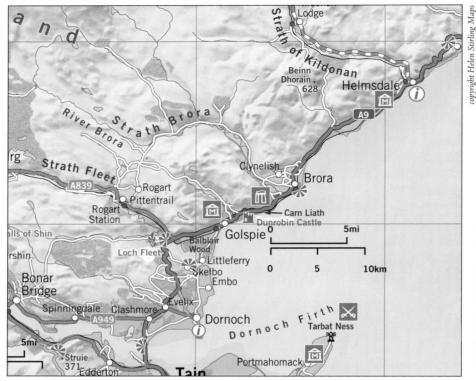

*copyright Helen Stirling Maps*

**SUTHERLAND** (ON *Sudrland*, South Land) covers 5,252km² with a population in 2011 of only 13,469, most of whom live on the fertile east coast. In Gaelic the southeast part is called *Cataibh*, referring to the Cat people who inhabited Caithness and Sutherland.

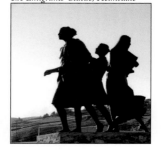

*The Emigrants' Statue, Helmsdale*

The east coast is mostly composed of Old Red Sandstone, but there are also Jurassic rocks exposed along the coast between Helmsdale and Golspie. In contrast to much of Caithness, the shores are gentle and low, with expansive sandy beaches backed by links.

Loch Fleet and the Dornoch Firth are large inlets from the sea with sand and mudbanks. They are fed by river systems running from the watershed far to the west. Waders and waterfowl feed and roost in large numbers, especially in winter.

The county town of Dornoch is an ancient settlement and a Royal Burgh with the only cathedral in the area. It is also home to the Royal Dornoch, one of the best and oldest golf courses in the world. Most of the other settlements are also on the coast and include Golspie, Brora and Helmsdale. Bonar Bridge at the Kyle of Sutherland and Lairg at the head of Loch Shin are at strategic crossroads.

Inland there is much evidence of former settlement. The Straths of Kildonan, Fleet and Oykel, as well as most of the remainder of the area was cleared of a large number of its indigenous people in the 19th century during the notorious

*Helmsdale from the South*

clearances. In recent times people have started to return but the remoter locations remain largely unpopulated.

There are many interesting places to stop and explore, seek out ancient sites, watch birds or enjoy spectacular scenery.

**Helmsdale** (ON *Hjalmundur's Dal*) is a pretty little village at the mouth of the River Helmsdale. For centuries it was an isolated Salmon fishing and curing station. In 1814 building of a new planned village and harbour was commenced by the Sutherland Estate for some of the families who had been displaced. The idea was that some would work small holdings near the village, while others would go to the fishing. The fine old Telford Bridge

was built in 1813 to carry the new road north. By 1819 this was completed over the Ord of Caithness. Communications were further improved by the arrival of the railway in 1871.

The harbour was developed in several stages from about 1818 coinciding with the development of Herring fishing. It was greatly enlarged again in the 1890s, but by the early 1900s the port and its curing sheds lay abandoned.

During the season over 200 vessels packed the basin. However, the advent of larger boats and then steam drifters in 1900 meant that catches were landed at bigger ports. Today a few inshore vessels fish for lobsters, crabs, prawns and shellfish. The riverside and harbour area

*Helmsdale Harbour*

is a very pleasant place for a stroll.

**The Emigrants' Statue** overlooks the river and harbour from the south side. This haunting sculpture commemorates the tens of thousands of people who were displaced

| EAST SUTHERLAND | |
|---|---|
| Balblair Wood | 147 |
| Ben Bhraggie | 148 |
| Brora | 144 |
| Carn Liath | 145 |
| Clynelish Distillery | 145 |
| Dornoch | 149 |
| Dunrobin Castle | 146 |
| Embo | 150 |
| Emigrants' Statue | 140 |
| Ferry Links | 147 |
| Glen Loth | 143 |
| Golspie | 147 |
| Helmsdale | 141 |
| History Links Museum | 150 |
| Kildonan Gold Rush | 143 |
| Last Witch Burning | 151 |
| Littleferry | 147 |
| Loch Fleet | 148 |
| Orcadian Stone Co | 148 |
| Portgower | 144 |
| Skelbo Castle | 149 |
| Strath of Kildonan | 143 |
| The Mound | 148 |
| Timespan Centre | 142 |

*Helmsdale by William Daniell (1815)*

son would inherit the estate. They were invited for dinner and served drinks laced with poison. However, her plot backfired and it was her own son who drank the poisoned wine and died. She then committed suicide to escape execution. The remains of the castle were demolished in the 1970s when the new bridge was built.

from the Highlands during the 19th century. The stone was commissioned by Dennis MacLeod, a local who became rich through gold mining in South Africa.

**Angling** The River Helmsdale is renowned for its Salmon and Sea Trout. The Salmon run starts in early spring and lasts until May or June, while Sea Trout and Grilse are best in June and July. There is an ex-

cellent tackle shop in Dunrobin Street.

**Helmsdale Castle** may well have originally been the site of a broch or a Norse stronghold. The building in the Daniell print dated from the 14th century. Its ignominious place in history was made in 1567, when Isobel Sinclair devised a plan to murder her nephew, the 11th Earl of Sutherland, his wife and son, so that her own

**Timespan**, near the Telford Bridge, has a permanent collection and changing exhibitions, an art gallery, a riverside café, and shop. Beside the river there are gardens with Scottish herbs, flowers and local geology. The multi-faceted collection illustrates many aspects of past ways of life with re-creations of a croft, byre, smithy, and shop. Other displays present the area's archaeology, geology and natural history.

The gallery holds exhibitions of the work of local, national and international artists. They often feature original works produced here by artists who have spent time in residence in the gallery.

**The Ice House** dates from the 1780s and is sited across the

*Helmsdale Harbour in the early 20th century*

*Dunrobin Street, Helmsdale*

*Timespan*

*Glen Loth*

old bridge from Timespan, below the War Memorial. Ice was gathered from a pond nearby and the chamber was filled via a chute. The structure was well insulated, so that the ice was available all through the Salmon season. There are good views of the river and village from the bridge and from the elaborate war memorial.

**Beach and Fossils** The coastline south of Helmsdale is an excellent place to seek Jurassic fossils. The boulder beds on the foreshore are rich in reptilian, coral and fish remains. Some Ammonites and molluscs may also be found. Exposures of Jurassic and Kimmeridgean rocks continue from here to Golspie.

This coastline has excellent examples of raised beaches.

These were formed when the relative level of the sea was higher than today, during and after the Ice Ages. Since then the land has risen, leaving these raised beaches well above the current shoreline.

**Archaeology** Like other areas, the Strath of Kildonan or Strath Ullie was cleared of its inhabitants for sheep farming in the 19th century. Evidence of settlement over thousands of years includes many chambered cairns, hut circles, standing stones, brochs and ruined homesteads.

**Glen Loth** A narrow and winding road runs north from Lothbeg to meet up with the main Strath Kildonan Road at Dal-Langal. It follows the Loth Burn through a remote and beautiful landscape.

Carn Bran (NC942122) is a ruinous broch near the south end. Clach Mhic Mhios (NC941151), stands on the moor overlooking the valley. At 3.3m high this is the largest and most spectacular standing

*Clach Mhic Mhios*

*Raised Beach South of Helmsdale*

*Brora Beach*

stone in Sutherland. It may be a marker for the winter solstice as it aligns with a notch in the hill to the southwest on an azimuth of 214° - that of the midwinter sunset.

**Portgower** is a small village on the A9 just south of Helmsdale which is worth stopping at to visit the beach, with its dramatic Fallen Stack of Portgower. Boulder beds are mixed with Kimmeridgean shales and set in a sandy rock. The con-

torted and confused rocks with many pools are aesthetically appealing, but the terrain is difficult to walk on.

Ammonites, molluscs, fish, coral and plant fossils can be found here. The shore south from Helmsdale is a good example of raised beaches. Be careful when crossing the railway line. The village itself was built as a result of the 19th century clearances. Park near the track which leads down to the

beach taking care not to block any entrances. There are fine walks along the shore here.

**Brora** (ON *Brua A*, Bridge River) in the parish of Clyne (G *cleonadh*, sloping) lies at the mouth of the River Brora. The early inhabitants would have been attracted by the fertile land of the coastal plain and fishing for Salmon and Sea Trout in the river. The long sandy beach stretches for nearly 2mi (3km) and is backed by dunes and machair.

Jurassic Rocks are exposed on the coast and river around Brora. There are interesting exposures on the low cliffs to the south of the village and on the cliffs along the river. Fossilised plants and molluscs are easy to find.

**Coal Mining** Most British coal is from the Carboniferous Period, but some is from the Jurassic Age. There are outcrops on the coast near Inverbrora. In c.1529 open cast quarrying was started near the coast. By the 17th century shafts were sunk. The coal was used to boil sea water in pans to make salt for the fishing industry.

*Brora has a small quay*

*Ice House, Brora*

*Floral Old Boat, Brora*

During the 19ᵗʰ century mining was expanded further. A brewery, brickworks and a distillery, all using local coal, were established. The mining was constantly plagued with spontaneous fires caused by pyrites in some of the coal layers. Operations ceased in 1975, but large reserves remain.

*Carn Liath, an Iron Age Broch*

**Clynelish Distillery** was established in 1819 by the Duke of Sutherland. The current distillery was opened in 1968 with six new stills, identical to the two originals. It is now owned by Diageo and produces a lightly peated, fruity, waxy malt. The Visitor Centre is open all year and offers a range of tours and tastings.

**Brora Golf Course** was designed in 1923 by the great James Braid as his most north-erly Scottish course. Golfers share their space with friendly cows on these attractive links, which in summer are covered by a sea of colourful wild flowers.

**Carn Liath** (G Grey Cairn) is a well preserved broch about 2mi (3km) north of Golspie off the A9. The walls are nearly 4m high, with an outside diameter of 19m. For access, park as indicated and take the signposted path. It was cleared out in the 1800s and a variety of items found, some of which are in Dunrobin Museum. The broch was excavated again in 1986.

The entrance, complete with side cell, intramural stairs and lower scarcement can all be seen. A small settlement, which was in use until about 400AD, surrounds the broch.

**Dunrobin Castle** (G *Dunrobin*, Robin's Fort) stands on a

*Scallop Fossil at Brora Beach*

*Old Clynelish Distillery*

*Clynelish has Distinctive Small Stills*     *Carn Liath Entrance*

*Dunrobin Castle from the Gardens*

bluff just north of Golspie. It has an enchanting fairytale appearance when seen from afar. Closer inspection reveals a huge multi period mansion house.

The oldest part of the building is a 14th century keep, but it is probably built on the site of a Norse fort, itself on an Iron Age broch. Additions were made during the 16th century, but most of Dunrobin visible today dates from the 19th century.

In 1835 Sir Charles Barry, the architect of the Houses of Parliament, was commissioned to build what Queen Victoria called "*a mixture between a Scotch castle and a French château*". In WW1 it was used as a naval hospital and in 1915 suffered serious fire damage.

Sir Robert Lorimer of the Arts and Crafts movement undertook major renovations in 1919 and made several major alterations in the style of the Scottish Renaissance. A grand staircase leads from the entrance to the public floor rooms, which have expansive views over the sea towards Moray and the Black Isle.

During the self-guided visit, the Dining Room, laid out as in the 1850s, the Drawing Room, saved from fire in 1915 and the Library with its 10,000 books are perhaps the highlights. There are a number of works by artists including Canaletto, Reynolds, Ramsay and Wright, as well as fine furniture and tapestries.

The gardens were laid out in French style in 1850 on the sheltered ground below the

castle. They supply the flowers for the arrangements within the rooms and also offer particularly good views of the front of the building.

The museum was originally built in 1732 as a summer pavilion. It houses an eclectic mixture of items and trophies from around the world, but probably its collection of Pictish symbol stones is of greatest interest. There are displays on geology, the Kildonan gold rush and coal mining at Brora.

The surrounding woods have many trails, which are open all year. There is a particularly fine circular walk from Golspie along the coast past old piers and the east gates of Dunrobin.

When the castle is open there are daily falconry displays on the lawn which feature Golden Eagles, Peregrines and other birds of prey. There are excellent opportunities to observe and photograph the birds.

Dunrobin is recorded as being a Sutherland fort in 1401 and is still in the family today. William of Duffus was made first Earl in about 1235 when

*Dunrobin Castle Drawing Room*

*Dunrobin Castle*

*Dunrobin Castle Library*

*Dunrobin Castle*

*Dunrobin Castle by William Daniell (1815)*

Sutherland was still a disputed Norse-Scottish territory. Today Lord Strathnaver welcomes visitors to the home of his ancestors.

**Golspie** (ON *Golls Baer*, Goll's Farm) is on the narrow coastal plain below Ben Bhraggie. The village is sheltered from the west and faces south to the Dornoch Firth. With an award winning sandy beach, nearby woodland and links, it is a very pleasant place to stop.

**Golspie Mill**, at the north end of the village, is one of the few water mills still in operation in Scotland. It was built in 1863, renovated in 1992 and is powered by the Big Burn. The mill produces peasemeal, beremeal, wholemeal flour, rye flour, and oatmeal. Products are stocked all over Scotland and may be ordered online.

**The Orcadian Stone Co** has a fascinating collection of, mainly, local fossils and minerals

## BALBLAIR WOOD

This mature Scots Pine plantation dates from 1905 and covers much of the north side of Loch Fleet. It replaced a much older wood destroyed by a severe storm around 1900. Ferry Wood has more variety, dating from the early 1800s, though much of it was replanted in the 1960s.

Three rare plants typical of Pinewoods grow at Balblair, One-flowered Wintergreen, Creeping Lady's Tresses and Twinflower. Common Wintergreen and Lesser Twayblade may also be found. These wild flowers indicate that Pinewoods have long been established here.

Birds typical of coniferous forest, which may be seen or heard in these woods include Crossbill, Siskin, Redstart, Treecreeper, Great-spotted Woodpecker, Buzzard and Sparrowhawk. Crested Tit have been seen here, but may not breed. The Capercaillie was formerly resident.

## FERRY LINKS

An area of exposed coastal heathland lies to the east of Balblair Wood, with an interesting variety of grasses and wild flowers adapted to this environment. Several rare species of butterflies and moths feed on the nectar from the flowers. In summer, Arctic, Common and Little Terns nest, while there are over 100 species of lichen and more than 50 species of fungi .

*Creeping Ladies' Tresses*

*One-flowered Wintergreen*
*Balblair Wood*

## LOCH FLEET NNR

Loch Fleet (ON *fljotr*, flood), the tidal estuary of the River Fleet, lies between Golspie and Dornoch. It has a diverse combination of habitats including both salt and freshwater mudflats, saltmarsh, Alderwoods, Pinewoods and sand dunes.

*Loch Fleet NNR from The Mound*

**The National Nature Reserve** here covers over 1,000ha and is managed to sustain its wealth of wildlife. Loch Fleet is the most northeasterly river estuary in Scotland. The varied surroundings include farmland, woodland and moorland. The unusual combination supports a wide range of wildlife throughout the year.

**Vantage Points** There are good vantage points on the A9 at the Mound car parks, all along the road which runs along the south side of the loch as well as from the Ferry Links and Balblair Woods.

**Residents** Common Seals haul out on sand banks and Otters are present, though rarely seen. Osprey breed here and are regularly seen fishing, while Buzzard are common and Sparrowhawk breed in small numbers. Curlew, Oystercatcher, Redshank, Shelduck, Widgeon, and Teal are present all of the year.

**Migrants** In autumn and winter Bar-tailed Godwits, Dunlin, Turnstones, and other waders are present. Greylag and Pink-footed Geese as well as many species of duck may be seen here. Some are in transit and some linger. It is always worthwhile stopping here to scan for birds.

built up over many years by Don Shelley. It can be found at the north end of the village and certainly warrants a visit. Fossils can be found at low tide among the Jurassic rocks below Dunrobin Castle.

**Golspie Golf Course** was designed by James Braid and opened in 1889. It offers a mixture of links, heathland and parkland, as well as fine views. It is just south of the village.

**Golspie Beach** stretches for nearly 3mi (5km) from Carn Liath to Littleferry. Families appreciate the sheltered areas near the village, while walkers, nature lovers and fossil hunters will all find much of interest.

**Ben Bhraggie** (394m) and its statue of the 1ˢᵗ Duke of Sutherland is a prominent landmark. The summit can be reached by a path leading from the centre of the village. There are fine panoramic views along the coast. The return route follows Dunrobin Glen and the Big Burn past a waterfall and small gorge.

**The Mound** was built between 1814 and 1816 under Thomas Telford as part of the road to the north. It is nearly 1,000m long with a bridge at the north end. Sluice gates prevent sea water travelling upstream, but allow Salmon and Sea Trout to pass by on the ebb tide. The structure has changed the ecology of upper Loch Fleet. A large area of willows and alders has developed due to a build up of silt in the shallow freshwater west of the causeway.

**Skelbo Castle** is a dramatic crumbling ruin overlooking Loch Fleet from the south.

*Skelbo Castle in the Mist*

*Dornoch by William Daniell (1815)*

It is in a strategic position to control the crossing at Littleferry and dates from at least the 12th century, but probably much earlier. The ruined keep, curtain wall and courtyard are 13th-15th century, while the nearby mansion house dates from c.1600.

The house deserves renovation and the ruins consolidation. Skelbo was an important strong point, perhaps the oldest reference being to Gilbert of Moravia (later Bishop of Caithness) being granted lands here in about 1211.

**Dornoch** (G *Dorn Eich*, horses hoof) is a lovely little town facing south and east across the Dornoch Firth. Major redevelopment during 1810-1815 by the Countess of Sutherland created the pretty cottages. The sandstone buildings fit

in well with the ancient Cathedral, giving the town a picturesque appearance reminiscent of a Cotswolds village.

**Dornoch Cathedral**  Gilbert de Moravia became Bishop of Caithness in 1222, and moved his seat from Halkirk to Dornoch. He started work on the Cathedral in 1224 at his own expense. The building was largely complete by the time of his death in Scrabster in 1245. The first service was held in 1239. Gilbert was a cousin of the 1st Earl of Sutherland.

Feuds during 1570 between the Earls of Caithness and Sutherland led to the MacKays from Caithness burning the Cathedral, which remained partially roofless for many years. In the early 18th century the church was re-roofed and the spire completed.

Finally, the Countess of Sutherland had the Cathedral re-built in 1835-1837. The nave was reconstructed without pillared aisles which did not please everyone. The interior is light and welcoming with several impressive stained glass windows. This ancient Cathedral has a special beauty and gives the whole town a stature far out of proportion to its size.

**History Links Museum** is a fascinating window on Dornoch's past. It has permanent exhibitions on the Cathedral,

*Dornoch Cathedral*

*Castle Street, Dornoch*

*Dornoch Beach and Firth*

was that monks and others from the monastery at St Andrews introduced the sport to their colleagues here. The oldest record of golf in Dornoch is 1616. Apparently the authorities frowned upon such activities as being unwarlike.

**Royal Dornoch Golf Club** acquired royal status in 1906. The present Championship course was laid out in 1886-1889 by Tom Morris Senior and by 1904 it was modified again to 5,960 yards. This course is said to be among the best 15 in the world.

During WWII an airfield was built over part of the course, but it was removed after the war. A second course, The Struie, is now a full 18 holes. Tom Watson, five times Open Champion, said 'it's the most fun I've ever had on a golf course'!

**Embo** was established as a fishing village during The Clearances in the early 19th century. Today there is no fishing but it is a popular holiday resort due to its lovely long sandy beach. There is a chambered cairn in the car park of the caravan site. It contained a number of

**DORNOCH DISTILLERY**

Phil and Simon Thompson, run the family owned Dornoch Castle Hotel. Their famous whisky bar specialises in old discontinued bottles at fair prices.

A small building in the castle grounds has been fitted out as a micro distillery. They have *"crammed a lot of functionality into a very small space."*

*"We'll be running a wee set of direct gas fired pot stills, 100l and 600l as well as a 200l column still. While laying down barrels of new make spirit we will also be applying our old school principles to experimenting with white spirits production with an initial focus on gin. We need to make a white spirit that is good enough to fund whisky production for the first few years. The better the white spirit does, the more barrels we can lay down for longer."*

Picts and Vikings, feuding clans and the shameful burning of Janet Horn. Donald Ross' workshop also features. He designed over 500 golf courses in the USA. Dornoch Light Railway and how Andrew Carnegie affected the town are also included in this little museum.

**Golf** Sir Robert Gordon, tutor to a young Earl of Sutherland and historian of the Earldom, wrote (1630): *"About this toun (along the sea coast) ther are the fairest and largest linkes, (or green fields), of any pairt of Scotland, fitt for archery, golfing, ryding, and all other exercise; they doe surpasse the feilds of Montrose or St Andrews."*

Scotland's ancient game has been played in some form on the Dornoch Links for hundreds of years. The tradition

*Dornoch Distillery*

*Donald Ross' Workshop*

*Harebell or Scottish Bluebell*

cist graves and had two chambers, but the confusion of stone slabs is hard to understand.

**The Dornoch Firth** separates Sutherland from Ross-shire. The bridge was opened in 1991. It shortens the drive north, although the route by Bonar Bridge and over Struie Hill is much more scenic. In former times the Meikle Ferry ran across the Dornoch Firth.

The dunes of the Cuthill Links and the estuary of the River Evelix are good places for bird watching. Ospreys regularly fish near here, while the mudflats and saltmarsh are excellent for waders and roosting waterfowl especially during migration times and winter. The varied habitats, also support a diversity of wild flowers.

While crossing the Dornoch Bridge it is recommended to stop at one of the laybys to take in the scene. There are expansive views westwards towards the mountains of Easter Ross. When the Whins (Gorse) are in bloom during April and May the scene can be glorious.

*Dornoch Firth from the Dornoch Bridge*

East of Dornoch Point, the Gizzen Briggs (ON *Gisnar Bryga*, leaky bridge, as in a dried-up boat) is a large sandbar, dangerous for boats, but accessible at very low tides. Common Seals lie up here in large numbers. The Dornoch Firth south of here is part of RAF *Tain* Bombing Range.

**Fairy Bridge** According to folklore, one may be able to glimpse fairies crossing the Firth from here on Cockle shell boats, with gossamer sails. They are also said to sometimes be seen building a bridge of fairy gold, hidden by a rainbow. Only those with open minds and all senses alert have any chance of seeing them. Anyone guilty of the Seven Deadly Sins will never be able to see our fairy friends.

## The Last Witch

Janet Horne was the last person to be tried and executed for witchcraft in Britain. In 1727 she and her daughter were arrested and jailed in Dornoch. They were accused of devilish crimes, like turning the daughter into a horse, and of getting Satan himself to shoe it. The mother was said to be senile, while the daughter had a deformity to her hands and feet.

At trial, Captain David Ross, sheriff-depute of Sutherland, found both guilty and condemned them to be burned to death the next day. Not being able to properly recite the Lord's Prayer was part of the evidence.

The daughter was released or escaped but Horne was stripped, tarred and paraded in a tar barrel through the town. At the burning site, it was said that she smiled and warmed herself before her incineration. A stone said to mark this site stands in a cottage garden in Littletown, but with the wrong date of 1722. In 1736 the Witchcraft Acts were repealed.

*Ferry Links Lichen-rich Heath*

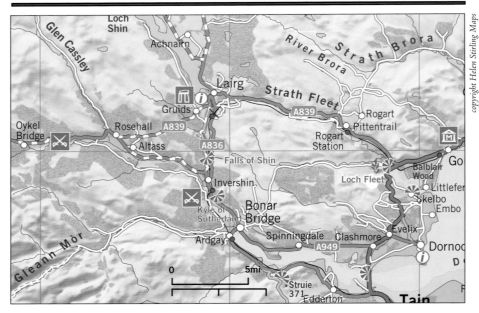

*copyright Helen Stirling Maps*

**LAIRG & BONAR BRIDGE LOOP** This c.36mi (56km) side trip loop follows Strath Fleet to Lairg from southwest of Golspie. It then passes through Invershin on the way to Bonar Bridge, from where either the north or south coast of the Dornoch Firth can be followed to rejoin the A9 at the Dornoch Bridge. The route mostly follows the North Highland Line railway.

**Rogart** (ON Red Farm), or Pittentrail, is in the middle of

Strath Fleet, which goes west from the Mound Rock to Lairg. This fertile valley is lush and green with a scattering of farms, houses and crofts. In comparison the surrounding area is ruggedly attractive with steep cliffs and rocky hills.

**St Callan's Church** sits in a prominent position with expansive views to the west over croftland and moorland. The present building dates from 1777, but is undoubtedly on the site of earlier churches.

The inside layout was changed around 1817. The kirkyard has many interesting tombstones.

**Battle of Torran Dubh** (G Black Hillock) In 1517 a ferocious battle was fought near Rogart between the Sutherlands under Alexander Sutherland and the Strathnavers under John MacKay. Sir Robert Will Gordon says that this *"was the greatest conflict that hitherto has been fought in between the inhabitants of these countreyes, or within the diocy of Catteynes, to our knowledge."*

**The Rogart Shirt** is a large woven woollen garment found in a grave near Springhill in Rogart. This russet brown shirt may date from the 14th century and is a rare example of a type of traditional tunic.

*Strath Fleet Autumn Colours*

*Strath Fleet near Rogart*

**Illegal Whisky** (G *uisge*, water, or *uisge beatha*, water of life) was a common product in the Highlands. Rogart was said *"to be entirely packed and crammed with whisky smugglers"*. Illicit stills were hidden in peat banks and in the hills. Before the building of the road to Lairg, Rogart was a relatively remote and isolated township.

Bere, an old fashioned type of Barley is an excellent food crop for humans and animals but is also a good source of malt for brewing and distilling. Malted Barley is much more nutritious and easier to store than fresh grain so there was undoubtedly a good supply after the harvest.

**John Alexander Macdonald** was the First Prime Minister of the Dominion of Canada. He served two terms and a total of 19 years. A cairn to his memory stands near Pittentrail, on the south side of the river. It is on the site of the home of

*Osprey*

*Common Buzzard*

| LAIRG & BONAR BRIDGE LOOP | |
|---|---|
| Achany Glen | 155 |
| Balblair Distillery | 159 |
| Bonar Bridge | 156 |
| Carbisdale Castle | 156 |
| Croick Kirk | 157 |
| Dalchork Bird Hide | 155 |
| Edderton Kirkyard | 158 |
| Falls of Shin | 155 |
| Hydro Electricity | 154 |
| Lairg | 154 |
| Ledmore & Migdale | 159 |
| Loch Fleet | 148 |
| Ord Archaeo Trail | 154 |
| Rogart | 152 |
| Sallachy Broch | 154 |
| Spinningdale | 159 |
| Strath Oykel | 156, 157 |
| Strathcarron | 158 |
| Struie Hill | 158 |

**LAIRG & BONAR BRIDGE SIDE TRIP LOOP**

**From the North** - 3mi (5km) west of Golspie on the A9 turn left onto the A839 signposted to Lairg at the Mound Rock. This road follows Strath Fleet to Lairg (15mi, 24km) at the south end of Loch Shin.

From here take the A836 south past the Falls of Shin to Invershin (7mi, 11km) where the rivers Shin and Oykel meet at the Head of the Kyle of Sutherland. Bonar Bridge is a further 3mi (5km) downstream.

**Three ways back to the A9**

1 - Follow the A949 along the north side of the Dornoch Firth to Clashmore on the A9 (11mi, 18km).

2 - Continue along the A836 by crossing the bridge and bearing left at Ardgay to reach the Meikle Ferry Roundabout at the south end of the Dornoch Bridge (11mi, 18km).

3 - Follow the A836 after Ardgay for 3mi (5km) then bear right onto the B9176 Struie Road which reaches the A9 between Alness and Evanton (20mi, 32km). Alternatively stop at the Struie viewpoint (NH653858) near the top of the hill (1.5mi, 2km) and return to the A836 as in 2.

**From the South** - simply reverse the sequence, starting north of Evanton, at Meikle Ferry or Clashmore.

*Lairg and Lower Loch Shin*

his grandparents, John and Jean Macdonald. Both families came from Rogart and although Sir John was born in Glasgow, the parish is proud of its connections with him.

**Lairg** (G *Lairg*, sloping hill) is the crossroads of Sutherland. Situated at the south end of Loch Shin, it is an ancient settlement site, with many Neolithic remains. Today it is renowned for its great annual sheep sale, the largest in Europe. At the main sale in August over 25,000 sheep may change hands.

This was one of the first areas of Sutherland where, from 1807, the people were cleared from the land to be replaced by sheep runs. The first general store was opened here in 1811, followed by an inn. The main

*Loch Shin Dam and Lairg*

street, Rogart Road, was built by 1816 and the village slowly developed.

With the arrival of the railway in 1868 and the development of proper roads, its position changed from remote to central. The Victorian fashion for outdoor sports such as fishing and shooting gave the village a boost in the late 1800s.

In 1919 Lairg was bought by Sir William Edgar Horne, who invested considerably in the area. In 1924 the village had its own diesel power station, one of the first in the Highlands.

**Hydro Electricity** Work on the Loch Shin dam started in 1954. The power stations were fully operational in 1959 and can generate 38MW. A small turbine is enclosed in the dam,

with most of the water being carried 5mi (8km) by tunnel to Shin Power Station at Inveran.

The dam is 427m wide and 12m high and raised the level of Loch Shin by about 11m. Fish lifts allow Salmon to migrate past the dam and diversion weir. The latter maintains the level of Little Loch Shin and allows water to continue to flow along the River Shin.

**The Parish of Lairg** formerly extended to the west coast. In a time when there were no roads, Loch Shin would have been an easy route to the northwest. It was MacKay country, like Strathnaver to the north, and the people did not take kindly to being ruled by the Earls of Sutherland, who were seen as incomers.

Tradition has it that St Maelrubha visited Lairg in the late 6th century and established a chapel. He is said to be buried at Skaill on the River Naver. There was a parish church here in 1222, probably on the site of the present kirkyard.

**The Broch of Sallachy** (NC549092) is the best preserved of several such Iron Age buildings around Lairg. It is accessed by a sign posted road off the A839 southwest of the village. The broch can be reached by following a track down to the loch shore.

Apart from the impressive situation, the walls stand to over 2m, surrounded by much

fallen rubble. The entrance with guard cell, intramural stairways, scarcement ledge and many other features can be examined. The views across Loch Shin to Lairg from here are lovely.

**Achany Glen** runs south from Lairg to the falls of Shin and Invershin. Many cairns, hut circles and burnt mounds litter the glen showing that it was well populated in the Bronze Age. There is a ruined chambered cairn at Grudie Bridge (NC571020). The chamber is visible and is surrounded by a ring of kerbstones.

**Dalchork Bird Hide** is approximately 2mi (3km) north of Lairg on the A836. It offers the chance to see Ospreys fishing on Loch Shin. Red and Black-throated Divers, Greenshank, Merlin, Hen Harriers

and even a White-tailed Sea Eagle have all been spotted from here.

**The Falls of Shin** is one of the great Salmon Leaps in Scotland, where the fish run upstream each autumn to spawn the next generation. There is access to observe the Falls from a platform. The *"Harrod's of the North"* was formerly owned by businessman Mohammed Al Fayed's Balnagowan Estate. It burned down in 2013. Kyle

*Ord North Chambered Cairn*

of Sutherland Development Trust is leading a replacement building project. The new centre is shaped like a Salmon and

### Ord Archaeological Trail

This trail starts at the Ferrycroft Centre, which has audiovisual displays covering archaeology, history and nature conservation. Events and activities are organised, and the Countryside Ranger gives advice on where to see wildlife and where to visit.

The trail takes in Neolithic chambered cairns as well as Bronze Age houses, cairns, and a burnt mound. There are fine views of Lairg and Loch Shin from Ord Hill (NC574055). In prehistoric times this hillside was cultivated farmland very different from today's landscape.

Ord North chambered cairn is a round cairn about 25m in diameter. It still stands to 2.5m and contains two cells. Ord South is ruinous. The Bronze Age ruins are less impressive in summer when they become overgrown; the colours are best in August with the heather in bloom.

*Northern Marsh Orchid*

*Sallachy Broch*

*Sallachy Broch*

*Salmon Leaping at the Falls of Shin*

and Maelbrigte, Thane of Moray. Sigurd was victorious, but died after being infected by the protruding tooth of his opponent's severed head. The Earl is said to be buried at Ciderhall, near Dornoch.

**The Battle of Carbisdale** was fought between Royalists led by the Marquis of Montrose and Scottish Government forces. Routed, Montrose escaped but was arrested at Ardvreck castle and later executed.

has exhibition space, a shop and a café.

The falls are most spectacular after heavy rain. Salmon may be seen here from late spring but the main run of breeding adults is in the autumn. There are several trails in the woods, which are mostly conifers, but include Aspen, Oak, Hazel, Alder, Birch and Rowan.

**Strath Oykel** is on the A837 route to the west. Invershin is

27mi (44km) from Ledmore Junction, north of Ullapool. This scenic was was built during 1821-1827. On a nice day it is a very pleasant drive despite the single track road. The Old Oykel Bridge dates from 1825. The rapids just up-river from here can be dramatic after heavy rain; Salmon may be seen running here from May onwards as the water warms.

This is the site of a battle between Earl Sigurd of Orkney

**Carbisdale Castle** overlooks the Kyle of Sutherland. It was built between 1906 and 1917 for the Duchess Blair, widow of the 3rd Duke of Sutherland. It was built in Ross-shire as she was refused land in Sutherland. In 1945 it was left to the Scottish Youth Hostels Association and until 2011was their flagship hostel. The SYHA sold it in 2015 for £1m.

The castle was home to King Haakon VI of Norway and his family during WWII. There is a good view of the Castle and the Kyle of Sutherland from the nearby railway station.

**Bonar Bridge** is at the south end of the Kyle of Sutherland, the confluence of the Salmon rich rivers of Carron, Oykel and Shin. Long a ferry point, in 1812 Thomas Telford chose it for the first of three bridges to cross here, and the village prospered until the Dornoch Bridge was opened in 1991.

Salmon were a major source

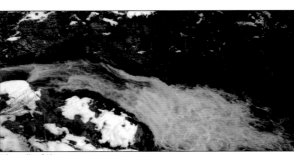

*The Falls of Shin*

*Oykel Bridge*

*Bonar Bridge from the South Bank, the third  Bridge , built in 1973*

of income here for centuries. They were caught in nets or traps on their way upstream and salted for export in wooden barrels until the early 19th century. Thereafter they were boiled in a brine pickle and exported in ice. Today the Salmon are only fished for sport.

**Croick Kirk** is 10mi (16km) west of Ardgay at the head of Strathcarron. This Thomas Telford designed Parliamentary Church was built in 1827.

Though remote, this place evokes more than almost anywhere else the poignant events of the 19th century clearances.

The clearance of Glen Calvie took place on 24th May 1845, when 18 families, comprising 80 people, were forcibly evicted from their crofts. They took shelter in makeshift booths in the graveyard and several left messages scratched onto the outside of the east window of the church.

**STRATH OYKEL
CLEARANCES, 1820**

The first Sutherland clearances happened in Strath Oykel in 1800, with riots in the final evictions here in 1820. Today a beautiful, fertile valley lies largely empty.

The Novar Estate had been inherited by Hugh Munro in 1805. By early 1820 he had decided to clear the people from the best land in favour of sheep. The first attempt at eviction having failed, Sheriff McLeod of Dingwall decided to use the militia.

On 2nd March 25 red-coats and 40 volunteers marched on Strath Oykel. A riot ensued made much worse by one militiaman who fired a live round into the crowd, killing a woman. The Sheriff decided to withdraw and await developments

In the end it was not the law but God that persuaded the tenants to give in 12 days later. The minister told them that the result of disobeying the law would be to burn in the fires of Hell. In May over 400 people left their ancestral valley, never to return.

*Bonar Bridge by William Daniell (1815), built 1812, washed away 1872*

*Croick Kirk*

*River Carron*

**Struie Hill** (G *an t-Srùidh*, Place of Streams, 371m) overlooks the south side of the Dornoch Firth. There are panoramic views from the viewpoint above Cagha Mor on the B9176. By taking a short walk to the top of the hill and then along the ridge a vista of the whole Firth can be taken in.

By this time public concern about the clearances was mounting, and a journalist from The Times was on hand to report on events. He had problems speaking to the people as they were Gaelic speakers. This raises interesting questions about the graffiti on the window panes.

Although some certainly date from 1845, others are from later years. They are all written in English in Victorian copperplate style. It also seems bizarre that the people did not shelter in the church because that would have been desecration, yet had no inhibitions about scratching the windows.

A ruined Iron Age broch lies just west of the church. It may have been a convenient source of stone and explain the siting of the building. Despite the questions, Croick Kirk remains a vivid and remarkable direct link to the brutal events of these times.

**Strathcarron** is a pretty valley which is well worthwhile visiting on its own account. There are several fine walks along tracks and through mixed woodland. Croick Kirk is open at all times to visitors.

The Struie Road was formerly the main road from Alness to Bonar Bridge. It was a popular short cut before the Dornoch Bridge was built but is now very quiet. Sadly the remote and once very popular Altnamain Inn is now closed. There are pleasant walks along the Strathrory River. The prominent hillfort of Cnocan Duin dominates this valley about two miles downstream.

**Edderton Kirkyard** is home to the eponymous Pictish cross-slab, a fine example of their symbol stones. The kirk itself dates from 1743 but is built on the site of a much older chapel. Clach Boarch (G Pointed Stone) stands in a field at Balblair Farm and may date from the Bronze Age. Later, Picts carved some of their symbols on the stone.

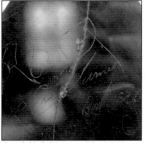

*Croick Kirk Messages May 1845*

*Croick Broch*

*Lone Piper on Struie Hill*

*Panoramic View of the Dornoch Firth from Struie Hill*

**Balblair Distillery** was founded in 1790 by John Ross, and run by his son until 1894. Since 1996 it has belonged to Inver House Distillers. The original water source, the Allt Dearg Burn, is still used in the production of this multi award winning Malt Whisky. Balblair is now released only as Vintage Whisky, each cask being selected for its optimum maturation point. The visitor centre is open all year for tours.

**Northern Shore** The alternative return route via the A949 to Clashmore runs along the northern shore of the Dornoch Firth and is also very scenic. It passes through Spinningdale which has changed little over the years. The village takes its name from the former spinning mill built in 1792. With no tradition of factory work and croft work to do, labour was a problem. It was not a success and burnt down in 1806.

**LEDMORE & MIGDALE FOREST**

This circular walk starts at a car park north of Spinningdale (NH668907). The route is on easy forest tracks and takes in Loch Migdale, Ledmore native woodland and the Migdale forest. There is an excellent viewpoint over the Dornoch Firth at A' Chraisg (NH646896, 186m). The total distance is c.6mi (9km).

*Edderton Pictish Symbol Stone*

*Balblair Distillery at Edderton*

*Old Postcard of Spinningdale*

Portmahomack has an attractive harbour and old girnels

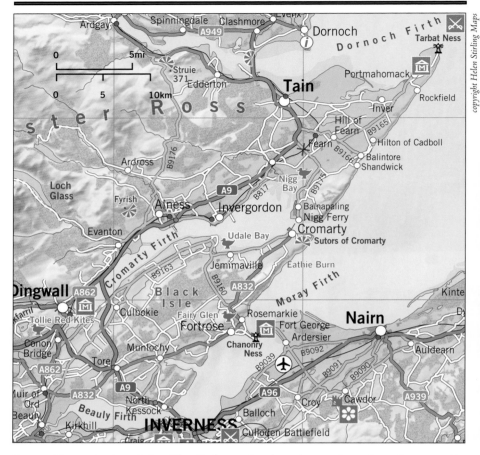

**Easter Ross** is bounded by the Dornoch Firth to the north and the Moray Firth to the southeast. It is split in two by the long, narrow Cromarty Firth. The climate is mild and dry, thanks to the uplands of Mid Ross to the west, which shelter the fertile farmland, small towns and villages.

The coastal plain is Old Red Sandstone making for rich soils which combine with the climate to be excellent for cereal growing. The east coast is cut off by the dramatic Great Glen Fault, continued north-eastward from the Great Glen.

There are outcrops of fossiliferous Jurassic rocks east of Nigg and again southeast of Cromarty. The Old Red Sandstone also contains many beds of fossil fish, first revealed by Hugh Miller. To the west Moine schists with granite intrusions predominate.

Settlements range from small towns like Tain, Alness, Invergordon and Dingwall to tiny coastal villages such as Port-mahomack or Cromarty. Inland there is the spa village of Strathpeffer and remote Garve. Most are ancient and have a long heritage, often dating from Pictish times or earlier.

Arts, crafts and heritage are well represented, with several good museums, galleries and potteries. In addition, many of the small towns and villages have retained interesting local shops which are a welcome change from the standard British high street.

Tain claims to be the oldest Royal Burgh in Scotland, having been granted a charter by Malcolm Canmore in 1066, which proclaimed the town as a Sanctuary, known as the *Girth o' Tain*. He is also said to have granted immunity from taxes on trading to residents.

St Duthac was born in Tain in the early 11th century, and was a highly venerated churchman in his own time and later. His shrine became one of the most visited pilgrimage sites in Scotland. James IV and James V visited it regularly, ensuring its continued popularity.

The Sanctuary granted in 1066 was enclosed by four crosses which marked the boundaries within which people could seek the protection of the Church. St Duthac died in Armagh and his body was buried in Tain in 1153.

In 1306 the Sanctuary was famously broken by the Earl of Ross when he and his men kidnapped Robert the Bruce's wife and daughter and handed them over to King Edward I of England. In 1428 a feud between Thomas MacKay of

*Tain Tolbooth dates from 1706*

Creich and Alexander Mowat of Freswick resulted in the former killing the latter in the chapel, which he then burnt.

**St Duthac Collegiate Church** dates from about 1370 and was extensively renovated in the 19th century. There are two hog-backed tombstones in the kirkyard, which may be Norse. The ruins of what could be the original chapel built to hold St Duthac's remains around 1153 are near the shore to the northwest. Another ruined chapel in the kirkyard is probably the one burnt in 1428.

**Tain through Time** is housed in an old schoolhouse in the kirkyard. It describes the life and times of James IV as well

as the miracles of St Duthac and the story of the Collegiate Church. The adjacent museum holds an interesting collection of local silverware. Tain was

| Easter Ross | |
|---|---|
| Alness | 170 |
| ANTA | 168 |
| Beatrice Oil Field | 167 |
| Black Isle | 172 |
| Black Rock Gorge | 171 |
| Cromarty Firth | 169 |
| Dalmore Distillery | 170 |
| D-Day Training | 168 |
| Edderton | 159 |
| Evanton | 171 |
| Fearn Abbey | 167 |
| Fyrish Monument | 171 |
| Glenmorangie Dist | 164 |
| Hilton of Cadboll | 166 |
| HMS *Natal* | 169 |
| Invergordon | 170 |
| Nigg Kirk | 167 |
| Nigg Bay RSPB Res | 168 |
| North Sea Mine Barr | 169 |
| Portmahomack | 165 |
| RAF *Tain* | 168 |
| Rockville | 166 |
| St Duthac Church | 163 |
| Shandwick | 167 |
| Tain | 163 |
| Tain Pottery | 164 |
| Tarbat Ness | 166 |
| Tarbat Discovery Cent | 165 |

*St Duthac Collegiate Church dates from 1370*

*Glenmorangie Distillery has very tall stills*

displays a wide range of contemporary work by Scottish artists. It has a reputation for showing outstanding pieces.

**Glenmorangie Distillery**, just to the north of Tain, was established in 1843 by William Mathieson in a former brewery. The nearby Tarlogie Springs provided a good water source. He installed two tall secondhand gin stills instead of the usual pot stills.

known since at least the 16th century for its gold and silversmiths, especially in the 1700s when men such as Hugh Ross produced outstanding work.

Most of present day central Tain dates from the 18th and 19th centuries. Building of the Tolbooth commenced in 1706. It was used as a prison and for secure storage of the town's documents and valuables. The mercat cross now stands

outside the front door. Tain Through Time hires out self guided audiovisual tours.

Tain is a slightly olde worldly, yet vibrant town centre, with a good selection of interesting independent shops. There are a number of excellent places to eat out as well as a good selection of accommodation.

**Arts and Crafts** Brown's Gallery opened in 1993 and

Today the distillery has eight tall stills. It was an early adopter of wood finishing, where the spirit is conditioned in a range of casks. These include barrels formerly used for Madeira, Port, Sherry or fine wines. Various distillery visits are run daily all year. These include the Original, the Signet and the Heritage Tours. A wide range of expressions of Glenmorangie is available in the shop.

**Tain Pottery** started in a derelict farm steading at Aldie in 1986. Situated just south of the town, it produces very attractive hand thrown and painted ceramics. Many of the designs reflect the beauty of local nature.

*Tain High Street*

*Tain was long famous for its silversmiths*

Two cups by Hugh Ross I

*Hog-backed graveslab*

**Portmahomack** (G *Port Mo-Cholaig*, Colman's, or Columba's Port) may claim some association with Columba. It is certainly the best harbour on the entire coast north of Burghead and has been in use as such for a very long time. The present pier was built by Thomas Telford in 1813-16.

*Portmahomack*

The larger warehouse or girnel was built in 1779 and the smaller by Lord Cromartie in the 17th century. They were used to store grain before shipment south. The village has many attractive 18th and 19th century houses which curve around the sandy bay. A cast iron drinking fountain celebrates the arrival of gravitation (piped) water in 1877.

**Tarbat Discovery Centre** in St Colman's Kirk tells the story of the Pictish settlement and monastery established here in the 6th century and flourished until it was destroyed in the 9th century. The church has at least six phases, the earliest dating from the 8th century. St Colman's was rebuilt in 1756 but abandoned in 1843 after the Disruption. From 1994, restoration of the church al-

lowed extensive excavation. The oldest burials within the church date from about 560AD, others are from 8th to the 11th centuries.

Excavations to the west of the kirkyard revealed a workshop, a barn, a mill and a ditch dating from the 8th century. Over 200 fragments of sculpture were found, as well as evidence for the large scale making of parchment from cattle hides.

This may have been used to make illuminated manuscripts like the Book of Kells.

Clay moulds, crucibles and glass studs were found in the workshops. Bronze, silver, gold and glass were being worked. Many parts of Pictish cross-slabs were also found, suggesting that large sculpted stones may have stood here, all dating from about 800AD.

*Pictish Carved Stone*

*Pictish Head*

*Bronze Pictish Queen*

*St Colman's Kirk, now Tarbat Discovery Centre*

Redwings, Wheatears, Pipits and other rarer species.

**Tarbat Peninsula** is mainly fertile farmland and has for long been known for its grain crops, first bere, then oats and barley. Nowadays a substantial amount of wheat is also grown. Alternating grazing and arable land, marshland, saltmarsh and heath make an interesting and varied landscape.

*Tarbat Ness Lighthouse*

**Tarbat Ness** The *Orkneyinga Saga* describes a battle at Torfness between Earl Thorfinn the Mighty and Karl Hundason in about 1035, where the Orkneymen won.

The lighthouse was established in 1830 and built by Robert Stevenson. The 41m tower has two wide red bands and is the third tallest in Scotland after North Ronaldsay and Skerryvore.

Tradition has it that there was a Roman camp at Brucefield Farm. Later, witches' covens were said to meet here. Mermaids may be seen offshore, but, Bottle-nosed Dolphins are more likely!

**Birds** Tarbat Ness is a good place for birds during migration times, especially seabirds on passage, including Manx and Sooty Shearwaters, Arctic, Pomarine and Great Skuas and others. Falls of passerines from Scandinavia sometimes occur. These may include Fieldfares,

**Rockville** is a small village just south of Tarbat Ness on this mostly rock bound east coast. It has a small pier built during the Herring Boom in the 1880s. Some Salmon fishing is still done here. Ballone Castle along the coast was abandoned about 1650, but has recently been restored.

**Hilton of Cadboll** is famous for its Pictish cross-slab, found

*Replica Cadboll cross-slab*

*Replica Cadboll cross-slab*

*Shandwick cross-slab*

on the shore in 1811. At present it is in the National Museum in Edinburgh, but a recently carved replica stands next to the ruined St Mary's Chapel near the beach. The base was found in 2002 during excavations and can be seen in the Seaboard Memorial Hall in Balintore.

**Shandwick** (ON *Sand Vik*, Sandy Bay) is famous for Clach a' Charridh, its large cross-slab which is over 3m high. It is now protected by a glass box which fails to take away from the intricate Pictish carvings.

**Fearn Abbey**, *The Lamp of the North*, was founded near Edderton in 1221 by Premonstratensians from Whithorn, but moved to its present location in 1238. It continued in use as the parish church after the Reformation.

*Fearn Abbey*

In 1742 the flagstone roof collapsed during a service, after the church was struck by lightning, killing many of the congregation. The Minister survived, being protected by the pulpit. It was rebuilt in 1771, incorporating some of the medieval walls and remains in use as the parish church.

**Nigg** (G *'n Eig*, the Notch, or gulley), at the southern tip of the Tarbat Peninsula, is another ancient Christian site. Nigg Old Church was rebuilt in 1626. It now houses the Nigg cross-slab, an 8th century Pictish masterpiece. Originally it probably stood overlooking the Cromarty Firth, one of at least four such stones on the peninsula.

The church itself is typical of Scottish kirks of the time with

the pulpit on the east wall, a laird's loft and a north wing. The kirkyard has many interesting tombstones, including the Cholera Stone, which dates from an epidemic of 1832.

**Nigg Fabrication Yard** is in sharp contrast to the tranquillity of the Old Kirk. In the 1970s it produced oil platforms for the production of North Sea Oil. Nowadays it is quiet except for the occasional construction of wind turbines for off-shore installation. The site has one of the largest dry docks in the world, and may well have a future in dismantling redundant North Sea structures.

**Beatrice Oil Field** The nearby Oil Terminal is operated by Talisman. It is the landfall of the pipeline from the Bea-

*Nigg cross-slab*

*The Cholera Stone, Nigg*

*Assembling offshore wind turbines at Nigg*

trice Field. The platforms are 15mi (24km) offshore from Dunbeath. The field was discovered in 1976 and the oil is sourced from Jurassic rocks. In 2006 two large wind turbines were installed here, each can produce 5MW. They may be the forerunners of a much larger windfarm.

**Nigg Bay RSPB Reserve** is a large sheltered area of saltmarsh, mudflats and wet grassland at the north head of the Cromarty Firth. The entrance to the car park for the Reserve is about a mile north of Nigg village. The nearby hide offers good views over various habitats. There are also several good vantage points along the B9175 as well as from the shore near Balintraid Pier on the west side. The road just west of Nigg Ferry terminal is

a good place to watch sea ducks in winter.

From October to March large numbers of waders, including Bar-tailed Godwits, Knots, Curlews and other species may be seen here. In summer, Lapwings and Redshanks breed. Many ducks winter here, including Pintail. The fields in the Tarbat Peninsula are home to large numbers of Greylag and Pink-footed Geese as well as Whooper Swans. Buzzards and Sparrowhawks are present all year.

**ANTA** is a design and architecture firm which is based near Fearn. It makes a unique range of stoneware pottery and weaves textiles on the site. Colours and designs are inspired by the Scottish landscape and traditional styles. The shop

has enticing displays of their products and the cafe serves good coffee and cakes.

**Tain Ranges** were developed in the 1930s to train pilots in bombing and dropping torpedoes. RAF Tain was established as a Fighter Sector Station in 1941. It was used as a forward base for bombers, most notably by Halifaxes trying to sink the Tirpitz in 1942.

In 1943 RAF Coastal Command took over the base. Beaufighters and Liberators were based here to carry out anti-submarine and anti-shipping patrols off Norway and Denmark. Some of the WWII buildings still remain. RAF *Tain* is still an operational air-to-ground weapons range and is regularly used by the RAF and other NATO airforces.

Fearn airfield was built by the RAF in 1941, but became HMS *Owl* in 1942. Its main use was as a torpedo school for pilots of Swordfish, Barracuda and other aircraft flown by the Fleet Air Arm.

**D-DAY landing training** was carried out in 1943-44 in an area around Inver, west of RAF Tain. Nearly 15 square miles was completely cleared of more than 900 people as well as nearly 10,000 head of livestock for several months.

Tarbat was judged the most suitable place to do combined operations training in Scot-

*The Cromarty Bridge from the Black Isle*

land. Beach assault, bombardment and inland tank operations were practised under realistic conditions, with intense firing of live ammunition.

Many units used the range over a period of about six months, but by mid March 1944 it had been closed down. Tarbat was ideally suited for practising beach landings and moving inland with tanks. The training here was valuable practice for the landings at Juno and Sword beach on D-Day. By mid 1944 the area had been cleared of ordnance and the people were allowed to return.

**Cromarty Firth** In WWI the Royal Navy used the Cromarty Firth as a base and refuelling station. HMS *Natal*, a Duke of Edinburgh class cruiser, blew up here in December 1915, with the loss of at least 390 crew, probably because of faulty cordite.

**North Sea Mine Barrage** In 1917 the US Navy requisitioned Dalmore Distillery as a mine depot, and built the nearby pier. Mines were shipped to Kyle of Lochalsh and transferred by rail to Invergordon. A

*Catalinas were based at Invergordon during WWII*

fleet of minelayers laid the barrage which extended 200nm from Orkney to Norway.

70,177 mines were laid, only to be cleared up again by the US Navy in 1919. Only about 30% of the mines laid in 1918 were discovered by the minesweepers. Up to 20 U-boats were damaged or lost because of the minefield. 24 million metres of wire rope and 10 million kg of explosives were used.

**Flying Boat Base** During the 1930s, Alness became a training base for flying boat crews. First of all, Saro *Londons* and *Stranraers* were based here. They were followed by *Sunderlands* and *Catalinas* By 1942, 22 crews were being trained each month. The base, along with Sullom Voe in Shetland, and Oban, provided long range flying boat patrols over the North Sea and North Atlantic.

*An American Mk6 mine*

*Natal Memorial Garden*

*Mines in storage at Invergordon*

*HMS Natal*

*Invergordon during WWI*

**Coast Defence** Extensive shore batteries were installed on the North and South Sutors in WWI and WWII. Significant remains still exist of these today and are worth exploring. A boom defence and inductive loop were also in place to protect against submarines and surface raiders. The naval base closed in 1956, but ships still refuel here.

**Invergordon** takes its name from Sir William Gordon,

*Alness Heritage Centre*

who owned land here in the 18ᵗʰ century. It was formerly known as Inverbreakie. The Cromarty Firth had, for long, been used as a safe anchorage before the Royal Navy started to see its potential in the early 19ᵗʰ century. By the mid-1800s it was established as a coaling station. During WWI fuel oil tanks, piers, dockyard facilities and the hospital were built.

The Navy considered Invergordon too vulnerable to air attack in WWII and reverted almost entirely to the heavily defended Scapa Flow. It did however remain in use until the 1950s, with a huge oil storage facility in the hill above the town from which ships still re-fuel.

Today many cruise liners visit the port, making use of its deep water and good facilities to provide passengers with
*Oil rigs and cruise ships at Invergordon*

tours of the North Highlands. Oil rigs are also often present, coming here for repairs, maintenance or decommissioning.

In 1971, construction of a large aluminium smelter, mostly financed by Highlands and Islands Development Board, was commenced by British Aluminium. At that time Government policy was the development of heavy industry. However the promise of low cost electricity from Dounreay and new hydroelectric power stations did not materialise and the facility shut in 1981.

Invergordon has a wide High Street with a good selection of small shops, as well as a range of places to eat and stay. The Naval Museum and Heritage Centre beside the British Legion has displays of artefacts and an archive. There are several old warehouses which date from the 18ᵗʰ century onwards.

**Alness** (G *Alanais*, bog, wet place or ON *A Ness*, Point of the River) has a long and pretty main street with a Thomas Telford bridge in the middle. The town regularly wins Scotland in Bloom and Britain in Bloom competitions due to its fine displays of floral art.

**Dalmore Distillery** was established in 1839 by Alexander Mathieson. It makes a range of award winning malts, which can be sampled in the Visitor Centre. To quote the website, *"Our esoteric, artisan approach has been passed down through*

*Alness has a pretty main street, bedecked with flowers in summer*

generations and remains to this day." The Distillery is signposted off the A9 in Alness.

**The Alness Heritage Centre** has displays of artefacts and wartime events as well as archives. Local books, crafts and knitwear are also on sale here. The genealogy unit has information for those seeking their ancestors from this area. It is situated in the main street.

**Evanton** is named after the son of the 19ᵗʰ century founder of the village. It is bypassed now by the A9 and so is spared the heavy traffic that formerly clogged every little village on this route north.

**The Storehouse** is on the A9 at Foulis Ferry just north of the Cromarty Bridge. It is a restaurant and tea-room with a farm shop.

### FYRISH MONUMENT

This bizarre but very impressive structure on Cnoc Fyrish (NH608698, 452m) was built for Sir Hector Munro in 1782. He had been the General in command of the British Army in India. It is modelled on the Gate of Negapatam, captured from the Dutch in 1781. There are wonderful panoramic views over Easter Ross and the Cromarty Firth all the way round to Ben Wyvis.

**Walk** There is a signposted carpark on a minor road off the B9176 northwest of Alness at NH627714. From here the waymarked Jubilee Path heads up to the monument. The total distance is 4mi (6km) along good paths.

### BLACK ROCK GORGE

This 36m-deep box canyon was cut by glacial meltwater through soft sandstone rocks. The River Glass flows at the bottom of this spectacular 1,000m-long gorge. It was used as one of the locations in the film *Harry Potter and the Goblet of Fire*.

Folklore alleges that the Lady of Balconie was enticed into the gorge by a strange man, who may have been the devil. Some say that her screams may still be heard coming from the depths, but nobody has seen her since.

**Walk** Park in the centre of Evanton where an information board indicates several walks. To reach Black Rock Gorge follow signs keeping to the west side to a second bridge which crosses the deepest section of this decidedly mysterious and somewhat creepy canyon. From here take a track, keeping left until a single track road, then turn right down the hill back to Evanton. This route will be muddy and slippery if wet. Distance 1.5mi (4km).

*Dalmore Distillery Visitor Centre*

*Fyrish monument old postcard*

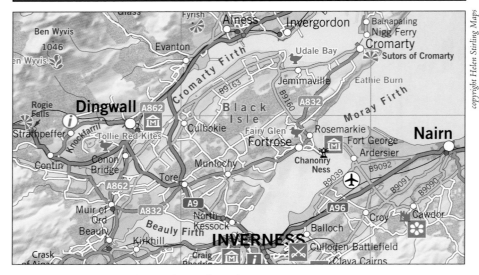

*copyright Helen Stirling Maps*

**THE BLACK ISLE** is neither black, nor an isle, but a long peninsula with the Cromarty Firth to the north and the Beauly and Moray Firths to the south. Conon Bridge, Muir of Ord and the A862 mark the western boundary.

Before the Kessock Bridge was opened in 1982, the main road north, the A9, wound its way laboriously around the Beauly Firth to Dingwall. Thus the previously isolated Black Isle suddenly became much more accessible. It makes a fine

*Big Vennel Street, Cromarty in the 19ᵗʰ century*

detour from the NC500, an option which will be enough to convince many visitors to return and explore it at leisure.

The A9 snakes rapidly south from the Cromarty Bridge to the Kessock Bridge and Inverness. Visitors should resist the temptation to by-pass this intriguing area.

**Geology** Most of the Black Isle is Middle Old Red Sandstone, which makes for fertile soils and good building stone so much in evidence. Of

greatest interest are the fishbeds which outcrop at Eathie and Cromarty. Fossil fish are found in shale beds. The rocks here date from Devonian times 391-370 million years ago.

These were closely studied by Hugh Miller of Cromarty in the 19ᵗʰ century. At Eathie, Jurassic shales hold Ammonite and Belemnite fossils. The east coast is formed by the Great Glen Fault.

**Farming** Agricultural improvement took root in the late 18ᵗʰ century on the Black Isle, and throughout the 19ᵗʰ century new breeds of stock and crops were introduced as well as innovative methods of growing them. Today's farmers are just as progressive, taking advantage of the fertile soils and benign climate to grow good crops of wheat and barley and to rear prime cattle as well as vegetables.

*Cromarty by William Daniell (1815)*

**North Kessock** (St Kessoc was Pictish and died c.560) is a tranquil little village on the southern tip of the Black Isle, by-passed by the busy A9 and yet a very good base from which to explore the area. A ferry operated to here from South Kessock since at least 1437 as part of the pilgrimage via Fortose and Nigg to Tain.

**Kessock Bridge** opened in 1982, and has a main span of 240m. It is designed to cope with high winds, floods and earthquakes as it straddles the Great Glen Fault. Its height allows shipping to pass.

**Ord Hill** to the northeast of North Kessock is topped by a vitrified Iron Age fort. It can be part of a circular walk from Craigton (just off the north end of the bridge on the south-bound A9). Several routes can be followed through the woods and minor roads here, with good views over Inverness, the Beauly Firth and the Bridge.

The west side of the Black Isle is a large glacial outwash plain, with fertile farms and small villages. The mountains of the Highlands are close by to the south and west. They help create the micro-climate which gives this area a special charm.

**Munlochy** (G *Bun lochaidh*, Head of the Loch, pronounced *"Mewchie")* is a small settlement at the head of Munlochy Bay, home to the Plough Inn, one of the smallest pubs in Scotland. Workers engaged in quarrying stone for Fort

| THE BLACK ISLE LOOP | |
|---|---|
| Avoch | 174 |
| Black Isle Brewery | 174 |
| Bottle-nosed Dolphins | 174 |
| Brahan Seer | 175 |
| Chanonry Ness | 175 |
| Clootie Well | 174 |
| Cromarty | 176 |
| Cromarty Bridge | 173 |
| Cromarty Courthouse | 178 |
| Eathie Burn | 178 |
| Fairy Glen | 176 |
| Fortrose | 175 |
| Groam House Museum | 176 |
| Hugh Miller | 177 |
| Kessock Bridge | 173 |
| Munlochy | 173 |
| Ord Hill | 193 |
| Red Kites | 179 |
| Rosemarkie | 176 |
| South Sutor | 178 |
| Udale Bay | 179 |

**THE BLACK ISLE SIDE TRIP**

The Black Isle has much to offer as a side trip from the NC500. Depending upon which direction is being taken around the route there are a number of options. Fortrose and Cromarty are the main villages with a good choice of accommodation, cafés and small shops.

Chanonry Point is one of the best places in Scotland to see Bottle-nosed Dolphins.

**Anticlockwise** - from Inverness take the A9 across the Kessock Bridge, then the 4th exit from the Tore roundabout onto the A832 sign-posted Cromarty. Then take the B9163 along the north coast to the roundabout on the A9 at the south end of the Cromarty Bridge. Turn right and head north on the A9. Dingwall can also be included by crossing the A9 and following the B9163 to Conon Bridge and following signposts to the town.

**Clockwise** - Follow the above route in reverse, taking in Dingwall before following the main road, the A862, then the A835 to the Tore roundabout. Return via the A9 to Inverness or via Muir of Ord and Beauly.

**Either Direction** From Muir of Ord turn right along the A832 to the Tore round-about. Return along the B9169 to Muir of Ord and continue west or north.

*Avoch from the harbour*

## BOTTLE-NOSED DOLPHINS

Bottle-nosed Dolphins are often seen in the Moray Firth which has a resident population of about 130. The best places to see them are from North Kessock, Chanonry Ness and around Cromarty. The best time to see them is during the first two hours of the flood tide.

Boat trips are operated from Cromarty, Avoch, Portmahomack and Inverness. They are most commonly seen in the summer when Salmon are running, or when shoals of Mackerel or Herring have come inshore.

Harbour Porpoises are also sometimes seen, but Minke Whales and White-beaked Dolphins may only occasionally be present.

George stayed here in the 1760s, which led to the growth of the village.

Munlochy Bay is a long, narrow inlet facing the Inner Moray Firth. Its large areas of sand, mudflats and surrounding saltmarshes are very attractive to birds, especially waders and waterfowl. Redshank, Oystercatcher, Ringed Plover, Dunlin, Curlew and Shelduck all breed here. Autumn sees the arrival of huge numbers of ducks, many of which overwinter. Geese and Whooper Swans pass through, or stay for the winter, roosting on the intertidal zone and feeding on fields.

**The Clootie Well**, (G *Fuaran nan Mhuiristean*, St Mary's Well, NH639536), near Munlochy, is of ancient origin. According to folklore, a gift of cloth had to be offered to its fairy before drinking the water. This ritual was supposed to restore health and give good luck. Christians took it over as St. Boniface's Well. Branches all around are covered with pieces of cloth which give a somewhat eerie feeling to the place. The best time to visit is on a cold, foggy day on your own. Traditionally it is visited on the first Sunday in May.

**Black Isle Brewery** was established in 1998. Its mission is to produce a range of top quality organic beers packaged in recycled materials. The barley and hops used are grown on organic farms, without artificial fertilisers or herbicides. The product can be tasted and purchased on the premises.

**Avoch** (G *Obh'ch* or ON *A*, river, pronounced "*Och*") was established as a fishing village in the early 17th century, when it was called Seatown. The harbour was built by Thomas Telford in 1814 at the same time as the village was expanded to house people displaced from the Highlands.

The *Ochies* fished locally for part of the year for Herring but

*Bottle-nosed Dolphin at Chanonry Ness*

*Bottle-nosed Dolphin at Chanonry Ness*

ranged as far as Caithness and Loch Broom. They were highly regarded as seamen. Avoch has attractive rows of mostly single storey cottages, separated by lanes leading down to the seashore. Ormond Hill lies to the west and, though wooded, offers fine views over the inner Moray Firth.

**Chanonry Ness** is a pebbly spit projecting about a mile into the Inner Moray Firth. St Boniface is reputed to have come here in the 7th century and established the first chapel in Rosemarkie. St Moluag may have been here earlier. The lighthouse, by Alan Stevenson, was first lit in 1846.

A ferry once ran from the slipway near the lighthouse to Ardersier. There was formerly a large Salmon fishery here but all that remains is the ice house, which was used to store ice for the preservation and shipping of the fish being exported.

Folklore says that a wizard joined forces with the fairies to build a bridge to Ardersier. This gossamer construction was well underway when a stranger wished the fairyfolk

*Chanonry Ness lighthouse*

God speed, after which they stopped work and returned to their homeland, some perhaps remaining in the Fairy Glen.

**Fortrose** is an attractive little town with fine sandstone houses surrounding its ruined 13th century cathedral. Only the south aisle and choir remain of what must once have been a very impressive building, as shown by the original outline. Although Cromwell's army is accused of its destruction, Lord Ruthven bought (or took) all of the lead off the roof in 1572. The nearby Chapter House is also 13th century.

This is a very pleasant place to take a wander through the pretty streets, admire views over the Moray Firth and explore the charming sandstone harbour, which has changed little in nearly 200 years.

*The Clootie Well*

## The Brahan Seer

A stone to the Brahan Seer, or *Coinneach*, stands at Chanonry Ness on the reputed site of his death. *Coinneach Adhair* was a 17th century clairvoyant who allegedly predicted many things. He was burnt here in a tar barrel as a witch in about 1660 on the orders of the Countess of Seaforth.

She wanted to know why her husband was staying so long in Paris. When the Seer informed her that the Earl was philandering with a French lady, his fate was sealed. Before his immolation *Coinneach* predicted that the Earl would be the last of his line, that his sons would die before him, and that one of his daughters would kill the other.

All four sons did pre-decease the father, and one daughter did die in a carriage accident while being driven by the other.

He is reputed to have made many other forecasts, such as the building of the Caledonian Canal, the North Highland Line and the Kessock Bridge.

*Remains of Fortrose Cathedral*

He died here in June 592. Curitan, who took the Latin name Bonifacius, was the first bishop and abbot here. He died here in c.630. Along with the Pictish monastic site on the Tarbat Peninsula, Rosemarkie was one of the most important Christian sites in Pictland.

St Boniface Fair was formerly held on his saint's day, 16th March until about 1830. It was revived in 1978 to mark the Silver Jubilee of Queen Elizabeth II and has been held in early August ever since. The Fair is set in the 1750s with participants dressed in period costume. The goods and entertainments on offer are those which would have been available at the time. It is held in Cathedral Square, which becomes a hive of colourful activity for the day.

**Rosemarkie** (G *Ros*, Point, *Marc*, Horse, Horseburn Point) is an ancient settlement on the north side of Chanonry Ness with a fine sheltered sandy beach. The village was another Salmon station, as attested by the icehouse near the shore. There is a fine sandy beach to the north of the burn, while a more variable one of sand and pebbles stretches all the way to Chanonry Ness.

St Moluag founded the great Pictish monastery at Rosemarkie in the late 6th century.

**Groam House Museum** is mainly dedicated to displays of the many sculpted Pictish stones which have been found in and around Rosemarkie. The intact Rosemarkie cross-slab takes pride of place. The Museum also houses the Bain Collection. George Bain (1881-1968) was a Caithness-born artist who made a lifelong study of Celtic designs on stone, jewellery and books.

**Cromarty** (G *Crom*, bent, *bath* sea, Curved Bay) is a delightful and unspoilt little village perched on a small headland protruding into the entrance of the Cromarty Firth. A visit here is a real treat.

The Romans called the Cromarty Firth *Portus Salutis*, and doubtless a Pictish settlement existed here, but no evidence has been found. A chapel was

### The Fairy Glen

From a carpark just northeast of Rosemarkie (NH735577) a path follows the Markie Burn through these enchanted woods. There are two fine small waterfalls which are spectacular after rain. A bridge crosses the burn at the head of the glen with steps back up to the road.

In spring children would gather wild flowers and scatter the petals on the pools for the fairies. Wild flowers including Primroses, Bluebells and Water Avens brighten the woods in spring.

Dippers and Grey Wagtails may be seen as well as Willow Warblers, Woodpeckers and Treecreepers. Ice from the millpond was used to replenish the Chanonry icehouse in winter. Today it is home to Herons and ducks; truly an enchanting place.

*The Fairy Glen*

*Cromarty from South Sutor*

established here in the 6th century by St Moluag but this and any carved stones have been lost due to coastal erosion.

The town has always alternately prospered and declined due to its location. By the 17th century it was one of the busiest ports in Scotland, trading in grain and salt fish with the Baltic, Holland and as far as the Mediterranean. Many emigrants left here for the New World. Cromarty prospered for a long time from the Herring fishing, partly due to the Guillam Bank, five miles to the east where 1,000 barrels a day were regularly caught.

In 1772 George Ross, owner of the Cromarty Estate, re-developed the harbour and set up a hand-weaving factory, which used hemp from Russia and which later became

a large ropeworks. Brewing, lace-making and manufacture of iron hand tools and nails also thrived. Many of those cleared from the land in the Highlands came here to work.

With the demise of these industries and the fishing, Cromarty declined in prosperity but in recent years many buildings have been renovated, nota-

*Hugh Miller*

### HUGH MILLER

Hugh Miller (1802-1856) was born in Cromarty, the son of a ship's captain, who was lost at sea in 1807. He trained as a stonemason and became very interested in the fossil fish which he found in the course of his quarrying work. He first found ammonites in Jurassic rocks at Eathie southeast of Cromarty.

Later, he travelled far and wide, the subtitle of one of his books was, *"Ten thousand miles over the fossiliferous deposits of Scotland".* He wrote widely on geology, politics and religion, his books being best sellers in their time.

His collection of over 6,000 fossils is in the National Museum. He was also a leading light in setting up the Free Church in 1843 and a fundamentalist. His seeming opposing religious beliefs and scientific discoveries caused him a psychosis which resulted in his suicide. He is buried in Grange Cemetery in Edinburgh

In a biographical review, he was recognized as an exceptional person by Sir David Brewster, who said of him, *"Mr. Miller is one of the few individuals in the history of Scottish science who have raised themselves above the labors of an humble profession, by the force of their genius and the excellence of their character, to a comparatively high place in the social scale."*

*Fortrose Harbour by William Daniell (1815)*

*Hugh Miller's House*

There is a good sandy beach on the northeast side and a smaller one to the west. There may even be the odd fossil left.

**South Sutor Walk** There are also several fine countryside walks in this area, including a coastal path from Cromarty to the South Sutor with its WWI and WWII gun emplacements. This viewpoint overlooks Cromarty with a panoramic view of the Cromarty Firth. The return distance is 3mi (4km).

bly by the National Trust, giving the town a new lease of life. All the same there is an air of graceful decay. Before WWII there were over forty shops; today only a few remain.

**Hugh Miller's House** is maintained by the National Trust and is well worth a visit. It was built in 1711. The sundial in the garden was carved by Miller. It retains a thatched roof and has displays related to his life and work as well as contemporary furniture.

**Cromarty Courthouse** dates from 1771 and has an audio-visual display of a 19th century trial and a realistic 1843 prison cell complete with occupant. The old Cromartyshire offices house the local museum and archives, where many original documents and facsimiles can be consulted.

**Cromarty Harbour** has changed little since the 1700s. Today it is home to a variety of pleasure craft. The basin is prone to silting due to the strong tidal currents which run through the entrance to the Cromarty Firth. The Admiralty Pier, built in 1914, is currently not in use.

**Nigg to Cromarty Ferry** runs seasonally between a slipway near Cromarty Harbour to Nigg. It carries two cars plus passengers and offers an interesting circular route to explore the Fearn Peninsula.

**Walks** Cromarty is a village where exploration on foot is essential. Apart from the narrow streets and limited parking, the many interesting 17th century buildings, narrow streets and closes can only be seen and enjoyed by walking.

To the south, Gallow Hill (156m) also offers a good view. By following the coast in a southwesterly direction several interesting features can be visited. These include, MacFarquar's Bed, a natural arch, and Marcus' Cave, one of a number along this coast. St Bennet's Well was another clootie well.

**Eathie Burn** (NH773641)is particularly lovely in early summer with its small waterfalls and wild flowers. It can be followed down to the shore where the remains of Eathie Fishing Station can be found. Outcrops of fossil bearing Jurassic rocks occur here which contain ammonites and belemnites.

*Cromarty Courthouse*

*Cromarty Courthouse Jail*

*Grey Heron*

*Laurie Campbell*

*Red Kite*

**Udale Bay** has an extensive area of mudflats and sand which is exposed at low tide. This is backed by saltmarshes. This RSPB reserve is best visited from late summer to April around high tide, when large flocks of birds may be seen roosting or flying. There is a bird hide west of Jemimaville.

Waders and waterfowl arrive here in huge numbers in autumn. These include Bar-tailed Godwit, Knot, Dunlin, Widgeon, Teal, Goldeneye and Pink-footed Geese. In summer, Lapwing, Redshank and Oystercatchers all breed along with Shelduck. Herons often patrol the shores, especially near high tide.

**St Michael's Chapel** The ruined St Michael's Kirk (NH706658) is also known as Kirkmichael Church. It over-

looks Udale Bay and the Cromarty Firth, on the north coast of the Black Isle. It was the parish chapel of Kirkmichael and Cullicudden from 1662 until 1767 when a new parish church was built at Resolis.

**Cromarty Firth** The B9163 follows the north coast from Udale to Conon Bridge. There are plenty of good places to stop and view the Firth, always dominated by Ben Wyvis in the western background. The

*Fossil Ammonite from Cromarty*

constantly changing light on water, sands and mudflats makes an interesting subject for photographers.

---

**RED KITES**

Red Kites were reintroduced to the Black Isle from 1989-1994 by the RSPB. From the original six birds, a population of over 50 breeding pairs has become established, raising about 90 young every year now. The adults are mostly sedentary, but the young range over a wide area of Europe, returning to their home areas in spring.

The birds build their nests high in trees, laying their eggs in April. Incubation takes about 32 days, and fledging about another 50. During this time the males do most of the hunting. These magnificent birds are very distinctive so keep looking.

Sadly they are vulnerable to poisons used to kill rats, and up to a third are killed in this way, as they are very good at finding rodents. It is estimated that over 200 Black Isle Red Kites have been illegally poisoned recently.

---

*Cromarty Firth*

*copyright Helen Stirling Maps*

In recent times the town has both suffered and gained as the main A9 trunk road now bypasses it via the Cromarty Bridge, opened in 1979. The nearby villages of Maryburgh, Conon Bridge and Muir of Ord were all on the main road north. All are quietly reviving and benefiting from a resurgent Inverness.

**Pictish Stone** Just inside the kirkyard of St Clement's stands an unusual stone carved with various Pictish symbols on both sides, but also featuring six cup marks, from earlier times. The markings are quite hard to distinguish.

**The Town Museum** is in the former Tolbooth, dating from 1730. The cupola was added in 1774 and the gables wings in 1905. The museum has a wide variety of documents and artefacts once held by the former Dingwall Town Council. Tableaux include an early 20th century kitchen and a local blacksmith's smiddy.

**Dingwall** (ON *Þing Vollr*, Field of the Thing or Meeting Place, popn. 5,491 in 2011) sits at the head of the Cromarty Firth and is sheltered from the west by hills. In Gaelic it is known as *Inbhir Pheofharain*, Estuary of the River Peffray. It was elevated to the status of a Royal Burgh in 1226 and prospered for nearly 400 years as the base of the Earls of Ross.

From 1707, as one of the six northern royal burghs, the town had one vote in the general election. Dingwall town council was allegedly notorious for corruption, and used money from bribes to build its Town House in 1730.

The building of proper roads and bridges in the early 19th century, and even more significantly, the arrival of the railway in 1862, made Dingwall prosper. It was the county town of Ross and Cromarty from 1843 until the reform of local government in 1975. It remains a regional centre of agricultural markets, retail, and professional services.

**Dingwall Canal** In 1817 a canal was built from the Cromarty Firth in an attempt to allow ships to reach Dingwall. Unfortunately the River Peffrey flowed though the canal and by 1840 it was having serious silting problems. The canal was dredged in 1868 but soon after abandoned. Today a walk along its banks is very pleasant. There are good views of the Cromarty Firth and Conon River Estuary.

*Dingwall Tolbooth is now the Town Museum*

*Dingwall and the Cromarty Firth from Knockfarril*

**Champion Haggis** Scotland's first champion haggis maker, Cockburn's of Dingwall has a high reputation. According to the *"Highland News"*, *"Seasoned sufficiently to keep things interesting for the palate, it boasts a nigh perfect melt-in-the-mouth consistency which, quite simply, I've never encountered elsewhere."*

**Chambered Cairn** At the Heights of Brae northwest of the town there is a Neolithic chambered cairn

*Pictish symbol stone*

(NH514615) above the road. Upright stones and traces of two chambers can be made out. There are lovely views over Dingwall and the Black Isle from here. The site can be reached by a side road off the A834 just west of Dingwall.

**Conon Bridge** developed after the opening of the Telford bridge in 1809. This was in turn replaced in 1969. The village grew up at the lowest fording point of the River Conon. With the rapid

| DINGWALL & STRATHPEFFER | |
|---|---|
| Champion Haggis | 181 |
| Conon Bridge | 181 |
| Contin | 182 |
| Dingwall Canal | 180 |
| Dingwall Museum | 180 |
| Eagle Stone | 185 |
| Fighting Mac Memorial | 183 |
| Heights of Brae | 181 |
| Knockfarril | 182 |
| Museum of Childhood | 185 |
| Pictish Stone | 181 |
| Pump Room | 182 |
| Strathpeffer | 183 |
| Þing Vollr | 181 |
| Tollie Red Kites | 182 |

**ÞING VOLLR**

The Þing took place on a mound located in the Cromartie Memorial carpark. Excavations have revealed possible stonework and an associated deep ditch which may have been linked to the sea.

In medieval times this site became the Moot Hill, where justice was dispensed and public meetings took place. The burgh court originally carried out proceedings here, much as in Norse times. Every Burgh of Baronry had to have gallows to hang male criminals and a pit to drown females.

**Cromartie Memorial** In c.1710 the First Earl of Cromartie, Sir George MacKenzie, had a 16m obelisk built on this mound. It was unstable and was demolished in 1917 and replaced by the current version in 1923. By making the site a mausoleum for the Cromarties, Sir George unwittingly also preserved this ancient Viking Þing.

*Strath Peffer from Knockfarril*

## GLENWYVIS DISTILLERY

*"The world's first 100% community-owned distillery. While we finish building it high on a hill overlooking Dingwall, we've set up GlenWyvis Basecamp down in the town itself – where you can learn all about GlenWyvis Gin, our plans for GlenWyvis Whisky, and our local heritage tours.*

*Today, with the support of the local community and our 2,600 founding members, GlenWyvis is truly ground breaking – a distillery owned by all. As the distillery build progresses, you can visit us at GlenWyvis Basecamp in our interim home in Victoria Restaurant on Dingwall High Street.*

*Here you can enjoy a tipple of GlenWyvis Gin and learn all about our limited edition malt whisky, Highland Inspiration, released to mark the laying of our foundation stone. Our dedicated GlenWyvis team members will be there to chat to you about what the distillery means for the local community, and how the community came together to secure its future. You may even choose to go out on one of our whisky heritage tours. But more than that, you will become part of the GlenWyvis community as we embark on making whisky history together. Who knows, you may even consider investing..."*

development of Inverness this former backwater has revived. The railway station reopened in 2013. Like many other villages around Inverness it is growing rapidly.

**Tollie Red Kites** (NH514563) is signposted off the A835,

*Red Kite*

*Glenwyvis Distillery logo*

about 3mi (4km) east of the Moy Bridge. This partnership between the RSPB and the Brahan Estate offers close-up views of Red Kites. The birds are attracted by food put out by volunteers at 14:30 in summer and 13:30 in winter.

**Knockfarril** (G *Cnoc Far-ralaidh*, High Stone Hill, 218m, NH503583) is a long narrow ridge overlooking Strath Peffer. It has an impressive Iron Age vitrified stone fort with three surrounding ditches on its east summit, overlooking Strathpeffer to the west and Dingwall to the east. It occupies a strategic position on this high ridge.

The fort was built of stone interlaced with timbers. When set on fire, the heat was sufficient to melt the rocks. It is easily reached from a car park overlooking Loch Ussie, about 2mi (3km) north of Tollie.

**Contin** is a small village on the A835 on the confluence of the Rivers Conon and Blackwater facing the fertile plains of Easter Ross. Westwards lies the wild scenery of the High-

*Fighting Mac MacDonald*

*Fighting Mac Memorial*

## "Fighting Mac"

In 1907 a prominent stone tower was erected to *"Fighting Mac"* Major-General Sir Hector MacDonald (1853-1903), a war hero. In 1871 he enlisted as a private in the Gordon Highlanders. He distinguished himself in Afghanistan, South Africa, Sudan and Egypt. He was *"one of only a few British Army generals who rose from the ranks on his own merit and professionalism."*

In 1902 he was made Commander in Chief of the British Army in Ceylon. Rumoured to be having homosexual relations with boys, he returned to London, but facing a court martial, he shot himself in a Paris hotel.

Thousands came to pay their respects at his grave in Edinburgh. A Government Commission reported later that year *"that there is not visible the slightest particle of truth in foundation of any crime, and we find the late Sir Hector MacDonald has been cruelly assassinated by vile and slandering tongues."*

*"Fighting Mac"* was a national war hero, especially in Scotland. The ultimate example of someone who rose from nothing to high rank through his own abilities. This may have been his undoing; sentiments in the British Army were tainted by his being a lowly Scottish outsider. Jealousy perhaps also played a part.

lands. It has the last filling station before Ullapool.

**Strathpeffer** is a charming and unique little village 2mi (3km) north of Contin. Wells have always had supernatural powers attached to them, and those around this village are no different. Here there are sulphurous wells of various strengths, and also chalybeate or iron-bearing waters, which were thought to be healthy.

*Vitrified Iron Age fort on Knockfarril*

*Strathpeffer Pavilion*

*Strath Conon looking southeast from the A834*

By the late 18th century people were starting to come here to partake of these waters. In 1777 the local minister wrote to the Commissioners of the Annexed Estate of Cromarty, describing the health benefits.

He suggested the development of accommodation for visitors. A number of people, including a Fortrose headmaster, a Kincardineshire tacksman and an Aberdeen doctor all claimed near miraculous cures from partaking of and bathing in these waters. Strathpeffer soon became part of a major Victorian health fashion.

This early tourism grew with the building of a wooden pump room in 1819. The present Pump Room was built in 1871, soon to be followed by The Pavilion, an elaborate concert hall, public gardens and a network of paths. Soon the Victorian passion for visiting spas developed into a major industry for tiny Strathpeffer, with the building of several large hotels and attractive little shops. It was all served by a branch railway line from Dingwall, which opened in 1885.

During WWI and WWII most of the hotels were requisitioned by the military; the Spa did not reopen in 1945. Fashions change in health as in other ways so taking of the waters was no longer popular in Britain. The village has recently undergone a renaissance

*Viking Lady*

*The Brahan Seer*

*The Pump Room*

*The Pump Room and a mud bath*

*Victorian shopping precinct*

*The Eagle Stone*

with the main spa buildings all having been done up. There is a new air of confidence.

**The Old Railway Station** is now the Highland Museum of Childhood, an interesting and different take on life in the north. It also has a little bookshop. Next door a cafe serves tasty food and excellent coffee. There is also a Fair Trade shop and several craft workshops here. The village has a wide range of shops, cafés and accommodation.

**The Eagle Stone** (G *Clach Tiumpan*, Sounding Stone) NH485585 stands on a small hill just northeast of the village, up a path with a somewhat small sign. This Class I Pictish symbol stone has a horseshoe

and an eagle on it and may date from the 7th century. The stone has been moved from its original local site lower down the strath. Tradition says this was to celebrate a clan battle in 1411 when the Munros beat the MacDonalds. The Brahan Seer, a 17th century man who made many prophesies said that if the stone were to fall for a third time bad things would happen to Dingwall.

**Walks** There are many walks around Strathpeffer suitable for every interest. These include woodland, riverside, small hills, mountains and several great viewpoints. The mild climate and varied landscape make this area appealing in every season and to all ages.

*Wooden Pictish carvings Highland Museum of Childhood*

*Strathpeffer train station today*

*Urquhart Castle is on Loch Ness, near Drumnadrochit*

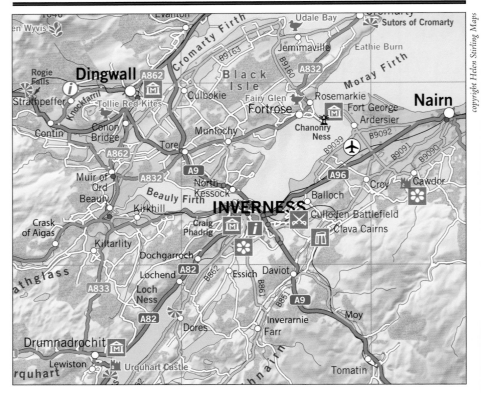

*copyright Helen Stirling Maps*

**EAST FROM INVERNESS** a series of varied visitor attractions, all close to the A96 trunk road to Aberdeen, make a fine and interesting day. The sites range from ancient burial cairns and a romantic castle, to the last battlefield site in the UK and a huge 18th century fort to an eclectic aviation museum.

**Balnuaran of Clava Cairns** (NH755444) are signposted off the B9006, east of Culloden. About forty of this type of chambered cairn survive around Inverness, with up to ten in the River Nairn Valley. These structures date from c.2000BC, the early Bronze Age, and are unique.

Clava-type cairns are round, ranging from 10m-17m in diameter. They feature a kerb of large upright stones, often with small quartz pebbles inserted between the slabs. Clava Northeast and Southwest cairns are passage graves with an entrance passage leading to a central chamber.

*Clava Northeast, passage from entrance*

*Cup marks*

*Clava Northeast - exterior with standing stones*

In both cases the kerb stones are up to 1m high and form a circle c.16m in diameter. The passage is 6m long, leading to a chamber nearly 4m across. The entrance passages face southwest precisely in the direction of the winter solstice sunset. Clava Southeast does not have a clear view of the horizon due to trees, but from within the chamber of Clava Northeast the setting midwinter sun illuminates several red stones on the back wall.

The central structure is a ring cairn, with no entrance passage. Upright slabs c.1m high surround most of this 17m diameter cairn. An inner kerb c.6m in diameter encloses the central area, which has no apparent access. Rays of small stones join the cairn to several of the standing stones.

Clava Northwest and Central cairns are surrounded by an outer ring of standing stones, ten and nine respectively. There is no evidence that Clava Southwest had such a design.

Cup marks can be seen on several of the stones in the entrance passages, kerb stones and standing stones which surround the cairns. Surveys, most notably by Professor Thom, have suggested possible

further solar alignments as well as to moonrise and moonset.

The chambers of the passage graves probably stood over 3m high, capped by large lintels. The ring cairn never had a roof, but clearly was part of a site of great importance to the people who built it. This place is an oasis of tranquillity, a world apart from the crowds at Culloden, a much newer place.

*Clava Ring Cairn, interior and surrounding circular cairn*

*Clava Southwest, interior showing kerb*

*The Battle of Culloden*

and marched south via Edinburgh to Derby before retreating north. The Jacobites occupied Inverness but were routed by vastly superior Government forces at Culloden.

With a reward on his head of £30,000, or over £1m today, Bonnie Prince Charlie went on the run. He spent months as a fugitive in the Outer Hebrides. He finally escaped to Skye, with the help of Flora MacDonald, and left for France on 20th September 1746.

**The Battle of Culloden**, on 16th April 1746, marked the end of the last catastrophic Jacobite rising of 1745-46. Several unsuccessful attempts to overthrow James II were made before the Glorious Revolution of 1688 when William of Orange and Mary, sister of James, were appointed monarchs. The deposed James fled to France.

There were abortive rebellions between 1689 and 1715 in favour of James, the *Old Pretender*. Finally, his grandson, Bonnie Prince Charlie, or the *Young Pretender*, had a disastrous and fatally flawed attempt.

Prince Charles Edward Stuart landed on Eriskay on 23rd July 1745. He raised his standard at Glenfinnan on 19th August

The main effects of the rebellion were the demise of the traditional clan system and the rapid development of commercial landlordism. This led to the clearances, emigration and the crofting system.

**Fort George** is at Ardersier 11mi (18km) northeast of Inverness overlooking the Moray Firth. It was built from 1757-1760 at the then vast cost of £200,000. This fort was built to oppose a threat that had long gone. It remains an army barracks for now. Much of the site is under Historic Environment Scotland and open to the public.

*Culloden Visitor Centre*

*Mortar round, grapeshot and balls*

*Jacobite glassware*

*Culloden Cairn*

*Vickers Valiant V-bomber*

*Cawdor Castle*

**The Highlander's Museum**, within Fort George, is the official regimental museum of the Queen's Own Highlanders and Lovat Scouts. There is a great deal here to interest military enthusiasts of all ages.

**Highland Aviation Museum** (NH763521) next to Inverness Airport has an outdoor static collection of aircraft, including the cockpit of a Vickers Valiant V-bomber. Indoors there are many interesting displays, including one on the pioneer civil pilot, Fred Fresson.

**Cawdor Castle** is on the B9090, signposted south off the A96. It was built by the Thanes of Cawdor in the 14th century to replace an older one in Nairn. Originally a four storey tower house, it was developed over the years into the multi period fairy tale castle of today. The gardens date originally from c.1600

### CULLODEN

The Battle of Culloden took place on the morning of 16th April 1746 on a cold day with sleet and rain showers. The well equipped British Army had greatly improved morale after previous defeats. The Jacobites were under equipped and poorly led with obsolete tactics.

After a failed Highland Charge into a hail of grapeshot and musket fire, it was all over in an hour. Of c.4,000 Jacobites c.2,000 lay dead or dying; Government casualties were c.300. Guerrilla tactics may have bought the Jacobites some time, but in truth their cause was doomed from the start due to lack of support from key clan chiefs.

The Culloden Visitor Centre (NH747449) is on the B9006 5mi (8km) east of Inverness. The immersive Battlefield Audio Guide is excellent.

*Bonnie Prince Charlie*

*Duke of Cumberland, British CIC*

*Fort George*

*The Highlander's Museum*

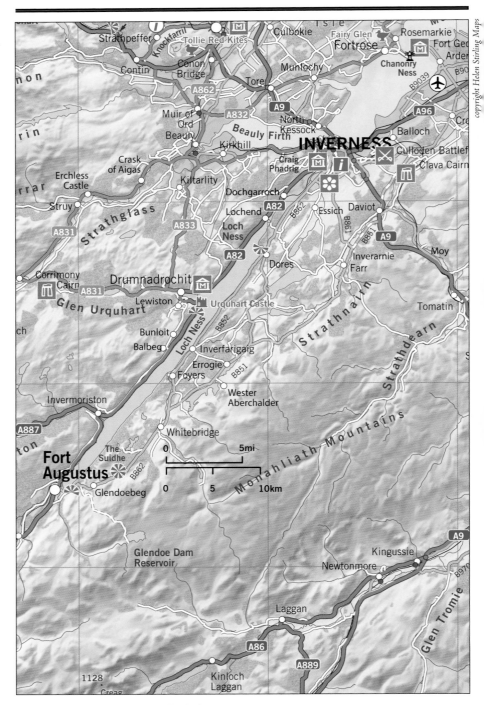

copyright Helen Stirling Maps

Strathpeffer · Knockfarril · Tollie Red Kites · Culbokie · Fairy Glen · Rosemarkie · Fortrose · Fort Geo · Arder

Contin · Conon Bridge · Munlochy · Chanonry Ness · B9039 · B90

Tore · A862 · A9

Muir of Ord · A832 · North Kessock · A96 · Cro

Beauly · Beauly Firth · Balloch

Kirkhill · INVERNESS · Culloden Battlef

Crask of Aigas · Craig Phadrig · Clava Cairn

Erchless Castle · Kiltarlity · Dochgarroch

Struy · Strathglass · Lochend · A82 · B862 · Essich · Daviot

A831 · A833 · Loch Ness · A9

A82 · Dores · Inverarnie · Farr · Moy

Corrimony Cairn · A831 · Drumnadrochit

Glen Urquhart · Lewiston · Urquhart Castle · Strathnairn · Tomatin

ch · Bunloit · Loch Ness · Strathdearn

Balbeg · Inverfarigaig

Errogie · B851 · Foyers

Invermoriston · Wester Aberchalder

A887 · Whitebridge · Monahliath Mountains

ton · The Suidhe · 0 · 5mi

Fort Augustus · B862 · 0 · 5 · 10km

Glendoebeg

Glendoe Dam Reservoir · Kingussie · A9

Newtonmore · B970

Laggan

A86 · A889 · Glen Tromie

1128 · Kinloch Laggan

SOUTHWEST FROM INVER-
NESS, Loch Ness and the Caledonian Canal have much to
offer. If approaching from Fort
William on the A82 there are a
number of essential stops along
this slow and busy road. The
loop around Loch Ness also
makes a good day's outing after
completing the NC500. Al-
ternatively take a boat trip.

*Loch Ness looking south*

Loch Ness is the largest body
of fresh water in the UK with a
volume of 7452m², a maximum
depth of 227m and a length
of nearly 23mi (37km). It is
surrounded by impermeable
Moine rocks which are mineral
deficient, making it infertile.

The Caledonian Canal runs
for 60mi (97km) from Clachnaharry Sea Lock in Inverness
to Corpach, near Fort William.
It was designed by Thomas
Telford and opened in 1822.
Only about one third is canal, the rest utilises Loch Ness,
Loch Oich and Loch Lochy.
The introduction of steam-
ships and railways in the mid
19th century made the canal a
popular visitor attraction.

The Loch Ness Centre & Exhibition is in the Drumnadro-

*Loch Ness Centre & Exhibition*

chit Hotel, 14mi (23km) from
Inverness on the A82. *"A portal
to the unique natural phenomenon that is Loch Ness"*, according
to Scottish Natural Heritage.

Although the Loch Ness Monster or Nessie occupies centre
stage, the exhibition covers
much more than this mysterious creature. Seven themed
rooms cover the geology, natural history, myths, legends and
history of Loch Ness. There

*Loch Ness Monster fake from 1934*

GREAT GLEN FAULT

The Great Glen extends for
over 60mi (100km) from
Inverness to Fort William.
It is part of a massive geological fault extending from
Shetland to Donegal formed
during the Caledonian Or-
ogeny c.600Ma. Broken in
two c.200Ma when North
America split off, it extends
for 300mi (480km) in northeast Canada. The fault separates the North Highlands
from the Grampians just as
further south the Highland
Boundary Fault separates the
Highlands from the Low-
lands.

## URQUHART CASTLE

Urquhart Castle is one of the most spectacularly sited and most visited castles in Scotland. The earliest records go back to the mid 13th century, but excavations suggest a major Pictish fort here by the 5th century.

*Urquhart Castle*

Hillforts in Glen Urquhart above Drumnadrochit and near Balnain show the strategic importance of this area in the Iron Age. Even older chambered cairns, cup marked stones, hut circles and field systems indicate much earlier settlement.

Urquhart Castle has a rich and complex history, its pivotal position being of interest to the Lords of the Isles, English and Scottish kings and their vassals. Later it became a fulcrum of clan warfare between the Frasers and the MacDonalds.

Finally, the gatehouse was blown up by Royalist forces in 1690 after a Jacobite siege. By 1770 the buildings were roofless ruins. The castle is now an interesting scheduled monument and a good visit.

Situated on Strone Point, with a 180° view of Loch Ness, Urquhart Castle is perfectly placed to control Loch Ness. Today the romantic ruins are one of the most visited sites in Scotland. During the summer it can get very busy here so it is better to come out of season, avoiding the crowds for a much better experience.

are several shops and a café. Boat trips run from nearby.

**Nessieland**, also in Drumnadrochit, is aimed at children and families. *"See for yourself the overwhelming evidence of Nessie's existence in the depths of Loch Ness. Imagine you are below the surface and taking part in one of the many Loch Ness investigations, what might you come face to face with."*

This is an ideal visit for families with curious children. There are many things to see and do inside and outside, mostly themed on the Loch Ness Monster. A family of Nessies stands outside. Visitors will either love it or hate it.

**Corrimony Chambered Cairn** (NH382303) is off the A831 8mi (13km) west of Drumnadrochit. The entrance pas-

sage of this Clava-type Cairn is aligned with the winter solstice sunset. The exterior is lined with large kerbstones; many pieces of quartz are scattered behind and between these uprights. The passage is c.7m long, leading to a chamber c.3.6m in diameter; the exterior diameter is c.15m.

The cairn is surrounded by a ring of 11 standing stones up to 2m high. There are cupmarks on the large capstone and one of the standing stones. This delightfully situated chambered cairn is rarely visited and nearly always tranquil in contrast to very busy Urquhart Castle. The Corrimony RSPB Reserve is home to the rare Black Grouse as well as Crested Tit and Crossbill.

**Fort Augustus** (G *Cille Chuimein*, after St Cummein of

*Urquhart Castle*

Loch Ness from Dores

Iona) is a small settlement at the south end of Loch Ness. After the 1715 Jacobite rebellion a fort was built here. It was completed in 1742, just in time to be captured in 1745. Little now remains of it. A Benedictine monastery operated on the site from 1876 until 1998. Fort Augustus has a series of five locks which are interesting to watch when vessels pass through. There are several restaurants, pubs and shops. The Caledonian Canal Centre *"allows visitors to learn about the Caledonian's rich history, grab a souvenir from a wide selection of Scottish gifts, or book activities"*

**General Wade's Military Road** from Fort Augustus follows the east side of Loch Ness. It was built between 1726 and 1732. After a lonely inland stretch with a fine viewpoint at Carn an t' Suidhe

(NH443104, 450m), the road hugs the coast from Foyers to Dores. This was part of a network of military roads designed to improve communications in the Highlands. They were to prove very useful to the Jacobites in 1745-46. Without substantial garrisons Wade's roads and forts were useless.

**The Falls of Foyers** tumble down a steep sided small gorge into Loch Ness. They are most spectacular after heavy rain. The nearby hydro electric power station is part of a major pumped storage system built in the late 1960s.

**Dores**, at the northeast end of Loch Ness, offers spectacular views the length of Loch Ness. Dores Inn is a popular pub and restaurant right on the shore. From here it is 8mi (km) back to Inverness on the B862.

Falls of Foyers

Jacobite Cruises

### LOCH NESS BOAT TRIPS

Jacobite Cruises operate boat excursions on Loch Ness all year. They leave from Inverness Bus Station, Tomnahurich Bridge, Dochgarroch Lock and Clansman Harbour, with visits to Urquhart Castle and the Loch Ness Exhibition Centre included in some tours.

*"Our aim is to help you create your own story of Loch Ness and ensure you get the most from what could be a once in a lifetime visit to this beautiful part of the world."*

Carn an t' Suidhe viewpoint on General Wade's Military Road

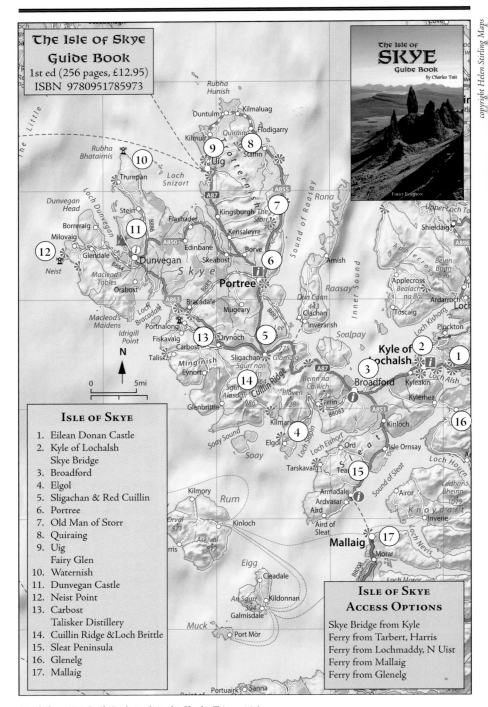

THE ISLE OF SKYE is well summed up by the noted *Sgitheanach*, Alexander Robert Forbes (1923), *"Nowhere among the Western Isles is there to be found such a combination of grandness and picturesque originality as in the Isle of Skye. It is past doubt that this island has long since been enthroned as the grandest of them all, the visible queen, whose place and title it would be mere wantonness of disaffection or caprice to dispute."*

The dramatic scenery of Skye includes the jagged Cuillin Ridge, which reaches 993m at Sgurr Alasdair and extends for 7mi (11km). The nearby Red Cuillin are more rounded in outline, but just as impressive. The Old Man of Storr and the Quirang form part of the Trotternish Ridge, another volcanic feature which extends the length of the peninsula. On a much smaller scale the Fairy Glen and Rha waterfalls offer quite magical experiences.

On the coast the majestic cliffs of Duirinish include Waterstein Head (296m) and Neist Point, while Kilt Rock is famous for its Dolerite columns. There are a few sandy

*The Cuillin Ridge from Loch Harport*

beaches, including Talisker Bay, Camusanary, Loch Brittle, Staffin and the Coral Beaches.

The visitor centres at Aros in Portree, Dunvegan Castle and the Clan Donald Centre are all excellent. Iconic Eilean Donan Castle near Kyle of Lochalsh is also an essential visit.

A visit to Skye makes an exciting addition to the NC500. The dramatic wild volcanic

scenery is in stark contrast to most of the North Highlands. Distances should not be underestimated here; Skye offers every type of accommodation and eating out experience from 5 star to basic. It is essentially an outdoors place and those making the effort to explore on foot will not be disappointed. The island ideally needs several days just to scratch the surface; you will either fall in love with it or hate it.

*Dunvegan Castle*

*Eilean Donan Castle*

*Portree*

*The Quiraing*

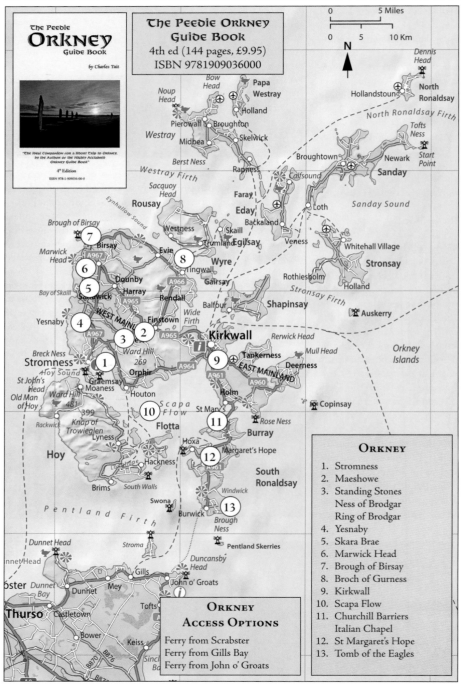

The Peedie
ORKNEY
Guide Book
by Charles Tait

"The Ideal Companion for a Short Trip to Orkney,
by the Author of the Highly Acclaimed
Orkney Guide Book"

4th Edition

ISBN 978-1-909036-00-0

The Peedie Orkney
Guide Book
4th ed (144 pages, £9.95)
ISBN 9781909036000

copyright Helen Stirling Maps

0          5 Miles
0      5      10 Km
N

**ORKNEY**

1. Stromness
2. Maeshowe
3. Standing Stones
   Ness of Brodgar
   Ring of Brodgar
4. Yesnaby
5. Skara Brae
6. Marwick Head
7. Brough of Birsay
8. Broch of Gurness
9. Kirkwall
10. Scapa Flow
11. Churchill Barriers
    Italian Chapel
12. St Margaret's Hope
13. Tomb of the Eagles

**ORKNEY**
**ACCESS OPTIONS**

Ferry from Scrabster
Ferry from Gills Bay
Ferry from John o' Groats

**ORKNEY** is just a short ferry ride from Scrabster, Gills Bay or John o' Groats in Caithness. The landscape is completely different to the North Highlands, with soft, fertile, green rolling countryside and low heather clad hills. Beef cattle rearing remains the biggest industry in this diverse economy.

The archipelago has the best archaeology in the whole of the UK, ranging uninterruptedly from the Mesolithic to the present. The Heart of Neolithic Orkney World Heritage Site includes Maeshowe, the Standing Stones of Stenness, the Ring of Brodgar and Skara Brae. These famous sites are just the best known of many.

The Ness of Brodgar is a huge Neolithic site which has excavations every year in July and August. There are daily tours during the season. In midwinter the interior of Maeshowe is lit up as the setting sun shines down its passage.

There is far more to Orkney than archaeology, with history going from the Vikings to the present. The Norse Cathedral of St Magnus dates from

*Ring of Brodgar midsummer sunset*

1137, while relics of WWI and WWII can be visited around Scapa Flow, most notably the Italian Chapel.

Locally produced food and drink are a major attraction. Apart from the famous Orkney beef, the shellfish, beer, whisky and even local potatoes are all world class.

The very varied coastal scenery ranges from the 351m St John's

Head and 137m Old Man of Hoy to gentle bays and glorious sandy beaches. In summer many thousands of seabirds breed on the cliffs, making Orkney a haven for birdwatchers.

Orkney makes an easy add on to the NC500 with two car ferry routes and a summer passenger ferry; ideal for a day trip.

*Maeshowe winter solstice*

*St Magnus Cathedral*

*Old Man of Hoy*

*Stromness*

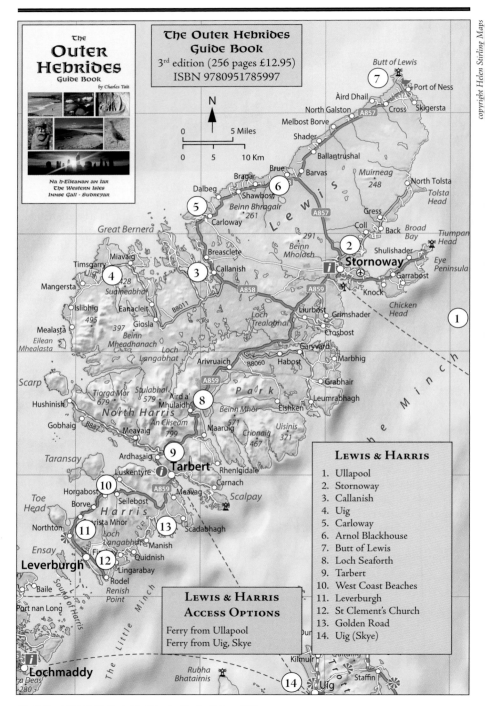

The Outer Hebrides
Guide Book
by Charles Tait

Na h-Eileanan an Iar
The Western Isles
Innse Gall - Suðreyar

## The Outer Hebrides Guide Book

3rd edition (256 pages £12.95)

ISBN 9780951785997

N

0        5 Miles

0      5       10 Km

Butt of Lewis
Port of Ness
Àird Dhail
North Galston — A857 — Cross — Skigersta
Melbost Borve
Shader
Ballantrushal
Brue — Barvas — Muirneag 248 — North Tolsta
Bragar
Dalbeg — Shawbost — Tolsta Head
Beinn Bhragair 261
Carloway — Gress
Coll — Back — Broad Bay — Tiumpan Head
Great Bernera — 291 — Beinn Mholach — Shulishader
Breasclete — Stornoway — Eye Peninsula
Miavaig — Callanish — Garrabost
Timsgarry — Knock — Chicken Head
Uig — 428 — Suaineabhal
Mangersta — A858 — A859
Islibhig — 495 — Eanacleit — B8011 — Liurbost — Grimshader
Giosla — 397 — Crosbost
Mealasta — Beinn — Garyvard
Eilean Mhealasta — Mheadhanach — Loch Langabhat — Marbhig
Arivruaich — B8060 — Habost
Scarp — A859 — Grabhair
Tiorga Mòr — Stulabhal — Aird a — Leumrabhagh
679 — 579 — Mhulaidh — Park
Hushinish — Beinn Mhòr — Eishken
Gobhaig — B887 — An Cliseam — Maaruig — Uisinis
Meavaig — 799 — Crionaig — 371
Taransay — Ardhasaig — 467
Luskentyre — Tarbert — Rhenigidale
Horgabost — Carnach
Toe Head — Borve — Seilebost — Meavag — Scalpay
Northton — Harris — Rista Mhor — Scadabhagh
Loch — Manish
Ensay — Langabhat — Fi — Quidnish
Leverburgh — Lingarabay
Baile — Rodel — Renish Point
Port nan Long
Lochmaddy
Rubha Bhatairnis — Kilmuir — Staffin — Uig

### LEWIS & HARRIS

1. Ullapool
2. Stornoway
3. Callanish
4. Uig
5. Carloway
6. Arnol Blackhouse
7. Butt of Lewis
8. Loch Seaforth
9. Tarbert
10. West Coast Beaches
11. Leverburgh
12. St Clement's Church
13. Golden Road
14. Uig (Skye)

### LEWIS & HARRIS ACCESS OPTIONS

Ferry from Ullapool
Ferry from Uig, Skye

**The Outer Hebrides** lie in a long line stretching 130mi (200km) from the Butt of Lewis to Barra Head. This route can be accessed from Ullapool or from Uig on Skye. The latter makes a highly satisfactory loop of a week or more.

Lewis and Harris is the biggest island in Scotland at 841mi$^2$ (2,179km$^2$). The north is mostly low lying peat bog, while the south is mountainous. The west coast has many wonderful beaches, separated by rugged rocky coasts.

The Ullapool ferry arrives in Stornoway, the only town in the islands. The new Museum nan Eilean in Lews Castle is an excellent place to start a visit here. Some of the famous Lewis Chessmen are featured here.

Of the many archaeological sites, the Callanish standing stones are by far the most spectacular. Apart from the main stone setting, there are at least four smaller circles in the area.

The remote area of Uig has one of the most spectacular beaches in the Outer Hebrides. Uig

*Callanish*

Bay, edged by green croftlands and backed by rugged mountains, is not to be missed.

Further north the well preserved Carloway Broch and nearby Gearrannan Village, followed by Arnol Blackhouse Museum are on the road to the Butt of Lewis.

From Stornoway the road heads south through increasingly rugged territory to

Harris. A steep incline shoulders the side of Clisham (713m) before descending to the village of Tarbert. Harris is a land of contrasts with its famous westside beaches and extremely wild east coast.

At the south end, Leverburgh is the departure point for boat trips to St Kilda. Slightly further stands the little Medieval St Clements Church, the oldest on the island.

*Rodel Church*

*Stornoway*

*Uig Bay*

*Seilebost*

LMS     INVERNESS     LNER

*1939s LMS/LNER railway poster*

from a huge number of European and long-haul cities. Inverness Airport is conveniently located to start a tour of the North Highlands and has car hire available on site.

There are onward connections from Inverness to Kirkwall (Orkney), Sumburgh (Shetland), Stornoway (Lewis) and Balivanich (Benbecula). Helicopter charter is also available.

Wick airport has more limited services but is a good arrival point for those exploring Caithness and the far north. Taxis meet scheduled flights and car hire is available locally.

**GETTING HERE** The North Highlands may appear remote from the perspective of southern Britain, Europe or overseas. In reality access is easy by air, rail, bus, car or ferry.

**Air Services** The main airport is at Inverness which has inbound flights from airports in England, Ireland, Amsterdam and other parts of Scotland. Several of these are hubs which have inbound flights

**Road** The North Highlands are easily accessible by road from the rest of Britain. The table below gives distances from some cities and

## DISTANCES AND AVERAGE DRIVING TIMES

### Inverness to

| | | |
|---|---|---|
| London | 555mi (893km) | 11h42m |
| Dover | 625mi(1006km) | 12h42m |
| Hull | 421mi (678km) | 8h42m |
| Edinburgh | 155mi (250km) | 3h34m |
| Glasgow | 170mi (274km) | 3h55m |
| Aberdeen | 104mi (167km) | 3h09m |
| Fort William | 64mi (103km) | 2h25m |
| Kyle of Lochalsh | 78mi (126km) | 2h18m |
| Ullapool | 57mi (91km) | 1h39m |
| Scrabster | 111mi (178km) | 2h48m |
| John o' Groats | 119mi (192km) | 2h50m |
| Durness | 104mi (167km) | 4h25m |

### Durness to

| | | |
|---|---|---|
| Kyle of Lochalsh | 152mi (245km) | 6h24m |
| John o' Groats | 93mi (149km) | 3h52m |

*Distances are by the most direct routes. Times may vary depending on traffic, time of day, weather, road works, drivers and vehicles.*

## INVERNESS AIRPORT FLIGHT OPERATORS

**Loganair** Benbecula, Dublin, Glasgow, Kirkwall, Stornoway, Sumburgh 0344 800 2855 loganair.com

**KLM** Amsterdam klm.com

**Flybe** Birmingham, Dublin, Manchester, 0371 700 2000 flybe.com

**easyJet** Bristol, Geneva, Gatwick, Luton 0871 244 2366 easyjet.com

**Jersey Travel** Jersey 01534 496 650 jerseytravel.com

**EasyJet** London Gatwick 0871 244 2366 easyjet.com

**British Airways** Heathrow 0844 493 0787 britishairways.com

**Aer Lingus** Dublin 0333 004 500 aerlingus.com

**Etihad** Manchester 0345 608 1225 etihad.com

**Cathay Pacific** Manchester 0208 834 8888 cathaypacific.com

*easyJet at Inverness Airport*

approximate driving times. Lands End to John o' Groats is 833mi (1341km) and will take about 16 hours by car. The many alternative methods may take considerably longer.

The main routes north from England are the M1/A1 to Edinburgh then M90 goes to Perth. Alternatively, take the M6 then the M74/A74 to Glasgow, then the M73 and M80/M9 to Perth. The A9 heads north from here to Inverness and Thurso.

The A9 from Perth north is a mixture of single and dual carriageways with some three-lane sections. When busy or in poor conditions this combination can be dangerous, drivers may become impatient and frequently pass in risky places. Average speed cameras cover the whole route.

There are many good places to visit which are bypassed by the A9. These include Pitlochry, Aviemore and other smaller villages as well as visitor attractions and interesting shops. Fuel and refreshment stops can also be found there. From Fort William the A82

follows a very scenic route via Loch Ness to Inverness. This is a rather slow and windy road. There are many suitable locations along Loch Ness to stop, take a break from driving and admire the view.

The A96 from Aberdeen can be a very slow road also and is usually busy with cars, trucks and agricultural machines. As with the other approaches to Inverness there are lots of interesting towns, villages and harbours along the way.

Just east of Inverness, Culloden Battlefield is the site of the defeat of Bonnie Prince Charlie and the Jacobites in 1746. The grim tale is told in a fascinating visitor centre.

**Train Services** into Inverness Railway Station are operated by First Scotrail. Details of the various lines are listed overleaf along with websites and telephone numbers for enquiries and booking. The two lines which run north and west from Inverness are very scenic and offer an alternative, slow paced introduction to the North Highlands.

**Bus Services** National carriers offer connections from every part of Britain, while there are local services provided by Stagecoach and a number of smaller companies. Details of national companies are listed overleaf. The Highland Council website has useful links to all forms of public transport in the area.

**Special Deals** There are many offers available for users of public transport in the Highlands. These change regularly and their availability and restrictions should be checked in advance.

*Ferry "Pentalina" to Orkney*

*Boat trip to Handa*

**Ports** There are several ports in the North Highlands from which ro-ro ferry services are run. These include routes to Orkney and the Western Isles which run all year round. There is also a summer passenger ferry from John o' Groats to Orkney.

A number of small passenger ferries operate in the summer months to places such as Cape Wrath and Handa, as well as between Cromarty and Nigg. Boat cruises are run from various places, including from Ullapool, Gairloch, Plockton, Kyle of Lochalsh, John o' Groats, and a few harbours on the Black Isle.

## TRAINS TO INVERNESS AND WITHIN THE NORTH HIGHLANDS

**Scotrail** runs services on four lines from Inverness Train Station:
**From the South** via Aviemore and Perth to Edinburgh and Glasgow.
**From the East** via Nairn and Elgin to Aberdeen.
**To the West** via the scenic Kyle Line to Kyle of Lochalsh.
**To the North** via the North Highlands Line to Thurso and Wick
scotrail.co.uk
0344 811 0141

**National Rail Enquiries** - Find the best-matched trains for your journey. Covers Britain's National Rail network with train operator and timetable information  View live departure and arrival information and make bookings.
nationalrail.co.uk
Tel  08457 48 49 50

**thetrainline.com**  For further details about UK trains, visit this site  for timetables and online booking.
thetrainline.com
Tel  0871 244 1545

## FERRIES FROM NORTH HIGHLAND PORTS

**NorthLink Ferries** daily ro-ro services from Scrabster in Caithness to Stromness in Orkney and from Aberdeen to Orkney and Shetland.
northlinkferries.co.uk
Tel 0845 6000 449

**Pentland Ferries** year-round ro-ro services from St Margaret's Hope in Orkney to Gills Bay in Caithness.
pentlandferries.co.uk
Tel 01856 831226

**John o' Groats Ferries** operate a summer passenger service between John o' Groats and Burwick in South Ronaldsay in Orkney.
jogferry.co.uk
Tel 01955 611353

**Calmac** year-round ro-ro services from Ullapool to Stornoway in Lewis. They also run services from Uig on Skye to Tarbert on Harris and Lochmaddy in North Uist as well as many other islands in the Hebrides; Mallaig to Armadale on Skye may also be useful.
calmac.co.uk
Tel 0800 066 5000

*Single track road with passing places*

*ScotRail Sprinter train on the Far North Line*

**Cycling** is not recommended on any of the busy main roads, but once in the North Highlands there is a huge choice of excellent quiet roads to explore the countryside at leisure. Bikes can be hired in Inverness as well as in many smaller places.

**Walking** Suggested walks are mentioned throughout this book. Most are not very long or strenuous, but proper gear should be worn as the terrain can be wet and/or rough. Ordnance Survey maps are strongly recommended, either paper or digital.

## Timetable Information: Traveline Scotland

For specific routes and transport modes, times or journeys, the company websites listed should be used. Traveline is open 24 hours, 7 days a week. *"We aim to provide accurate, up to date and impartial timetable information to get you to your destination by the quickest public transport mode."*

*"On the Plan your Journey page you can select which mode or modes you wish to travel by. When it is needed, full information on connections will be given to make transfers as smooth as possible."*

travelinescotland.com
Tel 0871 200 22 33

### Highland Council

Highland Council website has information and links to local transport providers - air, rail, bus, taxis and ferries. Timetables are available at Visitor Information Centres as well as transport terminals.

highland.gov.uk/info/1523/public_and_community_transport/transport_and_streets
Tel 01349 8666065

## Bus Services To Inverness and in The North Highlands

**Megabus** is a Stagecoach company and operates budget bus services throughout Britain including from Edinburgh, Glasgow, Dundee, Perth, and Aberdeen to Inverness.
megabus.com
Tel 0900 160 0900

**Scottish Citylink** operate buses between Inverness and destinations all over Scotland. Visit their website for timetables. You may be able to benefit from the Explorer Pass with offers for unlimited travel between certain dates. Discount tickets (Smart Cards) are available for students aged 16-25.
citylink.co.uk
Tel 0871 266 33 33

**Stagecoach** operates on local routes all over the North Highlands as well as all over Britain. Stagecoach in the Highlands offers a wide range of tickets to help you make the most of travel in your area.
stagecoachbus.com
Tel 01463 233371 (Inverness office)

## What to See & Do in The North Highlands

The North Highlands has a huge range of things to see and do. Whatever your interest, whether it be archaeology, history, nature, arts or culture there is something special for everyone.

**Museums** There are a number of museums, ranging from the Inverness Museum to many specialist village heritage centres. All are interesting and staffed by enthusiastic people who love to tell the story of their island or parish.

**Nature** enthusiasts will be happy as the North Highlands is a year round destination for bird watchers. The area is also famous for wild flowers, including several rare orchids as well as mammals such as Red Deer and cetaceans.

**Walkers** find the area very welcoming, with a huge selection on offer, long distance and shorter. Suggested routes are included throughout the book as well as in the Itineraries Section. A wide selection of walking books is available. Tour guides also lead groups in many places.

**Cyclists** will find the quiet roads very enticing. There are plenty of steep hills, and frequently strong headwinds. There is no better way to observe the life of the countryside than on an ambling bike ride.

**Activities** There are many to chose from, including walking to water sports, horse riding to hiking, fishing to surfing, shooting and hill walking. Sea trips to Handa and other offshore islands are also on offer from several operators.
*Loch Assynt and Quinag*

**Coastline** For many the prime attractions of the North Highlands are the many stunningly beautiful beaches, dramatic mountains, lochs and lonely moorlands. There are no traditional seaside facilities and entertainments here, just miles and miles of amazing sandy strands. Those who prefer quiet coves or rugged cliffs will not be disappointed either, even in the winter.

**Year-round Attractions** The North Highlands is a destination which will reward the visitor at any time of year and in any weather. That so many visitors come back time and again is testament to the place, but also to the welcome afforded by the inhabitants.

**Accommodation** This guide specifically does not include detailed information about accommodation, eating out or shopping as these are well covered by annual tourist guides or websites and subject to frequent change. The North Highlands offers everything from five star hotels, self catering and bed & breakfast, to campsites.

**Eating Out** ranges from top class restaurants to very good pubs. An excellent range of local produce including prime Highland beef, lamb, and seafood as well as vegetables in season, is on offer. Few are disappointed.

**Shopping** The many small settlements have largely retained their local shops. These include butchers, bakers, fishmongers, clothing shops, bookshops, hardware stores, newsagents and other interesting businesses.

### Visitor Information Centres
visitscotland.com
The Visitor Information Centre in Inverness is open all year, while those in Assynt, Durness and John o' Groats are seasonal.

Other information sources include visitor attractions, museums, local shops, accommodation providers and rural post offices. Books, maps and guides are available from VICs, local bookshops and visitor attractions, as well as online.

## ARCHAEOLOGY

## ARCHAEOLOGY & HISTORY
## CASTLES & DUNS

## BEST BEACHES

## BOAT TRIPS

**Cape Wrath Ferry & Minibus**
(*Seasonal, Operating Hours, Fare Payable*)
capewrath.org.uk  Tel 01971 511246
visitcapewrath.com  Tel 01971 511284 ................105

**Handa Ferry**, Roger Tebay
(*Seasonal, Operating Hours, Fare Payable*)
handa-ferry.com  Tel 07780 967800 ......................94

**EcoVentures**, Victoria Place, Cromarty IV11 8YE
(*Seasonal, Operating Hours, Fare Payable*)
ecoventures.co.uk  Tel 01381 600323................174

*Handa Boat Trip*

**Cruise Loch Ness Ltd**, By Canal Swing Bridge, Caledonian Canal, Fort Augustus PH32 4BD (*Seasonal, Operating Hours, Fare Payable*)
cruiselochness.com  Tel 01320 366277 ................195

**Dolphin Spirit** Inverness Marina, Inverness, IV1 1SU (*Seasonal, Operating Hours, Fare Payable*)
dolphinspirit.co.uk  Tel 07544 800620 ................174

**Hebridean Whale Cruises**, Pier Road, Gairloch, Wester Ross IV21 2BQ (*Seasonal, Operating Hours, Fare Payable*) hebridean-whale-cruises.co.uk
Tel 01445 712458......................................................69

**Gairloch Marine Life Centre & Cruises,** Charleston Harbour, Pier Road Gairloch, Wester Ross IV21 2BQ (*Seasonal, Operating Hours, Fare Payable*)
porpoise-gairloch.co.uk  Tel 01445 712636...........69

**'Sealife' Booking Office**, Pier Road, Gairloch Harbour, Gairloch, Wester Ross  IV21 2BQ (*Seasonal, Operating Hours, Fare Payable*)
glassbottomboat.info  Tel 01445 712540 ..............69

**Jacobite Cruises**, Dochgarroch Lock, Dochgarroch, Inverness-shire IV3 8JG (*Seasonal, Operating Hours, Fare Payable*)
jacobite.co.uk  Tel 01463 233999 ..........................195

**Kylesku Boat Tours**, Kylesku Hotel, Sutherland, IV27 4HW (*Seasonal, Operating Hours, Fare Payable*)
kyleskuboattours.com  Tel 01971 502 231.............88

*Stoer Viewpoint*

*Coigach, Wester Ross*

**Shearwater Cruises**, 1 Royal Park, Ullapool, Wester Ross IV26 2XT (*Seasonal, Operating Hours, Fare Payable*) summerqueen.co.uk  Tel 01854 612472 .................78

**Seascape Expeditions**, Shore Street Ullapool, IV26 2 (*Seasonal, Operating Hours, Fare Payable*) sea-scape.co.uk  Tel 01854 633708............78

**Summer Isles Sea Tours**, Achiltibuie, Wester Ross IV26 2YG (*Seasonal, Operating Hours, Fare Payable*) summerisles-seatours.co.uk Tel 07927 920592 .....78

## Brewery

**Black Isle Brewing Company**, Black Isle, IV8 8NZ (*All Year, Opening Hours, Tours*) blackislebrewery.com  Tel 01463 811871

## Castles & Gardens

**Attadale Gardens, Strathcarron, Wester Ross IV54 8YX** (*Seasonal, Opening Hours, Entry Charge*) attadalegardens.com  Tel 01520722603 .................50

**Castle of Mey, Mey, Caithness KW14 8XH** (*Seasonal, Opening Hours, Entry Charge*) castleofmey.org.uk  Tel 01847 851473..................124

**Cawdor Castle**, Cawdor, Nairn IV12 5RD (*Seasonal, Opening Hours, Entry Charge*) cawdorcastle.com  Tel 01667 404401 ...................191

*Bealach na Ba, Applecross*

**Dunrobin Castle**, Golspie, Sutherland KW10 6SF (*Seasonal, Opening Hours, Entry Charge*) dunrobincastle.co.uk  Tel 01408 633177...............146

**Eilean Donan Castle**, Dornie, Kyle of Lochalsh IV40 8DX (*Seasonal, Opening Hours, Entry Charge*) eileandonancastle.com  Tel 01599 555202............196

**Inverewe Gardens**, Poolewe, Wester Ross IV22 2LG (*Seasonal, Opening Hours, Entry Charge*) nts.org.uk  Tel 0844 493 2158 ..................................69

**Inverness Botanic Gardens**, Bught Lane, Inverness IV3 5SS (*All Year, Opening Hours, Free Entry*) highlifehighland.com Tel 01463 713553 ................41

**Kerrachar Gardens**, Kylesku, Sutherland IV27 4HW (*Seasonal, Opening Hours, Entry Charge*) nwhgeopark.com.........................................................87

**Urquhart Castle**, Drumnadrochit, Inverness IV63 6XJ (*All Year, Opening Hours, Entry Charge*) historicenvironment.scot  Tel 01456 450551........194

## Distilleries

**Balblair Distillery**, Edderton, Tain, Easter Ross IV19 1LB (*All Year, Opening Hours, Charge for Tours*) balblair.com  Tel 01862 821273.............................159

**Clynelish Distillery**, Brora, Sutherland KW9 6LR (*All Year, Opening Hours, Charge for Tours*) discovering-distilleries.com  Tel 01408 623000....145

**GlenWyvis Distillery**, 1 Upper Docharty, Dingwall, Easter Ross IV15 9UF glenwyvis.com  Tel 01349 862005182...................182

**Dornoch Distillery**, Dornoch Castle, Dornoch, Sutherland IV25 3 SD dornochdistillery.com  Tel 01862 810 216............150

**Dunnet Bay Distillery**, Dunnet, Caithness KW14 8XD (*All Year, Opening Hours, Charge for Tours*) dunnetbaydistillers.co.uk  Tel 01847 851287 .......123

**Glen Ord Distillery**, Muir of Ord, Easter Ross IV6 7UJ (*All Year, Opening Hours, Charge for Tours*) discovering-distilleries.com  Tel 01463 872004......45

**Glenmorangie Distillery**, Tain, Easter Ross IV19 1PZ (*All Year, Opening Hours, Charge for Tours*) glenmorangie.com  Tel 01862 892043 ..................164

**Old Pulteney Distillery**, Huddart St, Wick, Caithness KW1 5BA *All Year, Opening Hours, Charge for Tours)*
oldpulteney.com Tel 01955 602371 .......................130

*Suilven and Lochinver*

### Nature

**Beinn Eighe NNR**, Kinlochewe, Wester Ross IV22 2PA *(Trails - All Year, Free Entry; Visitor Centre - Seasonal, Opening Hours, Free Entry)*
nnr-scotland.org.uk Tel 01445 760254............. 60,63

**Orcadian Stone Company**, Main St, Golspie, Sutherland KW10 6RA
*(All Year, Opening Hours, Entry Charge to Museum)*
orcadianstone.co.uk Tel 01408 633483 ..............147

**RSPB Forsinard Flows**, Forsinard, Strath Halladale, Sutherland KW13 6YT *(Reserve, All Year; Visitor Centre, Seasonal, Opening Hours, Free Entry)*
rspb.org.uk Tel 01641 571225 ..............................115

### Museums

**Caledonian Canal Centre**, Ardchattan House, Canalside, Fort Augustus PH32 4BA
*(Seasonal, Opening Hours, Free Entry)*
visitinvernesslochness.com Tel 01320 366493.....195

*Urquhart Castle*

# NORTH COAST 500 - PLACES TO VISIT

*Urquhart Castle, Loch Ness*

**Castlehill Heritage Centre**, Castletown, Thurso Caithness KW14 8TG (*All Year, Opening Hours, Free Entry*) castletownheritage.co.uk ...............................124

**Clan Gunn Heritage Centre**, Old Parish Church, Latheron, Caithness (*Seasonal, Opening Hours, Free Entry*) clangunnsociety.org........................................135

**Dingwall Museum**, High Street, Dingwall, Ross-shire, IV15 9RY (*Seasonal, Opening Hours, Free Entry*) dingwallmuseum.co.uk  Tel 01349 865366...........180

**Dunbeath Heritage Centre**, Dunbeath, Caithness KW6 6ED (*Seasonal, Opening Hours, Entry Charge*) dunbeath-heritage.org.uk  Tel 01593 731233.........36

**Gairloch Heritage Museum**, Gairloch, Wester Ross IV21 2BP (*Seasonal, Opening Hours, Entry Charge*) gairlochheritagemuseum.org  Tel 01445 712287....66

**Groam House Museum**, Rosemarkie, Black Isle, Easter Ross IV10 8UF (*Seasonal, Opening Hours, Free Entry*) groamhouse.org.uk  Tel 01381 620961.....176

**Highland Aviation Museum**, Unit 9, Inverness Airport IV2 7XB (*Seasonal, Opening Hours, Entry Charge*) Tel 01667 461100 ....................................191

**Highland Museum of Childhood**, The Old Station, Strathpeffer. Easter Ross IV14 9DH (*Seasonal, Opening Hours, Entry Charge*) s620947988.websitehome. co.uk  Tel 01997 421031 ......................................185

*Inverness Museum Pictish carved stone*

**History Links Museum,** The Meadows, Dornoch, Sutherland IV25 3SF (*Seasonal, Opening Hours, Entry Charge*) .historylinks.org.uk  Tel 01862 811275..150

**Hugh Miller's Cottage**, Church St, Cromarty Black Isle IV11 8XA (*Seasonal, Opening Hours, Entry Charge*) nts.org.uk  Tel 0844 493 2158 ................177

**Laidhay Croft Museum**, Dunbeath, Caithness (*Seasonal, Opening Hours, Entry Charge*) laidhay.co.uk  Tel 01593 731270 .........................136

**Pump Room**, Strathpeffer, Easter Ross IV14 9DY (*Seasonal, Opening Hours, Free Entry*)...................183

**Strathnaver Museum**, Clachan, Bettyhill, Sutherland KW14 7SS (*Seasonal, Opening Hours, Entry Charge*) strathnavermuseum.org.uk  Tel 01641 521418 ....111

**Russian Arctic Convoy Museum** seasonal exhibition c/o Poolhouse Hotel, Poolewe, Wester Ross, IV22 2LD russianarcticconvoymuseum.org ....................70

**Tain Through Time**, Tower St, Tain, Easter Ross IV19 1DY (*Seasonal, Opening Hours, Entry Charge*) tainmuseum.org.uk  Tel 01862 894089 ................163

**Tarbat Discovery Centre**, Tarbatness Rd, Portmahomack, Easter Ross IV20 1YA (*Seasonal, Opening Hours, Free Entry*) tarbat-discovery.co.uk  Tel 01862 871351 .............165

**Timespan Museum & Arts Centre**, Dunrobin St, Helmsdale, Sutherland KW8 6JA (*All Year, Opening Hours, Entry Charge*) timespan.org.uk  Tel 01431 821327 ......................142

**Torridon Deer Museum**, Torridon, Wester Ross IV22 2EZ (*All Year, Opening Hours, Free Entry*) nts.org.uk  Tel 0844 493 2158 ................................60

**Waterlines Visitor Centre**, Lybster, Caithness KW3 6DB (*Seasonal, Opening Hours, Free Entry*) Tel 1593 721520.............................................135

**Wick Heritage Museum**, 20 Bank Row, Wick KW1 5EY (*All Year, Opening Hours, Entry Charge*) wickheritage.org  Tel 01955 605393 .....................130

## WALKS

# Boat Trips, Museums, Nature & Shopping

### Visitor Attractions

**Caithness Horizons**, High St, Thurso KW14 8A
(*All Year, Opening Hours, Free Entry*)
caithnesshorizons.co.uk  Tel 01847 896508..........122

**Culloden Battlefield Visitor Centre**, Culloden Moor,
Inverness IV2 5EU (*Seasonal, Opening Hours, Entry
Charge*) nts.org.uk  Tel 01463 796090 ..................191

**Eden Court Theatre**, Bishops Rd, Inverness IV3 5SA
(*All Year, Opening Hours, Entry Charge*)
eden-court.co.uk  Tel 01463 234234 .......................39

**Fort George**, Ardersier, Inverness IV2 7TD (*All Year,
Opening Hours, Entry Charge*)  historicenvironment.
scot Tel 01667 460232.............................................190

**Inverness Museum & Art Gallery**, Castle Wynd,
Inverness IV2 3EB (*All Year, Opening Hours, Free
Entry*) highlifehighland.com  Tel 01463 237114 .... 38

**Kiltmaker Visitor Centre**, 4-9 Huntly St, Inverness
IV3 5PR (*All Year, Opening Hours, Free Entry*)
highlandhouseoffraser.com  Tel 01463 222781 ......38

**Loch Ness Centre & Exhibition**, Drumnadrochit,
Loch Ness, Inverness IV63 6TU (*All Year, Opening
Hours, Entry Charge*)
lochness.com  Tel 01456 450573 ...........................193

**Nessieland**, Drumnadrochit, Loch Ness, Inverness
IV63 6TU (*All Year, Opening Hours, Entry Charge*)
nessieland.co.uk  Tel 01456 450342................194

*Glen Ord Distillery*

### Visitor Information Centres

**Assynt Visitor Centre,** Lochinver, Sutherland IV27
4LX (*Seasonal, Opening Hours, Free Entry*)
discoverassynt.co.uk  Tel 01571 844194.................84

**Durness iCentre**, Sango, Durness, Sutherland IV27
4PZ  (*Seasonal, Opening Hours, Free Entry*)
visitscotland.com  Tel 01971 509005.....................98

**Inverness iCentre**, Castle Wynd, Inverness IV2 3BJ
(*Open All Year, Opening Hours, Free Entry*)
visitscotland.com  Tel 01463 252401.....................37

**John o' Groats Tourist Information Centre**, County
Road, John o' Groats, Caithness KW1 4YR
(*Seasonal, Opening Hours, Free Entry*)
visitscotland.com Tel: 01955 611373.....................126

**Thurso iCentre**, Caithness Horizons, High Street,
Thurso, Caithness KW14 8AJ (*Open All Year, Opening Hours, Free Entry*)
visitscotland.com  Tel 01847 893155...................122

*Sinclair & Girnigoe Castle, Wick*

Dunrobin Castle & Gardens, Golspie

# HISTORY & CULTURE

## SOME OLD NORSE PLACENAME ELEMENTS

| Map; Old Norse. English | Map; Old Norse. English |
|---|---|
| a, o, or; *a*, burn | ler-; *leir*, clay |
| aith; *eið*, isthmus | ling; *ling*, heather |
| os; *austr*, east | mel-; *mel*, sandbank, dunes |
| ayre; *eyrr*, gravel beach | moll; *mol*, shingle beach |
| bodha; *boði*, submerged reef | moul, mull; *muli*, muzzle, lip |
| -back; *bakki*, banks | mous-, muss-, -mo; *mor*, pl.mos, |
| -bàgh, -way; *vagr*, bay | moor |
| -bhat, water; *vatn*, water | muckle; *mykill*, large, great |
| big; *bygging*, building | myre; *myri*, wet meadow |
| -bost; *bolstaðr*, farm, dwelling | -nis; *nes*, nose. point |
| burg, borve, borgh; *borg*, fort | nev; *nef*, small headland |
| broch-, breck-; *brekka*, slope | noup; *gnup*, peak |
| broad, *breiðr*, wide, broad | pap-; *papa*, priest, monk |
| brett-; *bratt*, steep | od-; *oddi*, sharp point |
| bro-; *bru*, bridge | -ord, -ort, -ford; *fjord*, wide bay |
| -bol, -bost, -pol; *bolstaðr*, house | òs-, -ose; *oss*, burn mouth, estuary |
| chule-; *sula*, gannet, solan goose | qui-; *kvi*, cattle pen |
| cleit; *klett*, low rock, stone house | ram-, ramas-; *hrafn*, raven |
| cnoc, cnap; *knap*, hillock | -ret; *reyy*, sheepfold |
| -cro; *kro*, sheepfold | ron-; *hraun*, rough, rocky |
| cumla-, -cuml; *kuml*, burial mound | ruadh-; *raud*, red |
| dail, dal, -dale, -dall; *dalr*, valley | russ-; *hross*, horse |
| jub-; *djup*, deep | saur; *sauðr*, sheep |
| eilean, -ey, -ay, -a; *ey*, island | scap-; *skalp*, ship |
| far-; *faer*, sheep | score; *skor*, ridge |
| fiska; *fiskr*, fish | -sta, -shader; *setr*, out-pasture |
| fladda; *flatr*, flat | selli-; *sel*, setter hut |
| -ford; *fjord*, wide bay | -shun; *tjorn*, small loch |
| fors; *fors*, waterfall | -skaill; *skali*, hall, house |
| foul; *fugl*, bird | skel-; *skal*, soft rock |
| garry, gearry; *garðr*, enclosure | sgeir, skerry; *sker*, skerry |
| geata; *gata*, gate | skalp-; *skip*, ship |
| geodha; *gja*, chasm, geo | slettr; smooth, sleek |
| -gill; *gil*, narrow valley, ravine | so-; *sauðr*, sheep |
| gra; *gra*, grey | stac, staca; *stakk*, pillar rock |
| graenn; *graenn*, green | staff; *stafr*, staff, column |
| grut-; *gryot*, gravel | storr; *staurr*, stack, rock pillar |
| hack-; *hagi*, enclosed pasture | sten-, -stain; *steinn*, stone |
| hall-; *hallr*, slope | -sta; *stadr*, homestead |
| ham, hamn-; *hafn*, harbour | suar-; *saur*, muddy, marshy |
| -hellya; *hellir*, cave | suar-; *svaðr*, sward, grassy |
| -hellya; *hella*, flat rock | teangue; *tangi*, tongue |
| hellya; *helgr*, holy | tote, -tobhta; *thopt*, site of dwell- |
| hest; *hest*, horse | ing, clearing |
| horn-; *erne*, White-tailed Sea Eagle | -ton, -town; *tun*, enclosure |
| idri-; *ytri*, outer | -val, ven; *fjall*, hill |
| -ist, -ista; *bolstaðr*, farm | varka-; *virki*, castle, fort |
| tolm; *holmr*, small island | vel-; *vollr*, valley |
| òb, tòb; *hjop*, shallow bay | -vaig, way; *vagr*, bay |
| -house, -ass; *ass*, ridge | water; *vatn*, water |
| kirk; *kirkja*, church | ùig; *vik*, bay |
| langa-, -land; *langr*, long | |
| lax; salmon | |
| -lee; *hlið*, slope | |

TOPONYMY, the study of placenames, provides a powerful view into the past, especially when written records are scant or non-existent. The North Highlands have a particularly rich and interesting selection of placenames.

Many derive from Old Norse (ON) while others are from Scottish Gaelic (G). There are others which are a mixture of both. A small number are much older. Some of the Norse names may of course be translations of older names, while many Gaelic names are clearly translations of Norse ones. T this results in tautology as in "Uig Bay" for example.

The first Ordnance Survey maps were surveyed after the Battle of Culloden in 1746. The army lacked proper maps of the Highlands and Islands from which to plan military roads and to seek out important Jacobites. George II ordered a military survey of the Highlands at a scale of 1:36,000. These form a snapshot of placenames in the 18th and 19th centuries.

Old documents, some of which go back to AD150, provide written evidence of the origins and evolution of toponyms in the past. Irish Annals, the work of clerics such as the Venerable Bede, Norse sagas and other ancient texts are good sources. Legal documents, contracts and other surviving archives provide much more detail.

The situation is confused at present because of the Scottish Government's policy to erect Gaelic roadsigns. In many cases the "new" names hide the "real" names and do not reflect the local usage. Further confusion is caused by placenames on maps not necessarily corresponding to these recent signposts. As if to further confound the visitor, modern Gaelic orthography has been applied to many names which are actually Norse.

Signposts may have one or more versions of a name, while maps can have either, both or something different again. Ordnance Survey coordinates are included for many sites of interest mentioned in the text for this reason. In general the original versions of names are used in this book rather than the "new" Gaelic translations.

Throughout this guide derivations are suggested for placenames. Many are obviously of Norse or Gaelic origin, while others remain tentative. They vary depending on which book, map or signpost is being studied. They also change over time, sometimes completely. Some useful books are suggested in the Bibliography.

The following two tables list Old Norse and Gaelic elements which it is hoped will help visitors to do their own deciphering. A study of local placenames add an extra dimension to the exploration of the NC500.

## SOME GAELIC PLACENAME ELEMENTS

| Gaelic | English | Gaelic | English |
|--------|---------|--------|---------|
| abhainn | stream, river | fada | long |
| acarsaid | anchorage, harbour | faing | sheep fank |
| achadh | ach, field | feannag | lazy bed |
| aird | ord, headland | fionn | white, fair, blessed |
| aiseag | ferry | fuaran | spring, green area |
| allt | burn or stream | garbh | rough |
| àth | ford | geal | white |
| athair | father | gille | boy |
| beag | little | glas | grey darker, green |
| bealach | pass, gap, gorge | gleann | glen, valley |
| beul | mouth | gob | beak, point |
| bodach | old man | gobha | blacksmith |
| -an | diminutive (lochan) | gorm | blue, green of grass |
| aonach | ridge | greian | bright, sunny |
| baile | bal-, township or village | grian | sun |
| bàn | blonde, pale | iar | east |
| beag | small | inbhir | inver, river mouth |
| beinn | ben, mountain | innis | meadow |
| bharpa | heap of stones | iolaire | eagle |
| bidean | tip, point | kille | church |
| bogach | bog | làirig | pass. |
| braigh | brae, upland | leac | rock ledge, stone slab |
| breac | brown trout, speckled | leana | green meadow |
| bruach | bank | leth | half |
| buchaille | shepherd | liath | grey lighter |
| buidhe | yellow | linnhe | pool |
| cailleach | old woman | loch | lake, bay |
| caladh | harbour, bay | lochan | small loch, tarn |
| camas | bay | long | ship |
| càrn | cairn, heap of stones | lùib | bend |
| caisteal | castle, fort | mac | son |
| ceann | head, headland | machair | fertile coastal plain |
| caol | kyle, strait, narrows | maol | bare round hill |
| chaolais | narrows | meadan | middle |
| cill | church, chapel | moine | moorland |
| clach | stone | mol | shingly beach |
| clachan | village | mòr | big |
| cladh | graveyard | muir | sea |
| claigeann | skull, head | poll | pool, pit |
| coille | woodland, forest | rath | fort |
| coire | corrie, cauldron, kettle | rathad | road |
| corran | point, sickle | ruadh | red, brown |
| crom | crooked | rubha | headland |
| cuidhe | enclosure, pen | scadan | herring |
| curach | bog, marsh | skòrr, skùrr | steep rocky hill |
| dail | riverside meadow | siar | west |
| darach | oak | sithean | fairy hillock |
| dearg | bright red | sneachd | snow |
| deas | south | sron | headland |
| donn | brown | teampall | church |
| druim | ridge | tigh, taigh | house |
| dubh | black | tioram | dry |
| dùn | broch, mound | tobar | well |
| eagach | notched | tràigh | beach |
| eaglais | church | tuath | north |
| ear | east | uaine | bright green |
| eas | waterfall | uaimh | cave |

7. Kylesku to

6. Ullapool to K

5. Gairloch to Ullapool p66

4. Shieldaig to Gairloch p58

2. I

3. Garve to Applecross p48

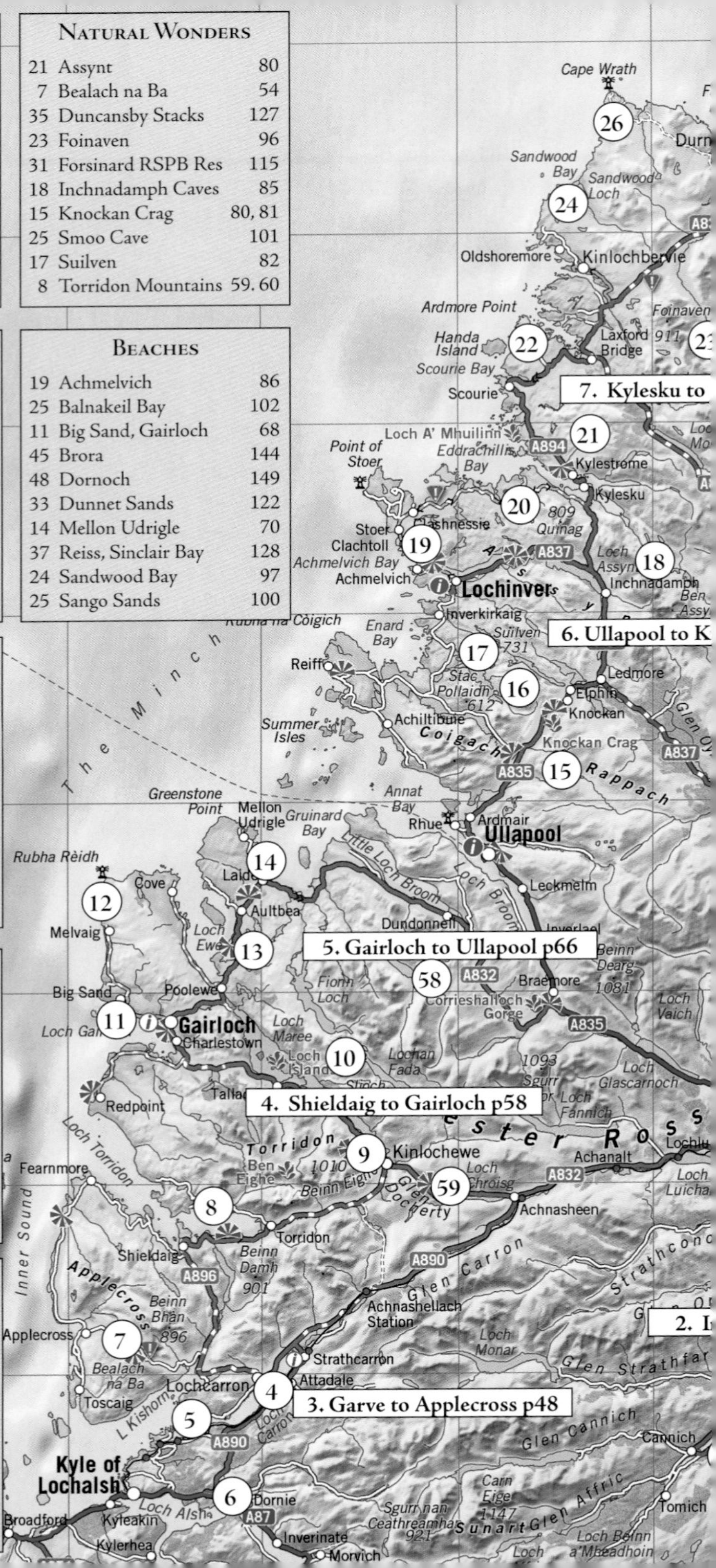

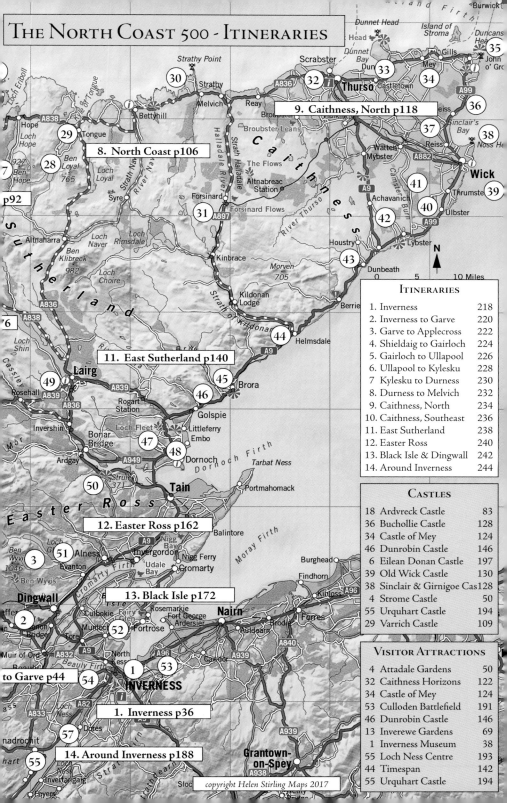

# The North Coast 500 - Itineraries

9. Caithness, North p118

8. North Coast p106

11. East Sutherland p140

12. Easter Ross p162

13. Black Isle p172

1. Inverness p36

14. Around Inverness p188

to Garve p44

copyright Helen Stirling Maps 2017

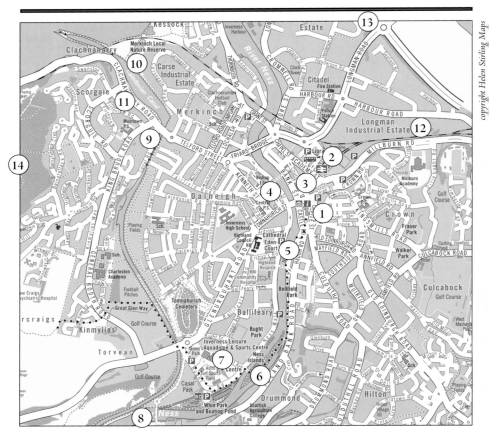

*copyright Helen Stirling Maps*

**INVERNESS CASTLE** marks the start and finish of the North Coast 500 route. This fast growing and dynamic small city is the capital of the Highlands and has much to offer the visitor. A stop to explore Inverness and its environs is an essential part of doing the NC500.

Although very few buildings are older than 19th century and the city centre has much brutal 20th century architecture, scratch under the surface and there is a quite different Inverness. From the Victorian Market with its quirky shops, to the many independent retailers, excellent cafes, restaurants and pubs, the city centre is welcoming.

There are plenty of places to park near the city centre, so leave the car and explore on foot. Inverness has a large selection of accommodation, ranging from luxury hotels to traditional B&Bs and camp sites. With over 100 restaurants, cafes and pubs there is something for everyone, including live music.

## INVERNESS CITY

## ORDNANCE SURVEY 1:50,000 & 1:25,000 MAPS
OS Landranger Map 26  Inverness & Loch Ness, Strathglass
OS Explorer Map 416  Inverness, Loch Ness & Culloden Fort Augustus & Drumnadrochit

## INVERNESS CITY

**1. Inverness Castle** (p36, *not open to the public*) overlooks the River Ness and Inverness from a prominent hillock. There are fine views over the city and Easter Ross as far as Ben Wyvis from the grounds. A statue of Flora MacDonald surveys the scene.

**Inverness Visitor Information Centre** (p37, *opening hours*), below the Castle stocks books, maps and brochures on the whole area; free maps of the NC500 and Inverness.

**Inverness Museum & Art Gallery** (p38, *opening hours, free entry*) is situated above the VIC. The displays are an excellent way to start to understand the geology, archaeology and history of the Highlands. The Gallery has regular exhibitions of contemporary Highland arts and crafts. Cobbs Tea House and interesting shop complete the experience.

**The Castle Gallery** (p38) opposite the Museum should be the first stop for collectors of contemporary fine and applied art.

**The Clach na Cudainn Stone** (p36) marks the ancient spiritual heart of Inverness. It rests rather inconspicuously below the Market Cross in front of the Town Hall, but it should not be underestimated.

**2. Inverness Train and Bus Stations** are conveniently situated in the town centre off Academy Street. **The Eastgate Centre** (p40) is Inverness' large town centre shopping mall. Even if not attracted by retail therapy, there are two large multi storey carparks. There is another mall east of the city at Inverness Shopping, off the A96.

**3. The Victorian Market** (p38) is in complete contrast to the Eastgate Centre, with a selection of interesting and eclectic shops. Visitors either love it or reject it out of hand, but it is unmissable.

**Leakey's Bookshop** (p40) in Church Street is said to be the largest secondhand bookshop in Scotland. Not to be missed on any account by bibliophiles.

**Old High St Stevens** (p40, *opening hours*) on the east bank of the River Ness, near the pedestrian bridge, dates partly from the 14th century. It is said to be the oldest building in Inverness. The *"Kirking o' the Cooncil"* takes place here every September.

**4. The Kiltmaker Visitor Centre** (p38) in Huntly Street on the west bank of the river explains the origins and history of the kilt. Kiltmakers can be seen at work and Highland Dress can be purchased or hired.

**5. Eden Court Theatre** (p39), which opened in 1976, is now the biggest arts centre in Scotland. Its cinemas, theatres, dance and drama studios host many performances annually.

**St Andrews Cathedral** (p39 *opening hours*) was completed in 1869. The interior is particularly impressive with Peterhead marble columns, a Caen stone reredos and alter as well as much fine stained glass, especially in the west window.

**6. The Ness Islands Walks** (p41) are a very pleasant surprise for visitors. An extensive network of paths and footbridges joins these attractive wooded islands.

**7. Inverness Botanic Gardens** (p41, *opening hours, free entry*) on Bucht Lane, near Inverness Leisure, are an Inverness secret; small, but impressive. A range of interesting propagated plants are on sale.

**Inverness Leisure** is a comprehensive sports centre which offers a huge range of activities. These range from swimming pools, a climbing wall and gyms to full outdoor sports facilities.

**8. Jacobite Cruises** (p195) operates a wide range of boat excursions on Loch Ness.

**9. The Caledonian Canal** (p42, 193) starts at Clachnaharry Sea Lock which leads to Muirtown Basin. The swing bridge and locks here are worth a visit.

**10. Merkinch Nature Reserve** (p42) is between the River Ness estuary and the Caledonian Canal sea lock. This area of coastal mudflats is excellent for waders and waterfowl, especially in winter.

**11. Ship Space** (p42), on Muirtown Basin has an interesting and unusual collection of nautical displays including a 1/10th scale model of *"Titanic"*.

**12. Longman Industrial Estate** has a wide selection of garages and other businesses. Of particular interest to NC500 explorers may be Halfords and Tisos.

**13. The Kessock Bridge** (p42) is part of the A9, the main route north to Wick and Thurso. There are excellent views over Inverness and the Beauly Firth from the pedestrian footpath across the bridge.

**14. Crag Phadraig** (p43, 172m) is a small hill just west of Inverness with a large vitrified fort, which was probably Pictish. Access is via King Brude Road, on the west side of Muirtown Basin.

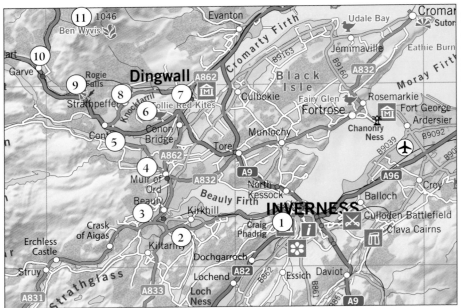

*copyright Helen Stirling Maps*

**INVERNESS TO GARVE**, the first section of the NC500, follows the route of the former A9 trunk road out of Inverness along the A862 along the south shore of the Beauly Firth to the eponymous pretty village, situated in a loop of the River

Beauly, has a spacious central square, graced with flamboyant floral displays in summer. With its range of shops, cafes and hotels, Beauly makes a good base from which to explore Easter Ross.

Photographers will find heaven at Ffordes, based in an old kirk at nearby Balblair, on the A831, just south of Beauly. This is one of the best stocked independent camera shops in the UK, with a vast array of new and secondhand gear.

The route continues through Muir of Ord, past Glen Ord Distillery to the A835 and then west to Garve. A short diversion to Tollie Red Kites and the hogback hill of Knock Farril, followed by the spa village of Strathpeffer makes an interesting side trip.

Rogie Falls on the Blackwater, northwest of Contin, are spectacular after heavy rain, but may be disappointing in dry weather. Salmon can be seen here whilst they are running in autumn, jumping in spectacular fashion as they negotiate the fast flowing waterfalls.

Garve is a quiet little hamlet with a train station and a few houses. It is the last village on the Easter Ross plain before the road climbs into the wild landscape of the Highlands.

The fit will chose to take a short side trip along the A835 towards Ullapool just to the north of Garve. The ascent of Ben Wyvis (1046m) affords panoramic views in all directions. The mountain is famous for its flora, fauna and avian wildlife.

## ORDNANCE SURVEY 1:50,000 & 1:25,000 Maps

Landranger Maps 26 Inverness & Loch Ness, Strathglass; 20 Beinn Dearg & surrounding area
Explorer Maps 416 Inverness, Loch Ness & Culloden Fort Augustus & Drumnadrochit; 431 Glen Urquhart
& Strathglass, Drumnadrochit & Muir of Ord; 437 Ben Wyvis & Strathpeffer, Dingwall

### INVERNESS TO GARVE

**1. Crag Phadraig** (p43, 172m) is a small hill just west of Inverness with a large vitrified fort, which was probably Pictish. Access is via King Brude Road, on the west side of Muirtown Basin, followed by signposted Forestry Commission paths.

**2. Lovat Bridge** (p44) was built across the River Beauly by Thomas Telford in 1814, the first of many bridges on the new road north to Wick and Thurso.

**3. Beauly** (p45) sits at the head of the Beauly Firth. This picturesque village, once on the main A9 north, is now a pleasant backwater, with many interesting shops and good places to stay. Most of the attractive sandstone buildings date from the 19th century. **Beauly Priory Church** was founded in 1230. The roofless ruins remain impressive, with ancient grave slabs and ancient Yew trees in the graveyard.

**Balblair Old Kirk** (p44) is home to the wonderful independent photography emporium of Ffordes as well as to a coffee shop and art gallery.

**4. Muir of Ord** (p45) is the venue of the annual Black Isle Show, held each August. The village developed at the crossroads of the Dingwall to Inverness and Black Isle to Contin roads.

**Glen Ord Distillery** (p45) is one of the few to still have its own maltings. The visitor centre is open all year. Tours (*entry charge*) include tastings of various expressions of the whisky.

**5. Moy Bridge** (p45) crosses the River Conon between Contin and Maryburgh. The surrounding fields are prone to flooding when the river is in spate. **Contin** (p182), at the junction of the A834 and A835, as well as the confluence of the Blackwater and the River Conon, marks the western extremity of the fertile plains of Easter Ross. This is the last filling station before Ullapool and Lochcarron.

**Strath Conan** (p46) is an exceptionally beautiful valley, remote and empty, having been cleared of people in the 19th century. In the 1950s a hydroelectric scheme flooded some of the remaining houses. It is at its best in spring when the Gorse is in full bloom, in late August with the Heather in flower and again in autumn when the colours are also spectacular.

**6. Knockfarril** (p182) is a long, narrow hogbacked hill between Dingwall and Strathpeffer, topped by an Iron Age vitrified hillfort. A path runs right along

the ridge. There are fine views over Ben Wyvis, Strathpeffer, Dingwall and the Cromarty Firth as well as to the south. Access is via the same junction off the A835 as the Tollie Red Kites. There is a car-park at the end of the road overlooking Loch Ussie.

**Tollie Red Kites** (p182), signposted off the A835 west of Maryburgh, is an RSPB maintained site. Red Kites are attracted here by food put out daily at 14:30 in summer and 13:30 in winter. The hide and outside viewing area afford excellent views of these spectacular birds of prey and other species.

**7. Dingwall** (p180) is the former county town of Ross and Cromarty. Founded by the Vikings, it has for long been a regional centre. With the opening of the road network in the early 19th century and the railways in the 1860s, it developed greatly. Today it is bypassed by the main A9 north, making it a fine town to visit, with little through traffic. The town retains most of its 19th century buildings and layout, largely without ugly 20th century development.

**8. Strathpeffer** (p183) developed as a spa village from the late 18th century, and once had its own branch railway line. Although few people now partake of the waters, it remains a popular destination and is an excellent base from which to tour the area.

**9. Rogie Falls** (p46) are signposted off the A835 northwest of Contin. Here the Blackwater transforms itself from a slow moving river into tumbling waterfalls, especially after heavy rain or when the snow on Ben Wyvis is melting. A suspension bridge affords especially good views of the falls and, in season, leaping Salmon.

**10. Garve** (p47) is a small hamlet just south of the junction of the A835 to Ullapool and the A832 to Lochcarron and Kyle of Lochalsh. The Kyle Line passes through Garve before turning west across the moors, ending ultimately in Kyle of Lochalsh. The road and railway line run parallel for much of this spectacular route.

**11. Ben Wyvis** (1046m, p47) stands in splendid isolation, the first of many Munros (mountains over 3,000ft or 914m) along the NC500. The route is described on page 47; although relatively straightforward, the area is very remote and all of the usual precautions should be adhered to.

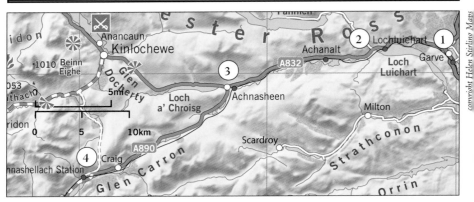

*copyright Helen Stirling Maps*

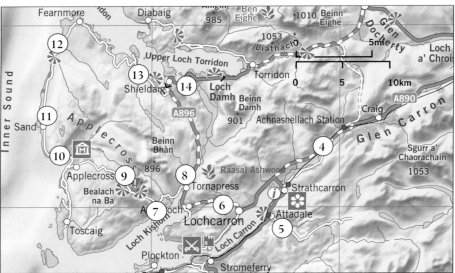

## Garve to Applecross via Lochcarron

| | | |
|---|---|---|
| 1. Garve | 9. Bealach na Ba | 54 |
|    Kyle Line | 48 |    Carn Glas Viewpoint | 54 |
| 2. Loch Luichart | 10. Applecross | 54 |
| 3. Achnasheen | 48 |    A' Chromraich | 55 |
| 4. Glen Carron | 49 |    Abbot Mor MacAogan | 56 |
|    River Carron | 49 |    Pictish cross slab | 57 |
| 5. Attadale Gardens | 50 | 11. Sand Mesolithic | 56 |
|    Kyle Line | 48 | 12. Viewpoint | 56 |
| 6. Lochcarron | 49 | 13. Upper Loch Torridon | 56 |
|    Strome Castle | 50 | 14. Shieldaig | 58 |
| 7. Loch Kishorn | 50 | | |
| 8. Raasal Ashwood | 51 | | |

**Garve to Applecross** After the junction north of Garve, the A832 passes Loch Luichart before striking west through Strath Bran to Achnasheen and Glen Carron. Apart from the last few miles to Lochcarron this is a very fast road through lonely lands.

After Lochcarron the route strikes inland to Loch Kishorn, whose shore it follows until the junction for the side road over the steep and spectacular hairpins of the Bealach na Ba (626m) to remote Applecross.

## ORDNANCE SURVEY 1:50,000 & 1:25,000 Maps

Landranger Maps: 25 Glen Carron & surrounding area; 24 Raasay, Applecross & Loch Torridon; 20 Beinn Dearg & surrounding area
Explorer Maps: 437 Ben Wyvis & Strathpeffer, Dingwall; 436 Beinn Dearg & Loch Fannich, Ullapool 429 Glen Carron & West Monar  Strathcarron & Attadale Forest; 428 Kyle of Lochalsh, Plockton & Applecross

### GARVE TO APPLECROSS VIA LOCHCARRON

**1. Beyond Garve, (p48)** at the A832/A835 junction bear left signposted Kyle of Lochalsh along the A832 through Strath Bran to Achnasheen. The route follows that of the early 19th century Parliamentary Road to Kyle of Lochalsh.
**The Kyle Line (p48)** runs parallel to the road all the way to Strathcarron. This railway is said to be one of the most spectacular in the UK.
**2. Loch Luichart** hydro electric scheme was one of the first of many to be built in the Highlands in the 1940s and 1950s.
**3. Achnasheen** (p48, 155m) is a remote hamlet with a train station, a nearby hotel and a cafe.
**4. Glen Carron** (p49) From the Achnasheen roundabout the A890 descends through Glen Carron to Lochcarron, passing attractive lochs with fine views to the southwest. These lochs are part of the River Carron, whose large estuary forms mudflats and salt marsh at the head of Loch Carron.
**5. Attadale Gardens** (p50, opening hours, entry charge) are a short (3mi, 4km) detour along A890 from Loch Carron. Established for over 250 years, there are several themed gardens. They even have their own train station.
**6. Lochcarron** (p49) is a pretty village which extends along the north shore of Loch Carron. The village prospered after the Parliamentary Road reached here in 1813 and even more when the railway reached Stromeferry in 1870. Lochcarron may be the only place in the UK where washing lines are placed on the foreshore.
**Strome Castle** (p50) is about 3mi (4km) southeast of Lochcarron along a narrow side road. A castle stood on this strategic site since Norse times. The gaunt ruins are all that remain. In 1602 the MacKenzies captured the castle from the MacDonalds and blew it up.
**7. Loch Kishorn** (p50) has a huge dry dock, which was the site of a major oil platform building in the 1970s. It may well be a decommissioning site in the 2020s for the many redundant North Sea oil rigs.
**8. Raasal Ashwood NNR** (p51), near the turnoff to Applecross, is an Ashwood growing on an outcrop of limestone. Hazel, Rowan and Willow also grow here. The wood is host to many species of lichen.
**9. Bealach na Ba** (p54) is the third highest road in Scotland, rising from sea level to 626m in 5.5mi (9km). With gradients of up to 20%, this single track road has many tight hairpins. It was opened in 1822 as one of the Parliamentary Roads. There is a spectacular view back down the pass from a parking place about 800m from the top of the pass.
Carn Glas Viewpoint (p54) at the top of the Bealach na Ba is one of several places to stop and admire the view over Inner Sound to Raasay, the Isle of Skye and the Cuillin Ridge on a clear day.
**10. Applecross** (p54) is one of the remotest settlements in the Highlands. The village nestles along the southeast side of the bay, with its hotel, camping site and small shop.
**Applecross Bay** has a large area of red Torridonian sand exposed at low tide. There are fine views to the Cuillin on Skye from the river mouth.
**A' Chromraich** (p55, 56) or The Sanctuary was founded in 673AD by the Irish monk, St Maelrubha. Only one intact Pictish cross slab remains in the kirkyard, along with a few broken pieces of another cross slab in the nearby Applecross Heritage Centre.
**11. Sand** (p56) is a beautiful sandy bay c.4mi (6km) north of Applecross Bay. A Mesolithic Age site was found here which dates from c.6000BC. Large numbers of shells, fish bones and stone tools were discovered, including bloodstone from Rum.
**12. Viewpoints** (p56) over Inner Sound and Loch Torridon abound  along the coast road to Shieldaig.
**13. The panorama over Loch Shieldaig** (p58) towards the Torridon Mountains is especially fine. The views from here are quintessential Northwest Highland scenery at its very best, requiring frequent stops. Perhaps the best panorama is from near Rhutoin, shortly before the junction with the A896.
**14. Shieldaig** (p58) is a strikingly situated planned fishing village, established in 1810. The road to Kishorn was built to facilitate the export of fish and shellfish, but the village was too remote to succeed as a fishing station. Today Shieldaig is popular with tourists. White-tailed Sea Eagles nest on Shieldaig Island and are often seen in the vicinity.

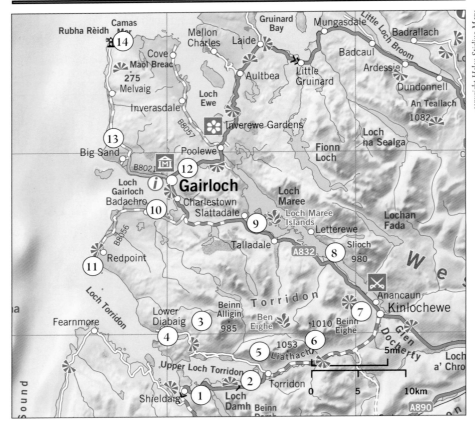

**Torridon to Gairloch** is one of the most scenically lovely parts of the NC500. The route follows the A896 and A832 past the dramatic backdrop of the Torridon Mountains. It then follows Loch Maree, one of the longest in Scotland. The loch is overlooked by the bulk of Beinn Eighe and the elegant peak of Slioch.

Towards Gairloch the scenery of Kerrysdale and Badachro becomes much more gentle, with picturesque harbours, beautiful sandy beaches and the pretty village of Gairloch itself. This is quintessential West Highlands at its best and merits a stay of a few days rather than a quick stop for lunch. The Gairloch area has a lot of secrets for the curious.

| Torridon to Gairloch | | | |
|---|---|---|---|
| 1. Shieldaig | 58 | 8. Loch Maree | 62 |
| Dubh-aird | 59 | Slioch | 62 |
| 2. Upper Loch Torridon | 58 | 9. Isle Maree | 64 |
| 3. Ben Alligin | 60 | Muc-sheilch Monster | 64 |
| 4. Diabaig | 60 | Slattadale Forest | 62 |
| 5. Torridon | 58 | 10. Badachro | 65 |
| Glen Torridon | 60 | Kerrysdale | 64 |
| Deer Museum | 60 | 11. Redpoint | 65 |
| Liathach | 60 | 12. Gairloch | 66 |
| 6. Coire Dubh Mor | 60 | Boat Trips | 69 |
| 7. Beinn Eighe NNR | 60, 63 | 13. Big Sand | 68 |
| Kinlochewe | 62 | 14. Rubha Reidh | 68 |
| Anancaun | 62 | Camas Mor | 68 |

## ORDNANCE SURVEY 1:50,000 & 1:25,000 Maps

Landranger Maps: 24 Raasay, Applecross & Loch Torridon; 25 Glen Carron & surrounding area; 19 Gairloch & Ullapool area

Explorer Maps: 428 Kyle of Lochalsh, Plockton & Applecross; Glen Carron & West Monar  Strathcarron & Attadale Forest; Torridon - Beinn Eighe & Liathach, Loch Maree, Kinlochewe & Gairloch

## TORRIDON TO GAIRLOCH

**1. Shieldaig** (p58) The single track coast road from Applecross joins the A896 just south of Shieldaig. **Dubh-aird** (p59) is one of several small headlands on the south side of Upper Loch Torridon. It can be reached by woodland trails starting near Loch Torridon Hotel and other places off the A896.

**2. Upper Loch Torridon** (p58) is dominated by the massive ridge of Liathach (1055m), which rears up seemingly vertically from sea level.

**3. Ben Alligin** (986m, p60) completes this spectacular skyline. There are several fine viewpoints along the A896, most of which benefit from a short walk from the car. The ever changing scene over the mountains and Upper Loch Torridon from above the beach is especially photogenic.

**4. Diabaig** (p60) a narrow side road winds along the north side of Upper Loch Torridon, overshadowed by Beinn Alligin and ending at Lower Diabaig. There are spectacular views from the steep pass of Bealach na Gaoithe (250m).

**5. Torridon** (p58) is a tiny settlement at the head of the loch with an interesting Deer Museum (p60) as well as an NTS Countryside Centre.

**Glen Torridon** (p60) is dominated by the bulk of Liathach to the northwest and Beinn Eighe to the northeast. There are many photo opportunities with the river or lochs in the foreground, all requiring short walks from the car.

**6. Coire Dubh Mor** (p60) is reached by a short walk from the main road. This spectacular corrie between Liathach and Beinn Eighe is idyllic on a summer's day but intimidating with snow and mist.

**7. Beinn Eighe NNR** (p60, 63) covers over 4,000ha of Caledonian Forest, mountain and moorland. There are woodland and mountain trails which start from the Visitor Centre near Kinlochewe. This Reserve should not be missed by nature lovers. **Kinlochewe** (p62) makes an ideal base from which to explore this area. Paths lead into the hills and around the shores of Loch Maree from here.

**Anancaun** (p62) is so named from the severed heads from the losing side of a clan battle. This small area of fertile ground at the head of the loch is full of wild flowers in summer.

**8. Loch Maree** (p62) is the largest in Wester Ross. It is said to have its own monster, the Muc-sheilch (p64). It is dominated by Slioch (980m,p62), which can be climbed from Kinlochewe.

**9. Isle Maree** (p64) is one of several islands on Loch Maree. It has long associations with Christianity. There are over forty islands on the loch. They have ancient Scots Pine and Juniper woodlands, protected from grazing. Loch Maree is an excellent place to observe Black-throated Divers.

**Slattadale Forest** (p62) has woodland trails with some fine views over Loch Maree. A small waterfall was named after Queen Victoria after her visit. This is only worth visiting after heavy rain.

**10. Kerrysdale** (p64) is a very attractive little valley on the A832 just south of Gairloch. From here the B8056 winds across beautiful remote countryside. **Badachro** (p65) is beautifully situated on one of the loveliest bays in Wester Ross. With a very popular Inn and quiet side roads this is a perfect place to dally.

**11. Redpoint** (p65) is at the end of the B8056. There is a fine walk around Red Point (42m) which takes in two beautiful red sandy beaches (3mi, 4km).

**12. Gairloch** (p66) is perfectly sited at the head of Loch Gairloch, sheltered by Longa Island. The village has much to offer the visitor, together with Charlestown, where the little harbour is situated. With a range of accommodation and shops this is a good base from which to explore Wester Ross.

**Gairloch Heritage Museum** (p66)is in the middle of the village. It tells the story of the area from early times to the present in a lively and interesting way.

**Boat Trips** (p69) are run from the pier to view wildlife including cetaceans, seals and birds. Gairloch is a particularly good location for dolphin sightings.

**13. Big Sand Camping Site** (p68) is one of the largest and best in the area. It is situated in a vast area of unspoilt sand dunes, overlooking the pristine beach of Caolas Beag, with exquisite views to the west.

**14. Rubha Reidh** (p68) is accessible via the Northern Lighthouse Board road from Melvaig, 3mi (5km). *No access to the lighthouse or its grounds.* **Camas Mor** (p68) is a delightful small cove 1.5mi (2km) east of the headland.

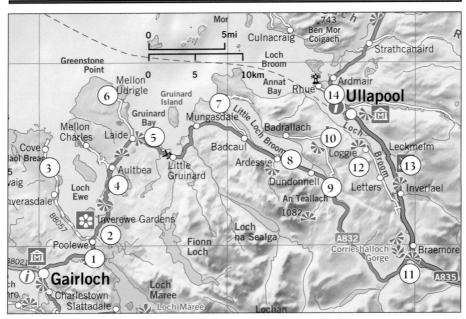

**GAIRLOCH TO ULLAPOOL**
This part of the NC500 route hugs the coast for much of the way except for the section between Dundonnell and Braemore. North of Gairloch there are grand views over Loch Maree, Loch Ewe and Gruinard Bay. Both sea lochs have wonderful sandy coves as good as any in the UK.

Little Loch Broom is dominated by the large mountain of An Teallach, whose grandeur can only be fully appreciated by taking a hike over the moor to its vast Corrie Toll. Much more accessible are the small falls at Ardessie and the side road to Badrallach on the north side of Little Loch Broom with its magnificent views.

Corrieshalloch Gorge and the Falls of Measach are near Braemore, at the junction heading north to Ullapool. These are spectacular after heavy rain or when snow is melting, when viewed from the pedestrian suspension bridge.

The A835 follows the east coast of Loch Broom to Ullapool, with lovely views opening up at nearly every turn. A short detour along the west side of the loch ends at Loggie, from where there is perhaps the best view of Ullapool.

Like most sections of the NC500, this part merits frequent stops, detours and short walks to fully appreciate the many splendours along the way. Those who do off piste will not regret it.

| GAIRLOCH TO ULLAPOOL | | | |
|---|---|---|---|
| 1. Tollie Viewpoint | 68 | 7. Little Loch Broom | 71 |
| 2. Poolewe | 68 | 8. Ardessie Falls | 72 |
| Inverewe Gardens | 69 | 9. Dundonnell | 72 |
| Pictish Stone | 68 | An Teallach | 72 |
| 3. Cove Road & Beaches | 70 | Loch Toll an Lochain | 72 |
| 4. Loch Ewe | 70 | 10. Badrallach | 72 |
| Mellon Charles | 70 | 11. Corrieshalloch Waterfall | 73 |
| Russian Convoy Mem | 70 | 12. Dun an Ruich Ruadh | 73 |
| WWII Loch Ewe | 70 | 13. Leckmelm Arboretum | 73 |
| 5. Gruinard Bay | 71 | 14. Loch Broom | 72 |
| 6. Mellon Udrigle | 70 | Ullapool | 76 |
| Camas a' Charaig | 70 | | |

## ORDNANCE SURVEY 1:50,000 & 1:25,000 Maps

Landranger Maps: 19 Gairloch & Ullapool area; 20 Beinn Dearg & surrounding area
Explorer Maps: 434 Gairloch & Loch Ewe; 435 An Teallach & Slioch, Kinlochewe & Achnasheen;
436 Beinn Dearg & Loch Fannich, Ullapool

## Gairloch to Ullapool

**1. Tollie Viewpoint** (p68) is on the A832 4mi (6km) northeast of Gairloch. From here there is a superb view right down Loch Maree.

**2. Poolewe** (p68) is at the head of Loch Ewe where the short River Ewe enters the sea. One of the few Pictish symbol stones found in Wester Ross can be seen in the graveyard (p68).

**Inverewe Gardens** (p69) are maintained by the NTS. They were created from a barren hillside by Osgood MacKenzie from 1862. With an amazing variety of plants, a Visitor Centre and Inverewe House this is an essential visit, best in early summer.

**3. Cove Road & Beaches** (p70). The B8057 follows the western shore of Loch Ewe through several small settlements and past a number of exquisite beaches.

**4. Loch Ewe** (p70) and Loch Eriboll were used as anchorages during WWII. In particular Loch Ewe was an assembly point for the Russian Convoys between 1942 and 1944. Remains of fortifications and a memorial stone are testimony to the brave crews of the 489 merchant ships that sailed from here.

**Viewpoints over Loch Ewe.** There are several fine viewpoints with carparks from which to take in panoramic views of this sea loch. The side road to Mellon Charles (p70) passes through a small crofting township and ends at the secret cove of Camas nan Geobhar.

**5. Gruinard Bay** (p71) is a large north facing bay dominated by Gruinard Island. From the carpark above Little Gruinard walk to the top of Creag Mhor (127m) for a superb view of the bay and its extensive part gravel, part sandy beach.

**6. Mellon Udrigle** (p70) is at the end of a side road which follows the west side of Gruinard Bay. The beach of Camas a' Charaig is perhaps the best in the whole of Wester Ross. Sheltered by low cliffs and a small headland and backed by dunes this little cove could easily be in the Caribbean on a fine day.

**7. Little Loch Broom** (p71) is a long narrow sea loch east of Gruinard Bay. Once again there are several fine viewpoints at which to stop and take in the scenery, as well as side roads to explore.

**8. Ardessie Falls** (p72) are accessed from a signposted carpark via a short path. As usual they are at their best after heavy rain or when snow is melting. The going is generally muddy, wet and slippery.

**9. Dundonnell** (p72) is at the head of Little Loch Broom. The River Dundonnell meanders over the small flood plain of Strath Beag which ends in salt marsh. Further up the valley the river becomes a raging torrent when in spate, with a series of fine, small waterfalls.

**An Teallach** (1062m, p72) is a vast ridge of jagged peaks, with nine over 950m. There is a fine viewpoint from the A832 southeast of Dundonnell above the waterfalls at a parking place (279m) on the road to Corrieshalloch Gorge and the A835.

**Loch Toll an Lochain and Corrie Toll** (p72) can be reached from a small carpark at Corrie Hallie (52m) south of Dundonnell House. A track goes for part of the way but this is mostly a hard 6mi (10km) walk across rough moorland to a splendid amphitheatre.

**10. Badrallach** (p72) is a remote settlement on the north side of Little Loch Broom. A narrow side road turns sharp right near Dundonnell House and follows the north side of Little Loch Broom. There are fine views to An Teallach and Little Loch Broom. A short walk from the summit (236m) to Loch Allt na h' Airbhe reveals fine views over Ullapool, Loch Broom and the Coigach.

**11. Corrieshalloch Gorge and Measach Waterfall** (p73) is at the junction of the A832 and A835. The River Droma cascades through this 61m deep box canyon before falling 46m as the Falls of Measach. There are fine views from a suspension bridge. The falls are at their best after heavy rain.

**12. Dun an Ruich Ruadh** (p73) is one of the best preserved brochs in Wester Ross. The side road to Letters starts just north of Corrieshalloch and runs through several small townships with increasingly good views of Loch Broom and Ullapool before passing this broch and ending at Dun Lagaidh.

**13. Leckmelm Arboretum** (p73) was planted in the 1870s and has been restored. This small plantation is well worth a visit for its old trees.

**14. Loch Broom** (p72) The A835 along the shores of Loch Broom offers increasingly fine views of Ullapool (p76) as it approaches the town.

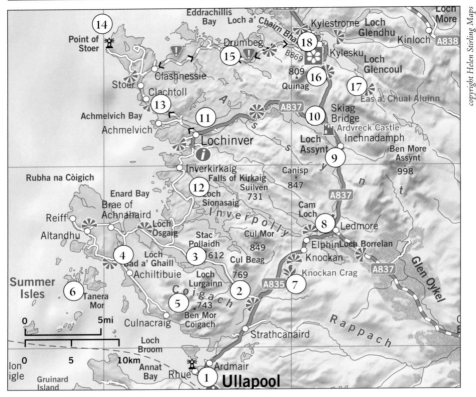

**Ullapool to Kylesku via Lochinver** is a highly varied part of the NC500 route. Initially it passes the Coigach, with its dramatic green mountains and deep blue lochs. A side trip leads to the remote township of Achiltibuie.

Knockan Crag is something of a geologist's paradise where visitors can get to grips with things like the Moine Thrust and see many fossils. Slightly further on Elphin is an oasis of greenery in the moorland.

Assynt is dominated by large mountains, including Suilven, Ben Mor Assynt, Canisp and Quinag. The village of Lochinver has much to offer the visitor, including a wonderful pie shop. The coastal route to Kylesku is a challenging and very narrow switchback road with beautiful views around every one of the many corners.

---

### ORDNANCE SURVEY 1:50,000 & 1:25,000 Maps
Landranger Maps: 19 Gairloch & Ullapool area; 15 Loch Assynt & surrounding area
Explorer Maps: 439 Coigach & Summer Isles, Inverpolly; 442 Assynt & Lochinver

---

## Ullapool to Kylesku via Lochinver

**1. Ullapool** (p76) is the main settlement in Wester Ross. Despite its summer bussle, it manages to retain its charm and welcome to visitors. Activity here centres on the busy harbour, with the ferry to Stornoway, fishing and tour boats coming and going. **Boat Trips** (p78) are run to the Summer Isles from Ullapool in summer. Seals, cetaceans and seabirds may all be seen.

**Rhue & Ardmair** (p78) There is a fine short circular walk around this small headland from the carpark next to the sign for Rhue. Climb to the top of Meal Mhor (165m) for fabulous panoramic views, especially at sunset. There are boat trips from Ardmair to the Summer Isles during the summer.

**2. The Coigach** (p78) is a verdant mountainous peninsula north of Loch Broom which is split in two by a deep loch filled glacial valley. There are fine views from several laybys on the A835 taking in Ben Mor Coigach (743m), Loch Lurgainn, Stac Pollaidh (613m) and Cul Beag (769m).

**3. Stac Pollaidh** (p78) is a steep but easy 500m climb from a carpark beside Loch Lurgainn. There are stunning views over the Coigach to the south and to Suilven and Inverpolly to the north.

**4. Achiltibuie** (p79) is a remote community at the end of the Coigach side road 14mi (22km) from the A835. With several fine beaches and a low coastline, this tranquil area offers fine walking. A ferry runs from Old Dornie jetty to Tanera More.

**5. Ben Mor Coigach** (743m, p79) overlooks Achiltibuie from the east. It can be climbed by a relatively easy, but very steep route, from the summit, route from the end of the road at Culnacraig (c.6mi, 10km, 4h).

**6. The Summer Isles** (p80) lie close offshore from Achiltibuie. Tanera Mor is inhabited with a cafe and holiday lets.

**7. Knockan Crag** (p17, 80, 81) is signposted off the A835 13mi (21km) north of Ullapool. Part of the North West Highlands Geopark, it is famous for elucidating the geology of the Moine Thrust, where older Moine Schist was pushed northwestwards over younger Cambrian and Durness Limestone. Fossil beds including Pipe Rock, Fucoid Beds, Salterella and Durness limestone can all be seen here.

**8. Elphin** (p81), just to the north of Knockan Crag, is a sudden patch of greenery caused by underlying Limestone rocks, after miles of bleak moorland.

**Cam Loch**, just to the north, forms a classic foreground to views of Suilven and Canisp.

**9. Inchnadamph NNR** (p82) is of great interest to geologists and botanists. Studies in the 19th century explained the Moine Trust. Limestone outcrops here support a diverse range of rare plants.

**The Bone Caves** (p85) are a series of Limestone caverns overlooking Allt nan Uamh south of Inchnadamph. Many animal and human bones were found here, dating from 4,500 to 47,000 years ago.

**10. Assynt** (p81) is a huge area which stretches from Elphin in the south to Kylesku in the north.

**Loch Assynt**, 16mi (25km) long and 80m deep is brooded over by Ben More Assynt. This loch has a dark, silent and lonely splendour.

**Ardvreck Castle** (p83) is near the south end of Loch Assynt. Now a ruin, it has a violent and sad history.

**11. Lochinver** (p84) is a thriving village and fishing port with an excellent harbour, overlooked by Suilven. The Assynt Visitor Centre, Lochinver Larder and Highland Stoneware should not be missed.

**12. Inverkirkaig** (p84) is c.2mi (3km) south of Lochinver along a narrow side road.

**The Falls of Kirkaig** (p85) are only 18m high but dramatic after heavy rain. They are 2mi (3km) upstream from Inverkirkaig.

**13. Achmelvich and Clachtoll** (p86) are on the very sinuous narrow side road northwest of Lochinver. Both have beautiful sandy beaches.

**14. The Point of Stoer** (p86) has a lighthouse. The road from Stoer had grand panoramic views towards the mountains to the south. The Old Man of Stoer is a 2mi (3km) walk from the lighthouse.

**15. Drumbeg** (p87) The route continues along a very narrow, twisty and hilly road via Clashnessie and Drumbeg to the main A984 south of Kylesku.

**16. Quinag** (808m, p88) is a large mountain which dominates the landscape around it in all directions.

**17. Eas a' Chual Aluinn** (p88) is a remote waterfall south of Kylesku with a drop of over 200m.

**18. Kylesku** (p88) is now bypassed by the main road. Boat trips run in the summer to the Kerrachar Gardens (p87) and to see the waterfalls as well as wildlife such as Golden Eagles and Otters.

**Loch Glencoul** (p88) is southeast of Kylesku. The flanks of Ben Aird da Loch very clearly show where older rocks cover newer strata in the Moine Thrust.

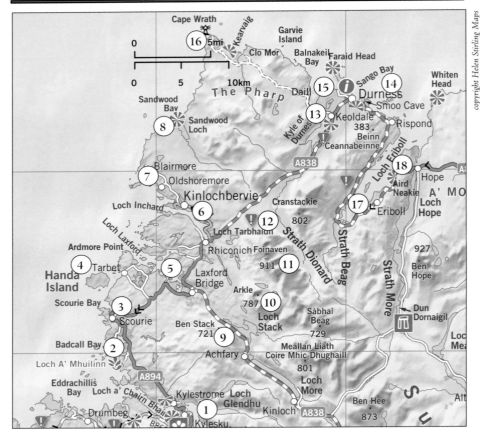

## Kylesku to Durness

**Kylesku to Durness**, the most northwesterly part of the NC500, is dramatically different from the whole of the rest of the route. Referred to as the "Lonely Lands", beautiful bays give way to dramatic Quartzite topped mountains and scattered lochs inland. The far northwest has the wide expanse of remote Sandwood Bay and the cliffs of Cape Wrath. Durness is an oasis of greenery due to its Limestone, made even more special by its lovely beaches and huge Smoo Cave.

## ORDNANCE SURVEY 1:50,000 & 1:25,000 Maps

Landranger Maps: 15 Loch Assynt & surrounding area; 9 Cape Wrath
Explorer Maps: 445 Foinaven, Arkle, Kylesku & Scourie;
446 Durness & Cape Wrath, Kinlochbervie & Rhiconich

## KYLESKU TO DURNESS

**1. The Kylesku Bridge** (p88) over Kylestrome was opened in 1984. It replaced a small ferry, transforming communications in the northwest.
**The X-craft memorial** (p92) at Kylestrome overlooks the bridge. It commemorates the miniature submarine crews who trained here in WWII.
**2. Badcall Bay** (p93) just south of Scourie is one of the most dramatically beautiful of many here.
**Loch a' Mhulinn NNR** (p93), just south of Badcall Bay, is the most northerly patch of mixed Oak woodland in Great Britain. It has many rare lichens.
**3. Scourie** (p93) is a small settlement at the head of a sandy bay. The coastline is of Lewisian Gneiss infiltrated by many igneous Scourian Dykes.
**4. Handa** (p94) is a delightful small cliffbound Torridonian Sandstone island reached by boat from Tarbat, north of Scourie. In summer it is home to thousands of breeding seabirds, including Puffins.
**5. Loch Laxford** (p94) is island strewn and strikingly beautiful, but only accessible by boat or on foot.
**6. Kinlochbervie** (p96) is a major white fish landing port, due to its proximity to the fishing grounds to the west. It is situated in a sheltered bay on Loch Inchard. There are fine views over Foinaven and Arkle from the road to Kinlochbervie.
**7. Oldshoremore and Polin** (p96) are two delightful beaches northwest of Kinlochbervie. Both are sheltered but Polin is the real gem.
**8. Sandwood Bay** (p97) is reached by a 4mi (6.5km) track across the moor from Blairmore. This 2mi (3km) expanse of exposed sandy beach is perhaps the best in the whole of the North Highlands.
**9. Ben Stack** 720m, (p96) and its dramatic cliffs, Leitir an Staca, overlook Loch Stack.
**10. Arkle** (787m, p94), on the north side of Lock Stack, forms perfect reflections on calm days, especially near dawn and sunset.
**11. Foinaven** (911m, p96) is covered in shattered white Quartzite scree which glitters in the sunshine, especially after rain. On calm days it is reflected in the lochs north of Rhiconich.
**12. Srath Dionard** (p97) is a dramatic glacial hanging valley on the north side of Foinaven, on the A894 road to Durness.

**Carnstackle** (801m, p96) overlooks Srath Dionard from the north and is the last in line of the high peaks on the west side of Loch Eriboll.
**13. The Kyle of Durness** (p97) is a beautiful long sandy estuary, surrounded by fertile Limestone rocks. The River Dionard flows into the southern end, forming extensive salt marshes.
**Keoldale** (p105) has a small jetty, from which the ferry to Cape Wrath departs in summer.
**14. Durness** (p98) may be one of the remotest villages in the UK, but it is also one of the most vibrant. It has a wonderful campsite, interesting shops and many services as well as beautiful beaches.
**Sango Bay** (p100) is the main Durness beach, with fine sands and several small stacks. To the east, Sango Beg (p104) and Traigh Allt Chaligeag (p104) are just as attractive, but less frequented.
**Smoo Cave** (p101) is a huge Limestone cave with the largest entrance of any in the UK. When the river, Allt Smoo, is in spate a huge waterfall enters the inner cave via a sink hole.
**John Lennon** (p101) had a cousin in Durness and spent many childhood holidays here. There is a small memorial garden to him next to the village hall.
**Balnakeil Craft Village** (p102) occupies a former military site on the way to Balnakeil Bay. An eclectic mix of interesting businesses can be found here.
**15. Balnakeil Bay** (p102) is at the mouth of the Kyle of Durness. Sheltered by Faraid Head, it forms a 1,500m crescent of sand, backed by high dunes.
**Faraid Head** (p103) is formed from erosion resistant Lewisian Gneiss and Moine Schist. Puffins breed on the cliffs. The clifftops and dunes harbour many rare plants including *Primula scotica* and orchids.
**16. Cape Wrath** (p97) can be reached during the summer by ferry from Keoldale, followed by a 12mi (19km) minibus ride to the lighthouse. The cliffs of Clo Mor at 200m are the highest on mainland UK.
**17. Loch Eriboll** (p106) is a huge glacially formed sea loch east of Durness, c.10mi (16km) long and up to 130m deep.
**18. Ard Neakie** (p107) on the northeastern shore is joined to the shore by a tombolo or ayre. The arched buildings are former lime kilns.

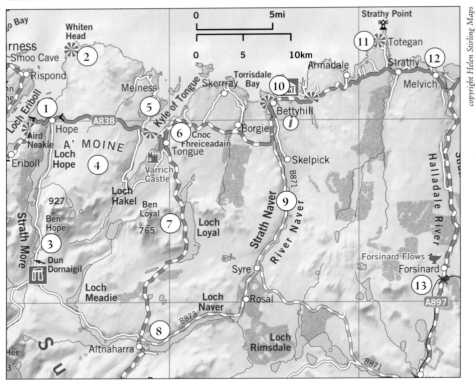

*copyright Helen Stirling Maps*

**The North Coast - Loch Eriboll to Melvich** is yet again entirely different to anything else on the NC500 route. Deeply incised sea lochs, including Loch Eriboll, the Kyle of Tongue and Torrisdale Bay are a major feature, along with sandy beaches and low cliff bound coasts.

In the west Ben Hope and Ben Loyal are dominant but further east the lonely valleys of Strath Naver and Strath Halladale are the major features, in turn giving way to the unique flat landscape of the Flow Country.

There are several small settlements at Tongue, Bettyhill, Strathy and Melvich. All offer facilities to visitors and interesting experiences for those who wish to explore the landscape, history and wildlife.

To those in a hurry the North Coast may seem like a place to flash past, but stop, look and open all your senses instead.

---

## ORDNANCE SURVEY 1:50,000 & 1:25,000 Maps

Landranger Maps: 9 Cape Wrath; 10 Strathnaver
Explorer Maps: 447 Ben Hope, Ben Loyal & Kyle of Tongue;
448 Strath Naver/Strath Nabhair & Loch Loyal, Bettyhill;
449 Strath Halladale & Strathy Point, Melvich & Forsinard

---

## NORTH COAST - LOCH ERIBOLL TO MELVICH

**1. Loch Eriboll** (p106) is a huge glacially formed sea loch east of Durness, c.10mi (16km) long and up to 130m deep.
**Ard Neakie** (p107) on the northeastern shore is joined to the shore by a tombolo or ayre. The arched buildings are former lime kilns.
**2. Whiten Head** (170m, p107) marks the eastern entrance to Loch Eriboll. Its striking white Quartzite cliffs gleam in the sunshine; the headland is a 5mi (8km) hike each way from Hope on the A838.
**3. Ben Hope** (927m, p108) is the highest mountain in the north. It can be climbed from Allnacaillich near Dun Dornaigil; total distance 5mi (8km).
**Dun Dornaigil** (p108) is an impressive broch, with walls still 6.7m high. It is situated below Ben Hope in Strath More on the side road to Altnaharra.
**4. A' Moine** (p107) is a large area of rolling hillocks and lochans between Loch Eriboll and Tongue from which Moine Schist takes its name.
**5. Melness** (p110) A side road just west of the Tongue causeway follows the west coast of Tongue Bay through Melness and a series of other small townships. There is fine beach and jetty at Talmine.
**6. Tongue** (p108) is a small settlement on the east side of the Kyle of Tongue, a long inlet which stretches c.5mi (8km) inland. The road crosses it via a causeway from where there are fine views.
**Varrich Castle** (p109) can be reached via a path from the village. This stronghold dates from Norse times and has sweeping views of the Kyle of Tongue.
**7. Ben Loyal** (764m, p109) is an eroded volcano with four sharp peaks south of Tongue. The route starts at Ribigill, 10mi (16km), 6 hours return.
**8. Altnaharra** (87m, p109) is a remote inland village which holds the record for the lowest temperature in the UK of -27C. This is a popular base for walkers, climbers, bird watchers and game shooters.
**9. Strathnaver** (p110) originally stretched from Kylesku to Caithness and was Clan Mackay country. **The Strathnaver Trail** covers 5,000 years of human settlement in this lovely but lonely valley.
**Clearances** (p113) Nowhere in the Highlands epitomises the Clearances quite like Strathnaver. The Sutherland Estate commenced clearing the people

from here in 1813, under their factor, one Patrick Sellar. Sheep ranching prospered for a time; today only lonely ruins, such as at Rosal remain, in a beautiful valley empty of people.
**Dunviden** (p112), north of Syre is an especially poignant site. Here people lived continuously from Neolithic times until the early 19th century. A chambered cairn, Bronze Age houses, a broch and an 18th century village all stand witness.
**10. Bettyhill** (p110) was created in the 19th century to accommodate families cleared from their lands. **Torrisdale Bay** (p111), at the mouth of the River Naver, is of exceptional botanical interest. Extensive sand dunes back beautiful sandy beaches and salt marshes here. Navermouth once supported a thriving Salmon netting industry but only ruins remain.
**Farr Bay** (p111), east of Bettyhill, has another lovely sandy beach backed by dunes. Here several rare species of bumblebees thrive.
**Strathnaver Museum** (p111) tells the story of the area, with archaeology, history and especially the clearances. The Farr Stone is an 8th century Pictish symbol stone and cross slab.
**11. Strathy Point** (p112) is the largest promontory on this coast. There are fine views from the lighthouse along the coast. *Primula scotica* and other maritime plants grow here; Puffins breed in summer.
**12. Strathy** (p112) has a small sandy beach, bound by cliffs on both sides, at the mouth of River Strathy. **Portskerra** (p113) was created as a fishing harbour during the clearances but is very exposed.
**Melvich** (p113) is on the estuary of the Halladale River. Here an expansive sandy beach is bound by low cliffs, where Puffins nest in summer. In former times this was a major Salmon fishing station.
**Old Split Stone** (p114) marks the border between Caithness and Sutherland.
**13. Strath Halladale** (p114) was never completely cleared like Strath Naver. Ruined brochs, isolated houses and modern farms dot the landscape. The River Halladale remains a classic Salmon river.
**RSPB Forsinard Flows Reserve** (p115) is unique, with a visitor centre in the train station and a landscape unlike any other.

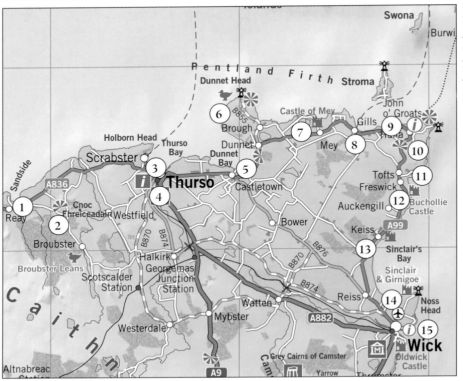

**CAITHNESS NORTH - REAY TO WICK** Caithness is completely different in character from most of the rest of the NC500. The underlying rock is Old Red Sandstone. The produces fertile soil is ideal for breeding cattle. The history is Norse rather than Scottish; as shown by the placenames.

Caithness has much spectacular coastal scenery, ranging from the high cliffs of Dunnet Head to the spectacular Duncansby Stacks. There are many fine sandy beaches from Sandside in the west to Dunnet Sands in the east.

The east coast is more rugged in places, except for Freswick and the vast Sinclair's Bay. There are many Iron Age brochs to visit between John o' Groats and Wick. Sadly most are dilapidated. Nevertheless they are interesting to explore since most are situated in good vantage points overlooking the nearby coast.

| CAITHNESS NORTH - REAY TO WICK | | | |
|---|---|---|---|
| 1. Reay | 120 | 7. Castle of Mey | 124 |
| Sandside Bay | 120 | 8. Gills Bay | 125 |
| Dounreay | 120 | 9. John o' Groats | 126 |
| 2. Cnoc Fhreiceadain | 120 | 10. Duncansby Head | 127 |
| 3. Scrabster | 122 | 11. Buchollie Castle | 128 |
| 4. Thurso | 120 | 12. Freswick | 128 |
| Caithness Horizons | 122 | 13. Old Keiss Castle | 128 |
| Old St Peter's Kirk | 121 | 14. Sinclair & Girnigoe Cas | 128 |
| 5. Dunnet Bay | 122 | 15. Wick | 129 |
| Castlehill | 124 | Wick Heritage Mus | 130 |
| Dunnet Bay Distillery | 123 | Old Pulteney Distillery | 130 |
| Mary Anne's Cottage | 124 | Old Wick Castle | 130 |
| 6. Dunnet Head | 124 | | |

---

## ORDNANCE SURVEY 1:50,000 & 1:25,000 Maps

Landranger Maps: 11 Thurso & Dunbeath; 12 Thurso, Wick & surrounding area
Explorer Maps: 450 Wick & The Flow Country, Lybster, Latheron & Dunbeath;
451 Thurso & John o' Groats, Dunnet Head

---

## Caithness North - Reay to Wick

**1. Reay** (p120) is the most westerly village in Caithness. From the west there are fine views over the Pentland Firth and Caithness from Drum Hollistan. **Sandside Bay** (p120) has a beautiful sandy beach, backed by dunes. The small harbour with its pretty houses is especially photogenic.
**Dounreay NPDE** (p120) is the site of major experiments in fast breeder nuclear power generation in the 20th century. The site is now being decommissioned.
**2. Cnoc Fhreiceadain** (p120) overlooks Dounreay. Two fine Neolithic chambered cairns are situated on the top of this small hill.
**3. Scrabster** (p122) has had a regular ferry service to Orkney since 1855. It is now one of the main fish landing ports in the UK.
**4. Thurso** (p120) is the largest town in Caithness. It grew due to the flagstone industry in the 19th century and the nuclear developments of the 20th century. **Caithness Horizons** (p122) is situated in the Old Town Hall.
**Old St Peter's Kirk** (p121) was founded in Norse times. Now roofless, it is of great interest due to its architecture and fascinating old memorials.
**Thurso Bay** (p122) is very popular with surfers. The fine sandy beach stretches to Scrabster. The Esplanade is a good place from which to watch the action.
**5. Dunnet Bay** (p122) faces northwest, with a huge arc of pristine sand, backed by extensive dunes. It is at its best during a major northwesterly storm.
**Castletown** (p124) was a major producer and exporter of Caithness flagstones for over a century. **Castlehill Heritage Centre** (p124) and the Flagstone Trail tell the story of this major industry.
**Dunnet Bay Distillery** (p123) is recently established. It produces acclaimed gin and vodkas, including Rock Rose Gin.
**Mary Anne's Cottage** (p124), on the east corner of Dunnet Bay, is a preserved 19th century croft with original fittings, furnishings and artefacts.
**6. Dunnet Head** (127m, p124), the most northerly point in mainland Britain, has fine views over the Pentland Firth to Orkney from near the lighthouse.
**7. The Castle of Mey** (p124) was the northern home the Queen Mother from 1952. The castle is

now looked after by the Castle of Mey Trust and is open to the public during the summer.
**8. Gills Bay** (p125) is the terminal for the vehicle ferry route to St Margaret's Hope in Orkney operated all year by Pentland Ferries.
**9. John o' Groats** (p126) has in recent years had an expensive makeover. It is the departure point for the passenger ferry to Orkney during the summer. With shops, cafes, accommodation and dramatic surroundings this is a place to dally in. To the east the Ness of Duncansby has fine sandy beaches.
**10. Duncansby Head** (p127) has some of the most spectacular coastal scenery on the whole NC500. **The Duncansby Stacks** should not be missed, regardless of the weather, or season. A short walk along these dramatic cliffs essential, 3mi, 4km, 2h.
**11. Freswick** (p128) has another fine expanse of sand, also backed by dunes. There are coastal brochs to visit at Skirza, Nybster and Keiss.
**12. Buchollie Castle** (p128) is one of the hidden gems of this coast. It is situated on a large sea stack at Kingans Geo, south of Freswick.
**13. Old Keiss Castle** (p128) is a dramatically sited romantic ruin, perched on the edge of cliffs north of Keiss Harbour. Facing east across the vast Sinclair Bay, this port is untenable in easterly gales.
**14. Sinclair & Girnigoe Castle** (p128) on Noss Head, northeast of Wick, is perhaps the most spectacular coastal castle in the UK. It is accessed via Staxigeo, with a carpark near the lighthouse.
**15. Wick** (p129) developed along the tidal Wick river from early times. In the 19th century it became the Herring capital of Europe. At the peak in 1862, 1,122 boats fished from here in the season.
**Wick Heritage Museum** (p130) is in Bank Row. It tells the story of the town, especially the Herring industry. This is a fascinating example of a local museum and well worth a good perusal.
**Old Pulteney Distillery** (p130) has unusually shaped pot stills. There is a visitor centre in Hubbart Street.
**Old Wick Castle** (p130), or the Old Man of Wick, is of Norse origin. It is the best preserved of several such buildings in Caithness.

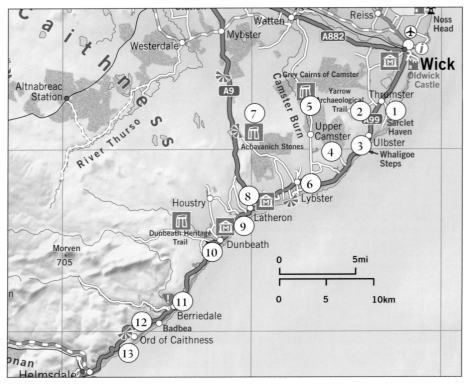

**Caithness Southeast - Wick to the Ord** South of Wick, Caithness takes on a somewhat different persona. The gentle agricultural landscape slowly changes to wilder Highland scenery, culminating at the Ord of Caithness.

From Wick to the Ord this is a hard, cliffbound coast with numerous small harbours, all exposed to the east. The familiar stories of the 19th century Clearances, followed by the Herring fishing boom are echoed in miniature here.

Southeastern Caithness is a paradise for all those interested in archaeology. Here there are numerous Neolithic chambered cairns and standing stones. Bronze Age houses, field walls and burnt mounds abound.

Iron Age brochs, mostly ruined and robbed out, seem to appear at every turn. A few, such as Dunbeath Broch have been conserved, perhaps because of being remote. Ruined medieval castles, abandoned crofts and later 19th century planned villages are everywhere. In many ways the 20th century development bypassed this area completely, leaving it unspoilt.

---

## ORDNANCE SURVEY 1:50,000 & 1:25,000 Maps

Landranger Maps: 11 Thurso & Dunbeath; 12 Thurso, Wick & surrounding area;
17 Helmsdale & Strath of Kildonan
Explorer Maps: 450 Wick & The Flow Country, Lybster, Latheron & Dunbeath;
444 Helmsdale & Strath of Kildonan

---

## Caithness Southeast - Wick to the Ord of Caithness

**1. Sarclet Haven** (p132) is one of many small fishing harbours on this exposed coast. Follow the side road from Thrumster to Sarclet to reach this gem for a coastal walk or a picnic.

**2. Yarrows Archaeological Trail** (p132) is signposted off the A99 just south of Thrumster. A circular walk takes in Neolithic chambered cairns, Bronze Age and Pictish houses as well as a splendidly preserved Iron Age broch.

**3. Whaligoe** (p132), at Ulbster, has 300 flagstone steps down to a geo where Herring were landed and shipped out. The steps can be treacherous when wet and great care should be taken. The curing house at the top is now the Whaligoe Steps Café.

**The Cairn o' Get** (p133) is signposted off the A99 at Ulbster. This small Neolithic chambered cairn has lost its roof and covering mound but the passage and chamber are intact and very interesting. There are several Iron Age brochs nearby.

**4. The Hill o' Many Stanes** (p133) is signposted off the A99 at Mid Clyth. This enigmatic site has over 200 stones laid out in at least 22 radiating rows. It may have been a lunar observatory around 2000BC.

**5. The Grey Cairns of Camster** (p133) are signposted off the A99 at West Clyth, near Lybster. They are superb examples of Neolithic chambered cairns with intact chambers. They are reached by boardwalks over boggy moorland. Camster Round has a 6m passage leading to its impressive chamber; Camster Long extends to over 60m, with two chambers.

**6. Lybster** (p134) was developed in the 19th century as a major Herring port. The village and pretty harbour were planned developments, designed to take advantage of the then booming fishery.
**Waterlines Visitor Centre** (p135) overlooks Lybster Harbour. Housed in a former fishing store, the Centre has exhibitions, regular events and a café.

**7. Achavanich Stones** (p134) can be reached via a side road southwest of Latheron, or via the A9 5mi (8km) north from Latheron. This unusual U-shaped stone setting comprises of c.40 of an original c.54 monoliths and overlooks Loch Stemster.

**8. Latheron** (p135), at the junction of the A99 from Wick and the A9 to Thurso, is a former monastic site. Pictish symbol stones have been found here. There are fine views northwards along the coast.
**The Clan Gunn Centre** (p135) is based in a former parish church. It tells the story of the clan from early times. There is an archive to consult and a shop.
**Latheronwheel** (p135) is another planned 19th century Herring harbour. Now quiet, over 50 boats were once based here. It is a lovely spot for a picnic.

**9. Laidhay Croft Museum** (p136) is a restored 19th century croft, just north of Dunbeath. With the dwelling house, byre and barn all under one roof and contemporary furnishings this is an interesting visit.

**10. Dunbeath** (p136) is another 19th century development, with a large natural harbour, exposed to the southeast. The harbourside buildings are especially attractive. Dunbeath was the birthplace of the acclaimed novelist, Neil M Gunn.
**Dunbeath Heritage Centre** (p136), in an old school overlooking the village, tells the story of the district. Brochs, the Clearances, Herring fishing and Neil Gunn are all featured.
**Dunbeath Strath Heritage Trail** (p137) follows Dunbeath Water upstream from the old Telford bridge. Dunbeath Broch is one of the best preserved in Caithness with 3m walls. The trail continues through ancient woodland to the Prisoner's Leap.

**11. Berriedale** (p136), with its steep hairpin bends, is passed in a few moments by the vast majority of visitors. This is greatly to their loss as a secret cove with old cottages and a small harbour lie hidden away from the busy main road.

**12. Badbea** (p137) was created for 28 families cleared from the nearby Langwell estate. The location, on steep ground above precipitous cliffs, was completely unsuitable for any kind of settlement.

**13. The Ord of Caithness** (198m, p137) marks the boundary between Caithness and Sutherland. This wild and ruggedly beautiful section of the NC500 is at its best when the Whin or Gorse is in full bloom. Fog frequently envelopes the Ord at any time of year, especially with an easterly wind off the sea, making progress slow and hazardous. In winter it is frequently blocked by snow, when the snow gates may be shut between Berridale and Helmsdale.

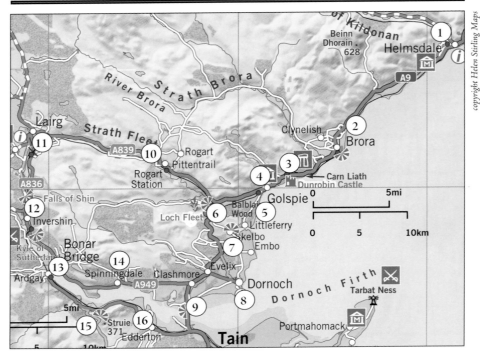

*copyright Helen Stirling Maps*

EAST SUTHERLAND stretches along the coast from Helmsdale to Dornoch, as well as inland to Bonar Bridge, Lairg and beyond. This is the most populated part of a vast area, much of which suffered greatly during the Clearances.

The numerous small villages all have much to offer the visitor who takes the time to seek out their charms. These range from abundant wildlife, a rich archaeological legacy, 19th century clearances and economic developments to a 19th century fairytale castle.

21st century retail therapy is also available in several of the villages, especially Dornoch, while malt whisky connoisseurs will not be disappointed. However the real charm of East Sutherland is the wonderful outdoors. Here it is easy to get away from the crowds and to enjoy solitude with only birds, wild flowers, insects and animals as company. So do try some of the diversions.

---

## ORDNANCE SURVEY 1:50,000 & 1:25,000 Maps

Landranger Maps: 16 Lairg, Loch Shin & surrounding area; 17 Helmsdale & Strath of Kildonan
21 Dornoch & Alness, Invergordon & Tain
Explorer Maps: 444 Helmsdale & Strath of Kildonan; 441 Lairg, Bonar Bridge & Golspie, Dornoch &
Brora; 438 Dornoch & Tain, Alness & Invergordon

---

## EAST SUTHERLAND - HELMSDALE TO DORNOCH WITH LAIRG LOOP

**1. Helmsdale** (p141) is a pretty village, mostly dating from the early 19th century, when it was developed as a Herring fishing station.
**Timespan Museum & Arts Centre** (p142) is a local museum, contemporary art gallery and creative hub focusing on the *Paradigm North*.
**The Emigrants' Statue** (p140) is a haunting reminder of the 19th century Highland Clearances. Strath of Kildonan (p143) or Strath Ullie is an interesting inland diversion.
**2. Brora** (p144) has a wonderful long sandy beach, where Jurassic fossils can be found at low tide.
**Clynelish Distillery** (p145) produces a lightly peated, waxy malt whisky. It can be visited all year round *(Opening hours, entry charge)*
**3. Dunrobin Castle** (p146) is dramatically sited just north of Golspie. Its enchanting fairytale appearance hides an interesting history and an opulent interior. *(Open April to October, entry charge)*
**Carn Liath** (p145) is a well preserved Iron Age broch, north of Golspie. With walls nearly 4m high and a surrounding settlement, it is a good visit.
**4. Golspie** (p147) stretches along a narrow coastal plain above another lovely beach. Jurassic fossils can be found here at low tide.
**Ben Bhraggie** (394m, p148) overlooks Golspie; there are excellent panoramic views from the summit.
**The Orcadian Stone Company** (p148) has a very impressive selection of fossils on display, *(Opening hours, entry fee)*. Flagstone products are also on sale.
**5. Balblair Wood** (p147) is a mature Scots Pinewood accessed from Golspie via the Golf Course road. Several rare plants and birds may be seen here.
**Ferry Links** (p147) forms the east coast here.
**6. Loch Fleet NNR** (p148) is a large tidal estuary north of Dornoch. A wide range of wildlife can be seen here throughout the year. Osprey breed locally.
**The Mound** (p148) was opened in 1816 to carry the Parliamentary Road northwards. A carpark at the north end is an excellent viewpoint.
**7. Skelbo Castle** (p149) is a gaunt and dramatic ruin overlooking Loch Fleet from the south.
**8. Dornoch** (p149) has a long history. This pretty little town has many warm coloured sandstone buildings, not least its 13th century Cathedral.

**History Links Museum** (p150) tells the story of Dornoch from early times until the development of golf in the 17th century. The story of Janet Horne, the last witch burnt in the UK is especially sad.
**Dornoch Distillery** (p150) is a newly established micro distillery attached to the Castle Hotel.
**9. Dornoch Bridge** (p150) was opened in 1991, avoiding a long detour round by Bonar Bridge.
**10. Rogart** (p152) is in the middle of picturesque Strath Fleet half way to Lairg on the A839.
**11. Lairg** (p154), the crossroads of Sutherland, developed despite the Clearances. The largest lamb sale in Europe is held here in August.
**The Ord Archaeological Trail** (p154) takes in Neolithic, Bronze Age and Iron Age remains.
**Hydro Electricity** (p154) was first generated from the 38MW Loch Shin scheme in 1959. Special arrangements allow Salmon to migrate past the dam.
**12. The Falls of Shin** (p155) is one of the great Salmon Leaps of Scotland. In the autumn Salmon can be seen running upstream here.
**Carbisdale Castle** (p156) was built for the widow of the 3rd Duke of Sutherland.
**13. Bonar Bridge** (p156) was on the main road north from 1812 until the Dornoch Bridge was opened. Situated at the head of the Dornoch Firth and the mouth of the Kyle of Sutherland, near the confluence of the rivers Carron, Oykel and Shin, it was for long a major Salmon station. Today it makes a pleasant base from which to explore East Sutherland and Easter Ross.
**14. Spinningdale** (p159) takes its name from an unsuccessful cotton spinning mill which operated here for a few years from 1792 to 1806.
**Ledmore & Migdale Forest Walk** (p159) starts north of Spinningdale and follows forest trails to a fine viewpoint over the Dornoch Firth.
**15. Struie Hill** (p158) offers dramatic views over the Dornoch Firth and Kyle of Sutherland. The B9176 was a former shortcut on the road north.
**16. Balblair Distillery** (p159), near Edderton, was established in 1790 and produces only vintage malt whiskies *(Open all year, admission charge)*.
**Edderton Kirkyard** (p158) is home to a fine Pictish cross slab. Another stands in a field at Balblair Farm.

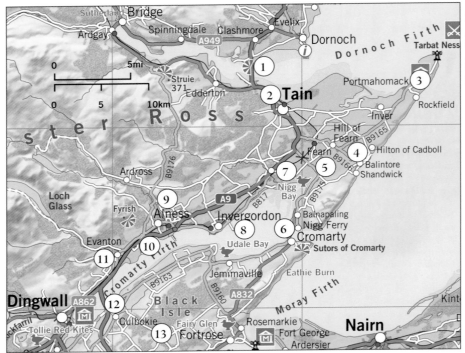

*copyright Helen Stirling Maps*

**EASTER ROSS** is Firth Country, separated from Sutherland by the Dornoch Firth and from Inverness-shire by the Beauly Firth. The Cromarty Firth splits the area in two.

Much of the area to the east of the A9 trunk road is prime agricultural land. To the west this soon gives way to the Highland interior, whose foothills dominate the view.

The coast from Invergordon to Evanton was largely taken over by the military in the 20th century wars. The Royal Navy had a huge base in WWI. In WWII the RAF had an airfield and flying boat base. The Royal Navy flew off carrier based aircraft here for training and maintenance.

The Oil Industry has used the deep water facilities here since the 1970s for oil rig building, maintenance, pipeline construction, oil rig storage and, soon perhaps, for decommissioning of oil rigs. In recent times Invergordon has become a popular stopover for cruise liners due to its deep water quay and facilities.

**ORDNANCE SURVEY 1:50,000 & 1:25,000 Maps**

Landranger Maps: 21 Dornoch & Alness, Invergordon & Tain; 26 Inverness & Loch Ness, Strathglass
Explorer Maps: 438 Dornoch & Tain, Alness & Invergordon; 437 Ben Wyvis & Strathpeffer, Dingwall;
432 Black Isle Fortrose, Cromarty & Dingwall

## EASTER ROSS

**1. Dornoch Bridge** (p150) was opened in 1991, avoiding a long detour round by Bonar Bridge. There are fine views from laybys on the bridge.

**2. Tain** (p163) is said to be the oldest Royal Burgh in Scotland, dating from 1066. The Sanctuary became a popular Medieval pilgrimage site.

**St Duthac Church** (p163) dates from c.1370, but a nearby chapel may have been built c.1153.

**Tain Through Time** (p163) tells the story of James IV and his pilgrimages to Tain as well as the town's famous gold and silversmiths.

**Glenmorangie Distillery** (p164), to the north of Tain, has unusually tall gin stills. (*Open all year for tours, entry charge for tours*).

**Tain Pottery** (p164) is just south of the town. It produces attractive and unique hand thrown ceramics.

**3. Portmahomack** (p165) is on the Tarbat peninsula, east of Tain. This attractive village was involved in exporting grain from early times.

**Tarbat Discovery Centre** (p165) is in St Colman's Kirk in Portmahomack. It tells the story of a major Pictish settlement and monastery established here in the 6th century with many artefacts from excavations.

**Tarbat Ness** (p166) with its lighthouse is on the northern extremity of the peninsula. This a good seawatching location during bird migration.

**4. Shandwick** (p167) is famous for its large 3m high Pictish cross slab, now protected under glass.

**Hilton of Cadboll** (p166) has a replica of another intricately carved Pictish cross slab found in 1811, and now in the National Museum.

**5. Fearn Abbey** (p167) was founded in 1221 by monks from Whithorn. The present church was rebuilt in 1771 after the old one was struck by lightning, killing most of the congregation.

**ANTA** (p168), near Fearn, is an interior design and architecture firm. They produce unique stoneware pottery and weave fabrics on the site.

**D-Day Landings Training** (p168) was carried out in WWII around Inver after the people and livestock were temporarily moved out. Beach assaults, live firing and inland operations were all practised.

**RAF Tain** (p168) has been a torpedo and bombing range since the 1930s. It is still regularly used by

RAF and other NATO airforces.

**6. Nigg Kirk** (p167) houses the Nigg cross slab, an 8th century Pictish symbol stone.

**The Beatrice Oil Field** (p167) was one of the first to be operational in the North Sea. Its terminal is at Nigg, where a pipeline comes ashore.

**7. Nigg Bay RSPB Reserve** (p168) occupies a large area of salt marsh, mudflats and coastal grassland at the north end of the Cromarty Firth. October to March is the best time to look for overwintering waders and wildfowl.

**8. The Cromarty Firth** (p169) is an a large area of sheltered water, with a narrow and easily defended deep water entrance from the North Sea.

**Invergordon** (p170) hosted a major Royal Navy base in WWI, but was too vulnerable to attack in WWII. The town still looks to the sea, hosting many oil rigs for maintenance or storage and increasing numbers of cruise liners in summer.

**9. Alness** (p170) is famous for its fine displays of floral art all summer. Bypassed by the busy A9, it is a very pleasant little town to visit.

**10. Dalmore Distillery** (p170) produces award winning malt whisky and has a visitor centre (*Open all year, admission charge for tours.*)

**The North Sea Mine Barrage** (p169) was laid by the US Navy in 1918 when over 70,000 mines were laid across the North Sea. Dalmore Distillery was used as a depot and long pier built.

**11. Evanton** (p171) is a pleasant little village nowadays. The WWII airfield, RAF Evanton, is now Deepwater Industrial Estate, serving the oil industry.

**Black Rock Gorge** (p171) is a 36m deep glacial box canyon at the bottom of a spectacular gorge. There is a fine short walk around this interesting feature.

**Fyrish Monument** (p171) overlooks the Cromarty Firth from Cnoc Fyrish (452m). This folly was built in 1782 for Sir Hector Munro, a British General.

**12. The Cromarty Bridge** (p180) opened along with new sections of the A9 in 1979, bypassing all of the small towns along the route.

**13. The Black Isle** (p172) is neither black, nor an isle, but a long peninsula, which forms the southeast coast of the Cromarty Firth.

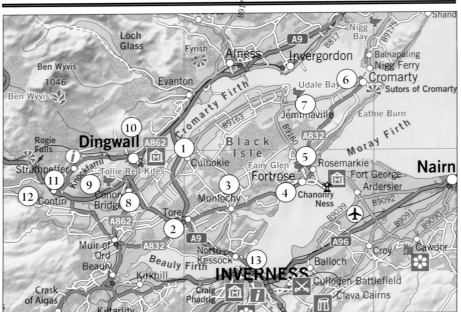

*copyright Helen Stirling Maps*

**The Black Isle** makes a very satisfying side trip to the main NC500 route. Neither an island, nor black, this is a long peninsula bound by the Cromarty Firth to the north with the Moray and Beauly Firths to the east and south.

Agriculture remains the main industry here, along with low key tourism. There is much to interest the visitor, ranging from Devonian fossils, to Pictish symbol stones and Medieval churches to Bottlenose Dolphins and rare birds.

Chanonry Ness, near Fortrose, is one of the best places to see Bottlenose Dolphins in the UK, if you survive the golf balls en route. Visitors are recommended to keep their eyes peeled skywards as Red Kites are common here and frequently perform aerobatics.

Cromarty, Fortrose and South Kessock are all good places to stay for a few days to explore Easter Ross, the Black Isle and the Inverness area. Boat trips run during the summer from Cromarty and Avoch to see the Dolphins and other wildlife in the Moray Firth.

The Black Isle is in many ways very like an island, with a slower pace of life, a more laid back attitude and with very welcoming people.

## ORDNANCE SURVEY 1:50,000 & 1:25,000 Maps

Landranger Maps: 21 Dornoch & Alness, Invergordon & Tain; 26 Inverness & Loch Ness, Strathglass; 27 Nairn, Forres & surrounding area
Explorer Maps: 432 Black Isle Fortrose, Cromarty & Dingwall

## BLACK ISLE, DINGWALL & STRATHPEFFER

**1. The Cromarty Bridge** (p180) opened along with new sections of the A9 in 1979; later the Kessock Bridge (p173) opened in 1982, along with another new section of the A9 across the Black Isle, completely transforming access to this formerly remote area.

**2. Tore Roundabout** (p173) is the main crossroads into the Black Isle, linking it with Dingwall, Conon Bridge, Muir of Ord and Wester Ross.

**3. Munlochy** (p173) is at the head of Munlochy Bay. This shallow bay is very attractive to waders and waterfowl at all seasons.

**Black Isle Brewery** (p174) is at Old Allangrange, near Munlochy. Established in 1998, it produces a unique range of beers using organic barley and hops. Much of the barley comes from its own farm.

**The Clootie Well** (p174) is on the A832 west of Munlochy. Also known as St Mary's Well, the branches of the surrounding trees are covered with pieces of cloth from those seeking better health.

**4. Fortrose** (p175) is an ancient settlement in a south facing nook, sheltered by Chanonry Ness. The village is built from warm coloured sandstone and has a charming 19th century harbour.

**Fortrose Cathedral** (p175) dates from the 13th century, but only the south aisle and choir survived the dissolution of the monasteries.

**Chanonry Ness** (p175) is a long shingle spit sticking out into the Moray Firth from Fortrose directly opposite Fort George.

**Bottlenose Dolphins** (p174) Chanonry Ness is one of the best places in the UK to get closeup views of Bottlenose Dolphins from the shore. The best time to see them is during the first of the flood tide.

**The Brahan Seer** (p175), or *Coinneach Adhair*, was a 17th century clairvoyant who was burnt in a tar barrel as a witch at Chanonry Ness in 1660.

**5. Rosemarkie** (p176) on the northeast side of Chanonry Ness was an important Pictish monastic site. Many Pictish stones have been found here.

**Groam House Museum** (p176) has displays of many sculpted Pictish stones. The Rosemarkie cross slab takes pride of place.

**The Fairy Glen** (p176) follows the Markie Burn through enchanted woods northeast of Rosemarkie.

There are two waterfalls and pools where children scatter petals in springtime for the fairies.

**6. Cromarty** (p176) is situated on the northern tip of the Black Isle. It prospered in the 18th century, but has been in slow decline ever since. This delightful little town has had a new lease of life recently.

**Cromarty Courthouse** (p178) features a realistic 19th century trial and prison cell.

**Hugh Miller** (p177), born here in 1802, was an early geologist and fossil hunter. He wrote extensively on geology, politics and religion. His house is maintained by the National Trust.

**The South Sutor** (p178) is a short walk from the town. There are fine panoramic views from here.

**7. Udale Bay RSPB Reserve** (p179) is a good place to view waders and waterfowl during autumn and winter. Around high tide is best.

**8. Conon Bridge** and Maryburgh straddle the mouth of the River Conon (p181). They are popular with Inverness commuters and retired people.

**9. Knockfarril** (p182), a long, hogbacked hill between Dingwall and Strathpeffer with fine panoramic views; access off the A835 as for Tollie Red Kites.

**Tollie Red Kites** (p182) is an RSPB maintained site. The birds are fed daily at 14:30 in summer and 13:30 in winter, affording excellent closeup views.

**10. Dingwall** (p180), bypassed by the main A9 north, is a fine town to visit. It retains most of its 19th century buildings and layout, largely without ugly 20th century development. Attractions include a Pictish Stone, the Fighting Mac Memorial, Dingwall Museum and Glen Wyvis Distillery. Dingwall offers numerous independent shops.

**11. Strathpeffer** (p183) developed as a spa village from the late 18th century; few people now partake of the waters, but it remains a popular destination. Attractions include the Eagle Stone, the Museum of Childhood and the Pump Room.

**12. Contin** (p182) is a small settlement at the confluence of the rivers Blackwater and Contin where the plains of Easter Ross give way to the Highlands.

**13. Kessock Bridge** (p173) is a quick route back to Inverness from the Black Isle for those who have already explored the Beauly Firth and Strath Conon.

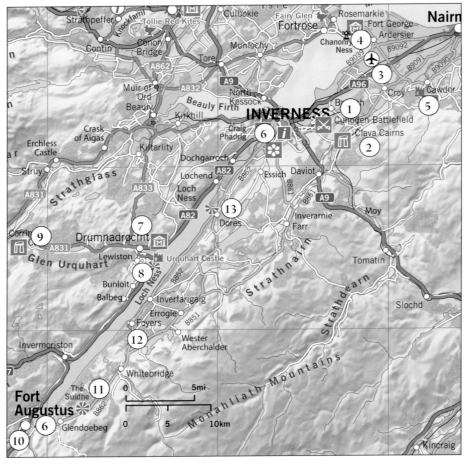

**Around Inverness** The NC500 starts and finishes in Inverness. Sadly many complete the route without spending any time in Inverness or exploring the hinterland.

To the east those interested in military history will enjoy Culloden Battlefield, Fort George and the Highland Aviation Museum. Cawdor Castle and Gardens is a multi period fairy tale castle, full of history.

The Loch Ness Circuit includes the elusive Loch Ness Monster, Urquhart Castle, the Caledonian Canal, Boat Trips and stunning views over the loch itself from many viewpoints.

| AROUND INVERNESS | | | |
|---|---|---|---|
| 1. Culloden Battlefield | 190 | Nessieland | 194 |
| 2. Clava Cairns | 188 | 8. Urquhart Castle | 194 |
| 3. Highland Aviation Mus | 191 | 9. Corrimony Cairn | 194 |
| 4. Fort George | 190 | 10. Fort Augustus | 194 |
| 5. Cawdor Castle | 191 | Loch Ness Boat Trips | 195 |
| 6. Caledonian Canal | 193 | 11. Suidhe Viewpoint | 195 |
| Loch Ness Boat Trips | 195 | 12. General Wade's Road | 195 |
| 7. Drumnadrochit | 193 | 13. Falls of Foyers | 195 |
| Loch Ness Centre | 193 | 14. Dores Viewpoint | 195 |

---

## ORDNANCE SURVEY 1:50,000 & 1:25,000 Maps

Landranger Maps: 26 Inverness & Loch Ness, Strathglass; 27 Nairn, Forres & surrounding area
Explorer Maps: 416 Inverness, Loch Ness & Culloden Fort Augustus & Drumnadrochit;
422 Nairn & Cawdor, Darnaway Forest, Ardersier & Culloden Muir

---

### AROUND INVERNESS

**1. Culloden Battlefield** (p190) is on the B9006, east of Inverness. The National Trust has an excellent visitor centre here. Self guided audio tours give a vivid impression of the events of 16th April 1746. This experience should not be missed (*Opening hours, entry charge, free to NT members.*).

**2. Clava Cairns** (p188), signposted off the B9006, are in complete contrast to Culloden. These round chambered cairns are unique to this area and date from c.2000BC (*free entry at all times*).

**3. Highland Aviation Museum** (p191) is next to Inverness Airport. It has an outdoor static collection of aircraft as well as an interesting small museum.

**4. Fort George** (p190) at Ardersier is a massive military fortification built after the 1745 rebellion. It remains in use as an army barracks. Much of the site is under Historic Environment Scotland and open to the public (*Opening hours, entry charge*).

**The Highlander's Museum** (p191) in Fort George is the regimental museum of the Queen's Own Highlanders and the Lovat Scouts. Their many engagements are well covered here.

**5. Cawdor Castle** & Gardens (p191) is signposted off the A96 on the B9090 southeast of Inverness Airport. This fairytale castle dates from the 13th century with many additions, while the gardens were started in c.1600 (*Opening hours, entry charge*).

**6. The Caledonian Canal** (p193) was designed by the engineer, Thomas Telford, and opened in 1822. The 60mi (97km) waterway follows the Great Glen joining Inverness with Fort William. Today it is a very popular visitor attraction. The Muirtown Basin and locks in Inverness make a good introduction to the operation of the canal.

**Loch Ness Boat Trips** (p195) are run by several operators. These include Jacobite Cruises, Loch Ness Cruises and Cruise Loch Ness. Details are included in the What to Do and See section p207.

**7. Drumnadrochit** (p193) is on Urquhart Bay on the estuary plain of the Rivers Coiltie and Enrick. There is a fine viewpoint over the village from a nearby Iron Age hillfort.

**The Loch Ness Centre & Exhibition** (p193), in the Drumnadrochit Hotel is *"A portal to the unique natural phenomenon that is Loch Ness"*. The Loch Ness Monster takes centre stage in this well designed exhibition, which will interest all of the family.

**Nessieland** (p194) is firmly aimed at curious children and their families. There are many hands on things to see and do. Children of all ages love it.

**8. Urquhart Castle** (p194) is one of the most spectacularly sited and popular castles in Scotland. With a rich and complex history dating back to the Iron Age due to its strategic location these romantic ruins are an essential visit. The castle gets very busy during the main tourism period; a far better experience can be had by visiting out of season (*Opening hours, entry charge*).

**9. Corrimony Chambered Cairn** (p194) is off the A831, west of Drumnadrochit. This Clava-type cairn is delightfully situated but rarely visited. The winter solstice sun sets down the passage.

**10. Fort Augustus** (p194) is at the southwestern end of Loch Ness. A series of five locks makes an interesting spectacle as vessels pass through.

**The Caledonian Canal Centre** tells about the rich history of the Caledonian Canal.

**Loch Ness Boat Trips** (p195) run to and from Fort Augustus from the dock on the canal.

**11. General Wade's Military Road** (p195) was built between Inverness and Fort Augustus in the 1720s to facilitate troop movements. These roads opened up the Highlands to trade, but also greatly facilitated the Jacobites in 1745-46. Later, they formed the basis for the building of the Parliamentary Roads built in the early 19th century.

**Carn an t' Suidhe Viewpoint** (450m, p195) is a short climb from the summit of the B862 northeast of Fort Augustus. There is a panoramic view of Loch Ness and over the remote Monadhliath Mountains.

**12. The Falls of Foyers** (p195) tumble down a small gorge into Loch Ness. A network of paths start from a carpark in the village.

**13. Dores** (p195) has spectacular views down the length of Loch Ness from an attractive small bay. Dores Inn is right on the shore; customers can enjoy their meals with a wonderful view.

During the research for this guide many books, periodicals, guides, maps and other publications were consulted. Websites and individuals were also useful. This bibliography is a distillation of some of them.

Useful leaflets, guides and small books are produced by Visitor Attractions, VisitScotland, SNH and others. Bookshops, Information Centres, Visitor Attraction Shops and Newsagents all stock them.

Starting with northcoast500.com, there are many useful websites about the North Highlands, individual areas and every type of business. Finally maps are essential to get the best out of the NC500 and are listed in full.

## ESSENTIAL BACKGROUND READING

| | | | |
|---|---|---|---|
| Scotland the Best 12th edition | Peter Irvine | Harper Collins | 2016 |
| Exploring the NC500 | David M Addison | Extremis Publishing | 2017 |
| The New Caithness Book | Donald Omand, Editor | North of Scotland Newspapers | 1989 |
| The Sutherland Book | Donald Omand, Editor | The Northern Times Ltd | 1982 |
| Wild Scots | Michael Fry | John Murray | 2005 |

## GENERAL BOOKS ON THE NORTH HIGHLANDS

| | | | |
|---|---|---|---|
| Scotland Highlands and Islands | Baxter, Winpenny et al | Ordnance Survey and AA | 1996 |
| The Empty Lands | Tom Atkinson | Luath Press Limited | 1986 |
| The Lonely Lands | Tom Atkinson | Luath Press Limited | 1985 |

## LOCAL GUIDES

| | | | |
|---|---|---|---|
| Loch Ness | Adrian Shine | Loch Ness Project | 2006 |
| Culloden | Lyndsey Bowditch et al | NTS | 2016 |
| Inverness | M Gerrard & D Dailey | Thomas Cook Publishing | 2011 |
| Inverness in Old Photographs | N Dalziel & J MacKenzie | History Press | 2011 |
| Urquhart Castle Souvenir Guide | Kirsty Owen | Historic Environment Scotland | |

## ARCHITECTURE

| | | | |
|---|---|---|---|
| Caithness Architectural Guide | Elizabeth Beaton | Rutland Press | 1996 |
| Sutherland, Architectural Guide | Elizabeth Beaton | Rutland Press | 1995 |
| Ross & Cromarty Architectural Guide | Elizabeth Beaton | RIAS | 1992 |
| Western Seaboard – Illus Arch Guide | Mary Miers | Rutland Press | 2008 |

## GENERAL BOOKS

| | | | |
|---|---|---|---|
| Scotland's Heritage: The Highlands | Joanna Close-Brooks | RCAHMS | 1986 |
| Rough Guide to Highlands & Islands | R Humphreys and D Reid | Rough Guides | 2006 |
| Scotland Highlands & Islands | Alan Murphy | Footprint Handbooks | 2001 |

## OUTLYING ISLANDS

| | | | |
|---|---|---|---|
| The Scottish Islands | Hamish Haswell-Smith | Canongate | 1996 |
| An Island Odyssey | Hamish Haswell-Smith | Canongate | 1999 |

## ARCHAEOLOGY - GENERAL

| | | | |
|---|---|---|---|
| Sutherland An Archaeological Guide | Robert Gourlay | Birlinn | 1996 |
| Ross & Cromarty A Historical Guide | David Alston | Birlinn | 1999 |

## ARCHAEOLOGY - NEOLITHIC & BRONZE AGE

| | | | |
|---|---|---|---|
| Neolithic and Bronze Age Scotland | P. J. Ashmore | Historic Scotland | 1996 |
| The Chambered Cairns of Caithness | J Davidson & Henshall | Edinburgh University Press | 1991 |
| The Chambered Cairns of Sutherland | A Henshall & J Ritchie | Edinburgh University Press | 1995 |
| Chambered Cairns of Cent Highlands | A Henshall & J Ritchie | Edinburgh University Press | 2001 |
| Landscape of Scotland, Hidden History | CR Wickham-Jones | Tempus | 2001 |

## ARCHAEOLOGY - IRON AGE

| | | | |
|---|---|---|---|
| Iron Age Britain | Barry Cunliffe | English Heritage | 1995 |
| In the shadow of the Brochs | B Smith and I Banks | Tempus Publishing Ltd | 2002 |
| Towers in the North Brochs of Scotland | Ian Armit | Tempus Publishing Ltd | 2003 |
| Scotland's Hidden History | Ian Armit | Tempus Publishing Ltd | 1998 |

## PICTS

| | | | |
|---|---|---|---|
| In Search of the Picts | Elizabeth Sutherland | Constable | 1994 |
| Field Guide to Pictish Symbol Stones | Alastair Mack | Pinkfoot | 1997 |
| Perceptions of the Picts | Anna Ritchie | Groam House Museum | 1994 |
| Pictish Symbol Stones | G Ritchie & I Fraser | RCAHMS | 1993 |
| The Art of the Picts | Henderson & Henderson | Thames & Hudson | 2002 |
| Picts, Gaels and Scots | Sally M. Foster | Historic Scotland | 1996 |
| Portmahomack monastery in Pictland | Tarbat Discovery Prog | HIE | 2007 |
| The Pictish Guide | Elizabeth Sutherland | Birlinn Limited | 1997 |
| The Picts A History | Tim Clarkson | Tempus Publishing | 2008 |
| Celtic Scotland | Ian Armit | Historic Scotland | 1997 |
| From Pictland to Alba 789-1070 | Alex Woolf | Edinburgh Univ. Press | 2007 |
| The Hill-Forts of Pictland | Ian Ralston | Groam House Museum | 2004 |

## VIKINGS

| | | | |
|---|---|---|---|
| Cultural Atlas of the Viking World | ed James G-Campbell | Time Life | 1994 |
| Social Approaches to Viking Studies | ed Ross Samson | Cruithne Press | 991 |
| The Orkneyinga Saga | Joseph Anderson | The Mercat Press | 1873 |
| Viking Scotland | Anna Ritchie | Batsford | 1993 |
| Westward Before Columbus | Kore Prytz | Norsk Maritime Forlag | 1991 |
| Iceland Saga | M Magnusson | Bodley Head | 1987 |
| Njal's Saga | Magnusson & Pálsson | Penguin Classics | 1960 |
| Northern Lights | AD Morrison-Low | National Museum of Scotland | 2010 |
| Orkneyinga Saga | H Pálsson & P Edwards | Hogarth | 1978 |
| The Norse Atlantic Saga | Gwyn Jones | Oxford | 1986 |
| The North Sea Earls | Ian Morrison | Gentry Books | 1973 |

## LORDS OF THE ISLES

| | | | |
|---|---|---|---|
| Somerled | John Marsden | Tuckwell Press | 2008 |
| Birlinn, Longships of the Hebrides | John MacAuley | White Horse Press | 1996 |
| The West Highland Galley | Denis Rixson | Birlinn | 1998 |

## CROFTERS AND THE LAND

| | | | |
|---|---|---|---|
| From the Land (As an Fhearann) | M MacLean & C Carrell | Mainstream | 1986 |

# NORTH HIGHLANDS BIBLIOGRAPHY

| | | | |
|---|---|---|---|
| Go Listen to the Crofters | AD Cameron | Acair | 1986 |
| Making of the Crofting Community | James Hunter | John Donald | 1976 |
| Who Owns Scotland Now? | Auslan Cramb | Mainstream | 1996 |

## HISTORY - EARLY TRAVELLERS

| | | | |
|---|---|---|---|
| A Description of the Western Isles | Martin Martin | Birlinn | 1698 |
| Journey to the Hebrides | Johnson & Boswell | Canongate | 1996 |
| Travellers in the Hebrides 1770-1914 | Derek Cooper | MacMillan | 1979 |
| The Hebrides of 1764 and 1771 | Rev J Walker | John Donald | 1980 |
| West Over Sea | DDC Pochin Mould | Acair | 1953 |
| The Yachtsman's Pilot to the W Isles | Martin Lawrence | Imray Laurie Norie & Wilson | 1996 |

## HISTORY

| | | | |
|---|---|---|---|
| Facing the Ocean | Barry Cunliffe | Oxford | 2001 |
| Hand to Mouth | Jane Cheape | Acair Ltd | 2002 |
| Third Statistical Account of Scotland | Alexander S. Mather, Ed | Scottish Academic Press | 1987 |
| Caithness  Wick 1794 | Sir John Sinclair | The Pentland Press | |
| Caithness Remembered 1999 | | N of Scotland Newspapers | 1999 |
| Lest we forget  The Parish of Canisbay | Anne L. Houston, Editor | Canisbay Parish Church | 1996 |
| Tales & Traditions of Caithness & Sutherland | | Lang Syne Publishing | 2005 |
| The Magic of Caithness | Ronald Thomson | N of Scotland Newspapers | 1998 |
| Life in Caithness & Sutherland | G Satterley, B McArdle | Paul Harris Publishing | 1983 |
| Memories of Caithness | Christopher J. Uncles | Stenlake Publishing Ltd | 2004 |
| Parish Life on the Pentland Firth | Morris Pottinger | Whitemaa Books | 1997 |
| Reay  Looking at the Past | Reay School Pupils | Reay School | 1991 |
| Historic Assynt | Malcolm-Bangor Jones | The Assynt Press | 2000 |
| Little Assynt Estate | R Noble, M Bangor-Jones | Culag Comm W Trust | |
| Rogart a Sutherland Crofting Parish | John Macdonald | The Byre | 2002 |
| The Province of Strathnaver | John R. Baldwin, Editor | SSNS | 2000 |
| A History of Lairg | Lesley Ketteringham | The Byre | 1997 |
| Durness Past and Present | Ronald Lansley | Caithness & Sutherland Ent | 1998 |
| Golspie's Story     Wilson Grant | The Northern Times Ltd | 1983 | |
| Tain Through The Centuries | R.W. Munro and J Munro | Birlinn | 1966 |
| A balance of Silver | Estelle Quick | Tain & Dist Museum Trust | 1997 |
| The Strath  Biography of Strathpeffer | Clarence Finlayson | St Andrew Press Edinburgh | 1979 |
| Action Stations - WWII airfields | David J. Smith | Patrick Stephens Ltd | 1983 |
| Iron Roads to the Far North & Kyle | Michael Pearson | Wayzgoose | 2003 |
| The Dam Builders  Power fm the Glens | James Miller | Birlinn | 2002 |

## NATURAL HISTORY- GEOLOGY & LANDSCAPE

| | | | |
|---|---|---|---|
| Geology, North Highlands of Scotland | Johnstone, Mykura | HMSO | 1936 |
| Exploring the landscape of Assynt | K Goodenough, E Pickett | BGS | 2004 |
| The Scenery of Scotland | W J Baird | NMS | 1988 |
| Hutton's Arse | Malcolm Rider | Rider-French Consulting Ltd | 2005 |
| The Highland Geology Trail | John L. Roberts | Luath Press Limited | 1990 |

## NATURAL HISTORY - GENERAL

| | | | |
|---|---|---|---|
| Natural History Highlands & Islands | FF Darling | Collins | 1947 |
| Highlands, Scotland's Wild Heart | S Moss & L Campbell | Bloomsbury | 2016 |

| Scotland After the Ice Age | ed Edwards & Ralston | EUP | 2003 |
| Beinn Eighe | Kenny Taylor | SNH | 2002 |
| Torridon, the Nature of the Place | Chris Lowe | Wester Ross Net | 2000 |

## NATURAL HISTORY - BIRDS

| Collins Bird Guide | Mullarney et al | HarperCollins | 2000 |
| Scottish Birds - Culture and Tradition | Robin Hull | Mercat Press | 2001 |

## NATURAL HISTORY - MARINE

| Guide to Sea & Shore Life | Gibson, Hextall & Rogers | Oxford | 2001 |
| Guide to Whale Watching | Mark Carwardine | New Holland | 2003 |
| The Natural History of Seals | W Nigel Bonner | Helm | 1989 |
| Whales Dolphins and Porpoises | Mark Carwardine | Dorling Kindersley Ltd | 1995 |

## NATURAL HISTORY - INSECTS

| Dragonflies and Damselflies | Brooks and Lewington | British Wildlife Publishing | 2004 |
| Moths of Britain and Ireland | Waring & Townsend | British Wildlife Publishing | 2003 |
| Butterflies and Moths | P Sterry, A Mackay | Dorling Kindersley | 2004 |
| Bumblebees of GB & Ireland | M Edwards, M Jenner | Ocelli | 2005 |
| Insects of Britain & Northern Europe | Michael Chinery | Harper Collins Publishers | 1993 |

## NATURAL HISTORY - FLORA

| Wild Flowers of Britain & Ireland | Blamey, Fitter & Fitter | A&C Black | 2003 |
| Orchids of Britain & Ireland | Anne & Simon Harrap | A&C Black | 2005 |
| Plants and People in Ancient Scotland | Camilla & James Dickson | Tempus | 2000 |
| Scottish Wild Plants | Lusby & Wright | Mercat Press | 2001 |
| Collins Scottish Wild Flowers | Michael Scott | Collins | 1995 |
| Plants and People in Ancient Scotland | C Dickson & J Dickson | Tempus | 2000 |
| Tree Guide | O Johnson &D More | Collins | 2004 |
| Wild Flowers of the N Highlands | K Butler & K Crossan | Birlinn | 2009 |

## PLACENAMES

| Reading the Gaelic Landscape | John Murray | Whittles Publishing | 2014 |
| Orkney Farm Names | Hugh Marwick | Kirkwall Press | 1952 |
| Place Names of the Highlands & Islands | Alexander MacBain | Grimsay Press | 1922 |
| Place-Names of Shetland | Jakob Jakobsen | Edinburgh | 1936 |
| Scottish Hill Names | Peter Drummond | Scot Mountaineering Trust | 1991 |
| Scottish Place-Names | WFH Nicholaisen | John Donald | 2001 |
| The Celtic Placenames of Scotland | WJ Watson | Birlin | 1926 |
| Place-Names of Ross and Cromarty | W.J. Watson | RCHS | 1976 |
| Place Names of the Highlands & Islands | Alexander MacBain | The Grimsay Press | 2003 |
| Gaelic in the Landscape | Ruairidh MacIlleathain | SNH | 2007 |

## WHISKY

| Scotland's Malt Whisky Distilleries | John Hughes | Tempus | 2002 |
| The Whisky Distilleries of UK | Alfred Barnard | David & Charles reprints | 1969 |

# North Highlands Bibliography

## SUGGESTED BACKGROUND READING

| | | | |
|---|---|---|---|
| Waverley | Sir Walter Scott | Caxton Publishing Co | 1829 |
| The Black Isle | Douglas Willis | John Donald Publishers Ltd | 1989 |
| The Glens of Ross-Shire A Guide | Peter D Koch-Osborne | Cicerone Press | 2000 |
| Gairloch and Guide to Loch Maree | J.H. Dixon | Edinburgh Co-op Printing Co | 1886 |
| The Castle & Gardens of Mey | Nick McCann | Heritage House Group Ltd | 2005 |
| Wick of the North | Frank Foden | N Scotland Newspapers | 1996 |
| Guide to Sutherland and Caithness | Hew Morrison | Spot on Printing | 2003 |
| Scotland's Edge Revisited | Keith Alliance | Harper Collins | 1998 |
| Northwest Highlands | Mendum, Merritts et al | SNH | 2001 |
| The Northern Highlands | Michael Scott | SNH | 2007 |
| The Northwest Highlands | D.J. Bennet, T. Strang | Scottish Mountaineering Trust | 1990 |
| Exploring Far North West of Scotland | Richard Gilbert | Cordee Ltd | 1994 |
| Firthlands of Ross and Sutherland | John R. Baldwin, Editor | SSNS | 1986 |

## OUTDOOR ACTIVITIES

| | | | |
|---|---|---|---|
| Cool Camping Scotland | McKelvie & McKelvie | Punk Publishing Ltd | 2007 |
| Backpacker's Britain: Volume 3 | Graham Uney | Cicerone Press | 2006 |
| Walks in the North-West Highlands | Chris Townsend | Aurum Press Ltd | 2007 |
| Walk Sutherland | Tom Strang | Sutherland Tourist Board | |
| Highland Walks: Skye to Cape Wrath | Hamish MacInness | Hodder & Stoughton | 1979 |
| Inverness, Loch Ness & NE Highlands | Neil Wilson | Jarrold Publishing | 1998 |
| Kyle of Lochalsh Walks | Terry Marsh | Jarrold Publishing | 2003 |
| Skye and the NW Highlands Walks | J Brooks and N Wilson | Jarrold Publishing | 1996 |

## SEA AND BOATS

| | | | |
|---|---|---|---|
| The Fringe of Gold | Charles Maclean | Canongate Publishing Ltd | 1985 |
| N & NE Coasts of Scotland & Orkney | ed Arthur Houston | Clyde Cruising Club | 2003 |
| Ardnamurchan to Cape Wrath | ed Arthur Houston | Clyde Cruising Club | 2006 |
| Stroma Yoles | Alastair R. Walker | The Orcadian | 2004 |
| Stroma | Donald Young, Editor | North of Scotland Newspapers | 1992 |
| A Wild and Open Sea | James Miller | The Orkney Press | 1994 |
| The Fishing Industry of Caithness | Iain Sutherland | Iain Sutherland | |
| Caithness & Sutherland Trout Lochs | Lesley Crawford | North of Scotland Newspapers | 1991 |
| Scrabster... the way forward | Ian Cassells | Cluny Publishers | 1993 |
| This Noble Harbour Cromarty Firth | Marinell Ash | John Donald Publishers | 1991 |
| Shipwrecks of the North of Scotland | R.N. Baird | Birlinn Limited | 2003 |

## ORDNANCE SURVEY MAPS

This guidebook uses 1:250,000 maps throughout the gazetteer section. In addition the OS coordinates of many localities are given. Free maps are available of the NC500 route, Inverness and the Inverness area. Road Map 1 will be found very useful in planning trips around the North Highlands. For more detailed exploring by car or bicycle the 1:50,000 Landranger Series is ideal, while walkers will find the extra detail on the 1:25,000 Explorer series very useful. Offline maps area available for free download from the Ordnance Survey. The Outdoors Great Britain offline maps can also be purchased for use on iPhones, iPads and Android devices. These maps use the GPS of the devices to show location and can record tracks.

## Road Map Series 1:250,000

| | |
|---|---|
| Road Map 1 | Northern Scotland, Orkney & Shetland |
| Road Map 2 | Western Scotland and the Western Isles |
| Road Map 3 | Southern Scotland and Northumberland |

## Landranger series 1:1,50,000

| | |
|---|---|
| Landranger | 9 Cape Wrath |
| Landranger | 10 Strathnaver |
| Landranger | 11 Thurso & Dunbeath |
| Landranger | 12 Thurso, Wick & surrounding area |
| Landranger | 15 Loch Assynt & surrounding area |
| Landranger | 16 Lairg, Loch Shin & surrounding area |
| Landranger | 17 Helmsdale & Strath of Kildonan |
| Landranger | 19 Gairloch & Ullapool area |
| Landranger | 20 Beinn Dearg & surrounding area |
| Landranger | 21 Dornoch & Alness, Invergordon & Tain |
| Landranger | 24 Raasay, Applecross & Loch Torridon |
| Landranger | 25 Glen Carron & surrounding area |
| Landranger | 26 Inverness & Loch Ness, Strathglass |
| Landranger | 27 Nairn, Forres & surrounding area |
| Landranger | 33 Loch Alsh & Glen Shiel |
| Landranger | 34 Fort Augustus & Glen Albyn area |

## Explorer series 1:1,25,000

| | |
|---|---|
| Explorer | 413 Knoydart, Loch Hourn & Loch Duich, Kyle of Lochalsh |
| Explorer | 414 Glen Shiel & Kintail Forest, Shiel Bridge, Morvich, Killilan & Kinloch Hourn |
| Explorer | 416 Inverness, Loch Ness & Culloden Fort Augustus & Drumnadrochit |
| Explorer | 422 Nairn & Cawdor, Darnaway Forest, Ardersier & Culloden Muir |
| Explorer | 428 Kyle of Lochalsh, Plockton & Applecross |
| Explorer | 429 Glen Carron & West Monar Strathcarron & Attadale Forest |
| Explorer | 430 Loch Monar, Glen Cannich & Glen Srathfarrar |
| Explorer | 431 Glen Urquhart & Strathglass, Drumnadrochit & Muir of Ord |
| Explorer | 432 Black Isle Fortrose, Cromarty & Dingwall |
| Explorer | 433 Torridon - Beinn Eighe & Liathach, Loch Maree, Kinlochewe & Gairloch |
| Explorer | 434 Gairloch & Loch Ewe |
| Explorer | 435 An Teallach & Slioch, Kinlochewe & Achnasheen |
| Explorer | 436 Beinn Dearg & Loch Fannich, Ullapool |
| Explorer | 437 Ben Wyvis & Strathpeffer, Dingwall |
| Explorer | 438 Dornoch & Tain, Alness & Invergordon |
| Explorer | 439 Coigach & Summer Isles, Inverpolly |
| Explorer | 440 Glen Cassley & Glen Oykel |
| Explorer | 441 Lairg, Bonar Bridge & Golspie, Dornoch & Brora |
| Explorer | 442 Assynt & Lochinver |
| Explorer | 443 Ben Klibreck & Ben Armine |
| Explorer | 444 Helmsdale & Strath of Kildonan |
| Explorer | 445 Foinaven, Arkle, Kylesku & Scourie |
| Explorer | 446 Durness & Cape Wrath, Kinlochbervie & Rhiconich |
| Explorer | 447 Ben Hope, Ben Loyal & Kyle of Tongue |
| Explorer | 448 Strath Naver/Strath Nabhair & Loch Loyal, Bettyhill |
| Explorer | 449 Strath Halladale & Strathy Point, Melvich & Forsinard |
| Explorer | 450 Wick & The Flow Country, Lybster, Latheron & Dunbeath |
| Explorer | 451 Thurso & John o' Groats, Dunnet Head |

# INDEX

# Index

# Index

7. Kylesku to Durness p92

6. Ullapool to Kylesku p76

5. Gairloch to Ullapool p66

4. Shieldaig to Gairloch p58

3. Garve to Applecross p48